Twayne's English Authors Series

EDITOR OF THIS VOLUME

Sylvia E. Bowman

Indiana University

Robert Lowth

TEAS 224

Robert Lowth

ROBERT LOWTH

By BRIAN HEPWORTH

York University

TWAYNE PUBLISHERS
A DIVISION OF G. K. HALL & CO., BOSTON

Library of Congress Cataloging in Publication Data

Hepworth, Brian.
  Robert Lowth.

  (Twayne's English authors series ; TEAS 224)
  Bibliography: p. 205–210
  Includes index.
  1. Lowth, Robert, Bp. of London, 1710–1787—
Criticism and interpretation.
PR3542.L43Z7   821'.5   77–15976
ISBN 0–8057–6695–2

To
Leyla in Istanbul

Contents

About the Author

Brian Hepworth was born in Yorkshire, U.K., and was educated in Quaker boarding schools in that county. After receiving a B.A. (Hons.) in English literature from London University, he spent some years in the Middle East, where he began an interest in the influence of the Orient on the Western sensibility which is reflected in this study of the leading Orientalist of the eighteenth century. Subsequently, Professor Hepworth taught at the Choate School, Wallingford, Conn., and earned his M.A. and Ph.D. at Harvard University.

Work at Harvard under the late Reuben A. Brower on the poetry of Edward Young — Lowth's fellow Wykehamist — directed Brian Hepworth's attention to the significance of Lowth in the work of other "Romantic" poets and critics, especially William Blake, William Collins, Thomas Gray, Christopher Smart, Joseph Spence, Joseph Warton, and Thomas Warton the Younger. It soon became clear that Lowth the Medievalist was indispensable also to the Gothic movement. Brian Hepworth's resolve while writing his Ph.D. thesis to produce later a full length study of Lowth — who has not yet been the subject of a book — finds its outcome in this present volume. The work has been greatly spurred by the current wave of interest in the theories of Giambattista Vico, with whose name Lowth's is usually linked.

Brian Hepworth has edited a selected edition of Edward Young (1975), and an anthology of critical texts, *The Rise of Romanticism: Essential Texts* which will shortly appear in the United Kingdom. He is at work on a novel set in the Middle East and on a large scale study of Time in eighteenth-century and Romantic literature. Brian Hepworth has taught at a number of universities in the U.S. and is presently a Professor of English in York University, Toronto.

Preface

The Oriental movement of the Enlightenment is perhaps the major tributary from which Romanticism arose. The eighteenth-century concept that a poet is a prophet and a prophet is a poet which clearly contains the matrix of the Romantic doctrine of "creative imagination"[1] finds its major definition in the pages of Robert Lowth's *De sacra poesi Hebraeorum praelectiones.*[2] In England, the definition of the poet as a prophet capitalized on the awareness of philosopher-psychologists George Berkeley, David Hume, and David Hartley; for these individuals believed that man's mind does not create uniquely a mirror image of a finite world but a novel artifact of infinity that is suggestive of futurity rather than of Mnemosyne, the Greek personification of Memory and the Classical mother of the traditional Western Muses.

Most specifically, it is through Robert Lowth that this mixture of the most modern descriptions of the mind and the set of poetic assumptions termed "Oriental primitivism" became available to Christopher Smart. This connection is dealt with in the chapter of the present book on Lowth's celebrated lectures and in the concluding chapter. Lowth is, of course, indispensable to an understanding of Romantic verse from Edward Young's *Night Thoughts* and William Blake's *Prophecies* to Samuel Taylor Coleridge's *Kubla Khan.* Lowth's "Orientalism" is an invaluable chapter also in the West's exotic fantasy (presently reaping its world harvest) of "the East," a fantasy which blossomed first in Biblical scholarship in the eighteenth century, which appeared in Samuel Johnson's *Rasselas* and William Beckford's *Vathek,* and which later gave to the English imagination such captives of the desert as T. E. Lawrence (of Arabia) and Charles Doughty.

In the past few years, Robert Lowth's name has been again mentioned in the most prominent places. In November 1976 *The New York Review* gave several inches of print to this eighteenth-century analyst of poetry.[3] In fact his appearance in twentieth-century thought is occasioned by a major rediscovery: that the image held by early Romantic writers of "original" man (although those origins were placed only five thousand years ago) is of overwhelming importance to the future of the race. The current revival of interest in Giambattista Vico (1668–1744) and in Johann von Herder (1744–1803), whose own work *The Spirit of Hebrew Poetry* borrowed from Lowth, touches inevitably, like Isaiah Berlin's *Vico and Herder* (1976)[4], on the most prominent English iconographer of "original" man, Robert Lowth; but, until this present publication, there has been no study of Lowth's background and his major works.

The following pages attempt to picture Lowth against the background of his family, school, and era; to suggest the importance of his political and professional ties and to indicate the sources of his early understanding of poetry in an investigation of his juvenile verse. They attempt also to account for his fight with William Warburton, Alexander Pope's literary executor; to analyze in detail his lectures on Hebrew verse; to explain the nature of his Medievalism in his *Life of William of Wykeham;*[5] to relate his famous *Introduction to English Grammar*[6] to his interests Medieval and Oriental, and to indicate the significance of Biblical translation in the late eighteenth century as seen in Lowth's *Isaiah, A New Translation.*[7] Contemporary critics' — including, surprisingly, John Wilkes' — evaluations of Lowth and his views of primitive poetry suggest Lowth's great significance not only for understanding Christopher Smart, his most important convert, but also for understanding in general the notions of "primitivism" and "originality" at the heart of the Romantic movement, especially in the verse of William Blake and William Wordsworth.

Not until the Bloomsbury Group of modern times has there been another cohesive literary nucleus as influential as the Wykehamist "pre-Romantics." From Winchester College and New College, Oxford — educational institutions both founded by William of Wykeham in the fourteenth century — there emerged in the eighteenth century a group of writers influenced by theories of Oriental and Medieval esthetics which included William Collins, Robert Lowth, Joseph Spence, Joseph Warton, and Edward Young; and their achievements, hitherto inadequately described, are of such importance that, without them, the rise of Romanticism is difficult to imagine. Robert Lowth was the most prolific theorist of this group. It cannot be too frequently stressed that Lowth's *Praelectiones* or *Lectures* contain the most comprehensive description of the nature of poetry at large that appeared in the mid-eighteenth century. In Lowth's works we gain entrance not only to the secrets of "pre-Romantic" verse but also to the climate of opinion at the highest levels of creative thought in England at one of the most crucial moments in the history of ideas and of esthetics.

I wish to thank Irvin Ehrenpreis for his constructive reading of this book at an early stage. Dr. John Walsh of Jesus College, Oxford, and Professor Ben Jones of Carleton University, Ottawa, made similarly useful observations which I found most valuable. Mrs. Pym Mannock of Oxford, who helped me in various matters of research, cannot be thanked enough for her part in this venture. The editor of this series, Sylvia Bowman has been encouraging throughout the writing of this book; and I thank her for her constructive aid. To Shirley Wiley, who showed that typing is a creative endeavor of the first importance, my thanks must be necessarily inadequate.

BRIAN E. HEPWORTH

York University, Toronto

Acknowledgments

The author wishes to acknowledge the special aid of the following in the making of this book: The Bodleian Library of the University of Oxford; Georg Olms Verlag, Hildesheim; The Osborne Collection of Early Children's Books, Toronto Public Library; Joan Carruthers, Chief Reference Librarian, Scott Library, York University; and the Minor Research Grants Committee, York University.

Chronology

1710 Robert Lowth born in the cathedral close, Winchester, son of Canon William Lowth.

1722 Lowth admitted as a scholar at William of Wykeham's St. Mary College in Winchester.

1724- As a schoolboy Lowth composes *The Genealogy of Christ,*
1729 in his friend Joseph Spence's terms, "an orientalism," and *Katherine Hill*, a "hill poem." Both poems are published, the latter in 1733.

1729 Enters New College, Oxford, Wykeham's other foundation. Begins research for Medieval biography of William of Wykeham.

1732 Death of Lowth's father.

1735 At twenty-five, a rising Wykehamist "star," Lowth is installed in living of Overton, Hampshire, by Benjamin Hoadly, Bishop of Winchester and Visitor of Wykeham's schools.

1741 Lowth elected to Professorship of Poetry at Oxford by the Masters of Arts of the University, the Wykehamists supporting him strongly.

1747 Lowth's poem, *Choice of Hercules* appears in Joseph Spence's *Polymetis.*

1748 Lowth goes with Henry Bilson-Legge to Berlin on behalf of the government.

1749 Lowth accompanies Lords George and Frederick Cavendish, sons of the Duke of Devonshire, the Whig leader, on the Grand Tour.

1750 Resigns Professorship of Poetry: appointed Archdeacon of Winchester by Bishop Hoadly.

1753 *De sacra poesi Hebraeorum praelectiones academicae* first published by Clarendon Press.

1754 Lowth awarded Doctor of Divinity by diploma by University of Oxford. Goes to Ireland with Lord Hartington, later the fourth Duke of Devonshire.

1758 Robert Lowth's *Life of William of Wykeham* published.

1762 Lowth's *A Short Introduction to English Grammar* published.

1765 Lowth wins his protracted battle with William Warburton ostensibly over the date of Job. After publication of Michaelis' edition of Lowth's *De sacra pöesi Hebraeorum* in Germany, Lowth elected Fellow of the Royal Society of Göttingen. Simultaneously elected Fellow of the Royal Society in London.

1766 The Rockingham government includes Lowth's friends. Lowth becomes Bishop of St. David's and then Bishop of Oxford.

1777 Attains bishopric of London.

1778 *Isaiah, A New Translation, with a Preliminary Dissertation* reasserts more strongly the principles of Lowth's lectures on sacred Hebrew poetry.

1783 Rockingham again in power. Lowth offered Archbishopric of Canterbury, but declines on grounds of sickness.

1787 *Lectures on the Sacred Poetry of the Hebrews:* translated into English by George Gregory.

1787 Lowth dies; buried in bishops' palace, Fulham.

CHAPTER 1

The Background and Times of Robert Lowth

I William Lowth

WILLIAM, the father of Robert Lowth, was born in 1660, the year of the Restoration; he was the son of a London apothecary who suffered in the Great Fire of 1666. William's grandfather, Simon Lowth, a country rector, helped to educate William, who entered Merchant Taylors' School at the age of twelve. But trade, less respectable then than now, continued to support the Lowth men. Robert's brother became a hosier, a dealer in and perhaps a manufacturer of underwear and stockings. We may detect what might today be termed "upward mobility" in the life of Robert Lowth; for, as well as becoming a European literary figure, he was appointed in 1777 Bishop of London, the city in which his grandfather had been an ill-fated pharmacist. Lowth's father proceeded from Merchant Taylors', one of England's greatest schools, which had educated the poet Edmund Spenser (1552?-99), to St. John's College, Oxford, where he earned the usual degrees, entered the Church, and became a Fellow of the college. The indispensable contribution which he made to his son's career was to become chaplain to the Bishop of Winchester, Peter Mew, and a canon of Winchester Cathedral in 1696 as a result of the conservative fervor of his writing.

The first published work of the elder Lowth was the *Vindication of the Divine Authority of the Old and New Testaments* (1692). Like the substantial promotion the work earned for its author, the title brings into focus a major conflict of the eighteenth century. Readers of John Dryden's *Religio Laici* (1682) recall the poet's alarm at the incursions of the Jesuit linguist, Father Simon, on the

15

foundation of Protestantism, the Holy Bible. The scientific establishment of the late seventeenth century provided an atmosphere
which weakened faith in the unseen and, in the form of the Royal
Society, directly encouraged research into the factual background
of the Scriptures. William Lowth's emphasis on the intervention of
God in the workings of Nature, or "revelation," was insistent. But
in this conservative churchman we find secular interests in Oriental
life or literary criticism which reveal for a moment disciplines distinctly different from that of theology. William Lowth's most
famous work was a *Commentary on the Prophets* (1714–25).[1]
Speaking of the phrase 'the rings and nose jewels,' Isaiah 3:21, the
elder Lowth observed,

The word may be translated *jewels for the face* or *forehead,* as it is
render'd *Gen.* xxiv. 47. *Ezek.* xvi. 12. But the same phrase is used *Prov.* xi.
22, where it certainly signifies a *nose-jewel;* and our interpreters translate
it to that sense, — *As a jewel of gold in a swine's-snout.* — St. *Austin,* in
his *Questions upon Genesis,* tells us, it was the custom of the women in
Mauritania to hang jewels in their nose; and the same custom is still
observed in *Persia, Arabia,* and other countries, as those who have travelled thither inform us. See Harris's *Collect. of Travels,* Part I. p. 207.[2]

Allusion to St. Augustine's authority is not unusual in a religious
work; but the one William Lowth made to Harris represents quite a
different influence. John Harris (1666?-1719), a scientific writer
and a topographer, was a member of the Council of the Royal
Society. His anthology of four hundred travellers writing in the
major European languages was perhaps the foremost collection of
voyages of his era,[3] a genre whose wisdom is questioned most con-
spicuously by Jonathan Swift (1667–1745) in *Gulliver's Travels*
(1726). William Lowth's allusion to Harris anticipates the later
eighteenth-century practice of viewing the Bible as a cultural docu-
ment to be mined for its anthropological truths about primitive
societies rather than as a guide to God's mysteries.

William Lowth's allusion to John Harris is a rare oasis in an
expanse of preaching, but another secular moment occurs in his
Commentary on Ezekiel. During the mid-eighteenth century, poets
were thought of as prophets and prophets as poets. The major
poets of the so-called pre-Romantic era, as well as the greatest of
the Romantics, saw Ezekiel as the greatest of Oriental poets. For
Robert Lowth, Ezekiel was the most sublime[4] of the prophets; and
one of the earliest purely literary comments in the eighteenth cen-

tury on the style of Ezekiel is made by his father, William Lowth. In his introduction to the Book of Ezekiel, William Lowth observes that René Rapin (1621-87), the French Classical critic, in his *Réflexions sur l'Éloquence* (1684) had termed Ezekiel's style "le Terrible," the terrifying, which Lowth, in terms common in discussions of "the Sublime," explains as "having something in it that strikes the reader with an holy dread and astonishment."[5]

Furthermore, Robert Lowth's father suggested a characteristic of Hebrew verse which his son found to be central in it forty years after. The harsh, the demeaning, and the unpleasant, William Lowth reported, were exaggerated and stressed too forcibly in Ezekiel, in order to produce a sense of overwhelming shock and power. The first century Classical critic Quintilian (*c*.35-*c*.95 A.D.) had described in general terms this kind of style, Canon Lowth of Winchester noted, as *"oratio quae rebus asperis, indignis & invidiosis vim addit"* (rhetoric in which bitter, unworthy and insulting images are given added strength).[6]

William Lowth's description of Ezekiel's "Sublime" differs in one major respect from his son's. William's world is a religious world in which higher truths are made available even by literary technique. The "Sublime" to which he alludes appears to be the "Sublime" attributed to the Classical writer Longinus who regarded the "Sublime" as a response to great moments of thought or feeling in literature or in other art in which the "noble" faculties of the soul are called forth by images which suggest the "nobility" of an inherently hieratic universe.[7] Robert Lowth later analysed the linguistic phenomenon of Hebrew poetry as purely subjective, psychological response that was in tune with contemporary philosophy.

A theological anticipation of another esthetic fashion of the later eighteenth century may be seen in William Lowth's warning: "one great use of the writings of the prophets, is to instruct us in the *signs of the times;* and tho' the warnings they give had a particular aspect upon their own age, yet they were likewise *written for our admonition, upon whom the ends of the world are come."*[8] In a non-doctrinal context, the image of vast destruction, such as that of the end of the world, became, frequently in conjunction with prophetic Oriental images, a major feature of the esthetic of the ruin. One thinks of the Earl of Shaftesbury (1671-1713) in whose *Characteristics* (1711) the end of the world is anticipated by travellers who view the North African Mt. Atlas;[9] of Edward Young

(1683-1765) in whose *Night Thoughts* (1742-45), an "imitation" of
Ezekiel, the end of Time is envisioned; or of Edmund Burke (1729-
1797), for whom one of the most esthetically delightful ideas was
the total destruction of the city of London.[10]

According to some testimonies, William Lowth was a greater
scholar than his son, Robert. His special interests were Josephus
(37-?100) and Clemens Alexandrinus (150?-?220). Especially on the
Jewish historian Josephus, for example, William Lowth contributed notes of great erudition to the monumental edition of 1720
edited by John Hudson (1662-1719).[11] Josephus, a Jewish historian
who was especially interested in the factual history of the times of
the Old Testament, neglected the history of Christianity and the
activities of Christ, treated David as a Greek lyric poet, and drew
an analogy between Moses and Plato. It is especially interesting
that in announcing to his Greek readers that the Hebrew arts flourished long before Greece and Rome, Josephus anticipated the
emphasis of English literary theory of the mid-eighteenth century.

We may conclude that Robert Lowth was born into a household,
in the cathedral close of Winchester in 1710, in which there was a
professional awareness of the factual accounts of the earliest ages
and an academic grasp by a leader in the field of the original
sources for a secular history of Biblical times. It is tempting to
speculate on the reasons why William Lowth did not himself publish any work on Josephus. It may well be that he was too timid to
risk accusations of Deism or irreligion which might endanger a
career founded on his *Vindication of the Divine Authority of the
Old and New Testaments.* Perhaps his son's achievement in non-
theological aspects of Hebrew culture was to some extent a reaction
against the timidity of his father.

II *Robert Lowth's Childhood and Youth*

To an extent rare among famous men, Robert Lowth might be
said to have been made by a city, by its institutions, and by its associations. That city is Winchester in the County of Hampshire, some
eighty miles from London, and some fifteen miles from the south
coast of England, and close to the seaport of Southampton. Not
until the Bloomsbury Group in the early twentieth century has any
single group of writers so influenced the course of English literature
as the small nucleus of men educated at Winchester College who
are to be counted among the most important early Romantics. The

greatest poet among these people was William Collins (1721-1759); but Edward Young, author of *Night Thoughts,* was also a product of Winchester. Joseph Spence (1699-1768), Professor of Poetry at Oxford before Robert Lowth, was a Winchester schoolboy, while the three celebrated Wartons — Thomas Warton the Elder (1688-1745), Joseph Warton (1722-1800), Thomas Warton the Younger (1728-1790) — who comprised the first family of Romanticism, were all affiliated to the group through the headmastership of Winchester College by Joseph, an alumnus, who was the author of early Romantic poems and of the highly influential *Essay on the Genius and Writings of Pope* (1756, 1782).

Winchester is a city with a peculiar attachment to the remotest past. It is within a few hours of Salisbury Plain and the monument of Stonehenge, possible center of Druid worship, which in the early eighteenth-century attracted much scholarly attention. Winchester itself, once a Roman camp, was the capital of King Alfred from 871 to 899; and King Arthur's Round Table is said to hang now in what remains of the Great Hall. The city was the scene of the rise to fame of one of the shrewdest of princes of the Medieval church, William of Wykeham (1324-1404), a close contemporary of Geoffrey Chaucer (1340?-1400). Starting life as an orphan without a family name, Wykeham served three kings of England, became the most famous of all Bishops of Winchester, and reached the heady pinnacle of political success as Chancellor of England. Wykeham, as a churchman unmarried, used his massive wealth in the founding of two institutions of learning named after his favorite saint. The one, St. Mary College of Winchester, was a boarding school devoted to training boys (as poor as Wykeham had been) for service to church and state; the other, St. Mary College of Winchester in Oxford, otherwise known as "New College," continued the education of Winchester graduates in the university milieu. It is clear that Robert Lowth inherited from his father a fundamental orientation to the "primitive" ages of Oriental or Hebrew culture. From William of Wykeham, the Medieval churchman who was his benefactor, and to whom he referred as a father, Lowth himself was a direct link with the Middle Ages in England, precisely at the time when Classical influences were waning in the imagination of English writers.

In Wykeham's detailed regulations for the running of his two schools, the Bishop of Winchester was the Visitor or chief inspector. Robert, as the son of the Bishop's chaplain William Lowth, might therefore expect, not only an easily arranged entry into Win-

chester College and later, New College — with the exception of
Eton and the similarly related King's College, Cambridge, the most
formidable educational combination of that, and quite possibly,
any age — but also the privileged attention of the clergymen who
were the two institutions' teachers. Lowth's mother was Margaret
Pitt, daughter of Robert Pitt "gentleman" of Blandford in Dorset.
We do not know much about her, but the appellation of Robert's
maternal grandfather, "gentleman," assures us that his father's
marriage had confirmed the family's movement away from metropolitan shopkeeping to genteel society where the middle classes
mingled with the aristocracy. There is little doubt that, endowed
with such advantages of background and education, any son of
Canon Lowth and his wife Margaret might well expect, if he possessed even ordinary "parts" or intelligence, to go far.

From material provided in 1756 for Joseph Warton when he
became an Usher or assistant at Winchester College by one Hollo-
way, the Senior Prefect of the school, we form some idea of learning at Winchester College in the mid-eighteenth century. From this
schedule, now in the archives at Winchester, we find that the boys'
day began at five o'clock and that chapel began at five thirty.
Morning school was held from six o'clock to nine; breakfast was
eaten at nine; and from nine thirty to eleven the boys studied in
their chambers. Lunch at twelve was preceded by an hour of "Middle School" and was followed by four hours of "Afternoon
School" which was interrupted by bread and beer at about three
thirty. Supper appeared at six, and there seems to have been some
food after this, as well as a study period which became known as
"Toy-time." Wykeham's foundation left provision for two pints of
beer for each boy each day.

There appear to have been three forms or classes, the Fourth,
Fifth and Sixth, and each had its own divisions. To select at ran-
dom, we note that on Monday morning the Sixth studied Virgil, on
Wednesday evening, Pliny and the *Orations* of Cicero. On Tuesday
and Thursday mornings, the Sixth studied Horace, Greek grammar, and geography. Along with the Fifth on Tuesday and Thursday evenings they studied Homer and Horace. On Friday evening,
the Sixth was engaged in a Greek task, or "homework"; on Saturday evening, the class took "Collections," tests which occurred
every three weeks. During "Cloister Time," a period of unsupervised study, the Sixth independently studied Demosthenes, the
Greek orator, Latin grammar and Homer.

At the other end of the scale, we note that the Seniors of the Fourth class studied Virgil on Monday and Wednesday mornings, the Middle Fourth read Ovid's *Metamorphoses* in a parallel text; the Juniors of the Fourth studied Latin grammar. At ten o'clock on these days, the Fourth-form Seniors studied Terence or "Fables," probably one of the many editions of Aesop available: such as Thomas Philipot's *Aesop's Fables in English French and Latin* (4th ed., 1703); the Middle Fourth Erasmus and "Fables"; while the Juniors studied the Latin grammars of Mathurin Cordier (1480-1564), teacher of Calvin, and Ovid's *Tristia*. The rest of the week seems to have followed along the same lines: Latin and Greek grammar, Ovid, Virgil, and Cordier. The Fourth underwent "Usher's Cloister Time," as opposed to the unsupervised "Cloister Time" of the Sixth. During this period, the Fourth was required to cope with the Latin of Quintus Curtius, Sallust, and Ovid's *Epistles*. There seems to have been a great deal of testing and composition and personal construing.

Among the books read by the Fifth form that are not mentioned in the studies of the other two forms, are Paterculus, the Roman historian, and Dionysius, the Greek grammarian. Some sense of the separate activities of the forms might be suggested by the assignments for the Easter week, during which there was no vacation but a change in the normal routine of the school. During this period, the Sixth read Juvenal, and the Fifth studied Greek grammar. In the evenings, the Seniors of the Fifth read Horace's satires and epistles; the Middle and Junior Fifth studied Terence.

Of peculiar interest in this list of studies is an absence of religious works. The school chapel, like the chapel at New College, was central in the life of the institution; but apart from the headmaster's talks in chapel and attendance at Winchester Cathedral (rebuilt by William of Wykeham in the fourteenth century) there seems to have been no formal religious instruction, a curious omission in a school founded by and run by the clergy and designed in part for the education of clergymen. The tolerance and the enlightenment of the period and the seeds of Robert Lowth's later humanistic, secular interest in theories concerning the nature of earliest man might be seen in the emphasis placed upon Hugo Grotius (1583-1645). On Sunday evenings the headmaster of Winchester expounded to the entire school the views of this Dutch Protestant thinker; and Grotius may be considered, along with Giambattista Vico (1668-1744) and Johann von Herder (1744-1803), as one of the era's major theorists on the nature of "primitive" societies and earliest man, on the literature of which Robert Lowth became the foremost English authority of the eighteenth century.

The sense that private study was strongly encouraged is suggested by one Winchester institution of some fame, the "scob." Each boy owned a box that was much like the top of a school desk, for it had fitted sides to it which could be raised to shield him from the distractions of the classroom. These boxes — known at Winchester as "scobs," a schoolboy version of "box" pronounced backwards — enabled the student to study in his own place and to be removed from temptation and note-passing. When he was called to the front of the class by his teacher, he apparently went up to the front with his "scob."

From this schedule prepared for Joseph Warton, we are left with three important conclusions: the school by and large was a Medieval monastery for adolescents; no vacations, except for a break of a few days after Whit Sunday, were granted; the curriculum, as we have seen, was almost entirely devoted to Latin and Greek in the original. The boys were forbidden to speak English. When one edits Spence's *Essay on Pope's Odyssey* (1726,27), Lowth's lectures on Hebrew poetry, Edward Young's *Conjectures on Original Composition* (1759), or Joseph Warton's *Essay on Pope* one is struck by a remarkable fact: not only did these men educated at Winchester allude with ease to passages and lines from minor as well as major Greek and Roman writers, but their knowledge of these writers was so intimate that they frequently constructed only from memory. Their less than accurate renderings of well-known lines, suggest that their minds accepted the languages of their adolescence almost as if they were part of the proverbial texture of their English.

Immured in their school during almost all their living hours, the boys worked a seven-day week and a sixteen-hour day, except for part of Tuesday and Thursday, their recreation days, when the young Wykehamists hunted badger, fished, and played cricket in the vicinity of Katherine Hill, a legendary landmark from which they could view large stretches of the local countryside and from which Lowth composed his own "hill poem" in the manner of Sir John Denham's *Cooper's Hill* (1642) and Alexander Pope's *Windsor Forest* (1713).

Our knowledge of life in Winchester school in the post-Renaissance era is supplemented by an unpublished Latin poem written by a schoolboy Robert Matthew, who is otherwise unknown. This poem, translated by A. K. Cook in his *About Winchester College,* [12] is of peculiar interest for our understanding of Robert Lowth in his formative years. From it we discover that there were seventy students who were controlled by eighteen seniors or prefects who were appointed from among them. There were also sixteen choristers who sang in chapel and who waited upon the Fellows or masters. Winchester, the choristers remind us, was to some extent a charitable foundation, the soul of whose Founder might benefit from the singing of youthful voices across the ages. As well as an organist, there were three chaplains and three clerks. The boys wore "dusky" wool gowns, made from the local wool, whose manufacture Wykeham had been keen to encourage. Lines 31–69 of Matthew's Latin poem describe the beginning of the day: "At five o'clock comes 'first peal,' and a prefect cries out *'Surgite;* stop snoring you sluggards, and get up.' We obey; put on gowns, breeches, shoes, hurry into line, and at 'bells down' chant a Latin psalm half-dressed.... At six the smallest bell rings, summoning us to School.... We pray for enlightenment, and then set to work on a 'verse-task' cudgelling our brains for a poem to fit our theme, bound to our 'scobs' as Prometheus was bound to his Caucasian rock." [13]

The Gothic building in which school took place was supported by four oaken posts. In the window seats, above the common herd, sat the prefects, who watched their schoolfellows. As Robert Matthew describes the setting, he poses pertinent questions:

On the northern wall is a map of the world; and on the eastern a table of Quintilian's Laws, the *Tabula Legum;* on the western *Aut Disce,* [either learn] with its symbols, offers three portions for your choice. Will you learn, quaffing the bitter draughts which Phoebus puts to your lips? Over the words *Aut disce* a mitre and a staff promise you a bishopric. Are you loath to learn, hating tasks and teachers' talk? Leave; over *Aut discede* [or get out] an inkhorn invites you to the law courts, a sword to the battlefield. Will you neither learn nor leave? There is a third alternative, the rod. — A little below the *Aut Disce* stands a pulpit for declamations. Here we fight our foes, hurling our scholastic weapons; but it is women's warfare, for we fight with tongues and not with hands. [14]

Matthew's poem adds three particular pieces of information of the greatest interest in a study of the Wykehamist pre-Romantics: William Collins, Robert Lowth, Joseph Spence, Joseph Warton, and Edward Young. The students were compelled to undertake first thing, every day, an exercise in what we would now term "creative writing." Each morning, before the sun rose, every student composed a poem on a set theme. Lowth's poems composed in his adolescence cleverly exploited the latest fashions and appeared in leading publications; he later became the most famous Professor of Poetry of his age. From this beginning at Winchester College, we must add, a significant revolution in poetic theory took place, not only through the agency of Robert Lowth but also through the firmly held poetic beliefs of his eighteenth-century school fellows who were strong-willed pioneers in an age previously characterised by neo-Classical poetic notions distinct from their own.

It is also fascinating to note that the miter and staff, the symbols of a bishopric, were painted on the wall of the school hall as the mark of the natural lot of a successful student who followed in the persevering footsteps of his Medieval patron. The famous command *Aut Disce, aut discede* — ... either learn or get out ... (the third choice: "be beaten!") — was reinforced with the less important emblems of the law, the inkhorn, and of the army, the sword. Clearly, it was assumed the boys were privileged and that the church, the law, the army, the nation in fact as Wykeham had intended, would benefit from their exertions. Law, of course, was as essential to the good government of the church's extensive institutions as of Wykeham's schools themselves. Lowth's legal skill was evident not only in his handling of the controversies surrounding New College that he alluded to in his *Life of Wykeham* but in his handling of the affair of "resignation bonds" as Bishop of London. But it is the clear promise that the first reward of attentiveness and application would be a bishopric which we must bear in mind as we view the boyhood of a man who became Bishop of St. David's in Wales, Oxford, and London.

Robert Matthew's schoolboy memories also convince us of the atmosphere of the arena in which learning was conducted. As it had been for William of Wykeham, academic distinction was of direct public usefulness; it was not the private retreat of unworldly gentlemen. In his lectures as Professor of Poetry at Oxford, Lowth persuaded his public of the finest points of his scholarship; and he was always ready to enter battle. The schoolboy's life at Winchester was dominated, we read in Matthew, by the pulpit of the school hall from which the boys declaimed and attacked each other — "warfare" and "battlefield" are the terms Matthew uses — in learned and literary controversy. In mature years, especially in the debate with William Warburton (1698-1779), Pope's executor, which was ostensibly about the date of Job, Lowth was a sardonic, superbly equipped public debater who used polished irony with devastating effect, a role which he had doubtless first rehearsed in the Winchester pulpit.

We can only conjecture about the effect of a Medieval boarding school on the imagination of a sensitive, gifted boy in the early years of the eighteenth century. Thomas Otway (1652-1685), the Restoration playwright and, perhaps most notably, author of the lugubrious *The Orphan* (1680) and the funereal *Venice Preserved* (1682), was an alumnus of Winchester College, as was Sir Thomas Browne (1605-1682), the author of the baroque *Urn Burial* (1658). It has been suggested that Edward Young, with Thomas Gray among the most notable of the "graveyard school" of poets of the mid-eighteenth century, absorbed his obsession with death in the funereal environment of antique Winchester College.[15] What is certain is that the major shift in English taste which occurred during the lifetime of Robert Lowth made Gothic architecture and literature fashionable and that Robert Lowth, educated through childhood and adolescence in fourteenth-century buildings, was well placed to appreciate the actual fabric and artifacts of The Middle Ages that were in the abbeys, monasteries and castles of England's "first ages."

Men who succeed in non-literary careers at the same time as literature are a rare phenomenon. Robert Lowth's critical acumen that is notable in his acclaimed lectures on Oriental poetry was instrumental in the building of his public career. Lowth's public success can be partly explained in terms of his successful connections, a benefit which Lowth enjoyed in stark contrast with his contemporary, Edward Young, the major poet of sensibility of the eighteenth century, who languished without preferment in a country rectory knocking humiliatingly on closed doors to the end of his long life. Among the famous alumni of Winchester College while Lowth was a boy at school, was Joseph Spence (1699-1768), who was eleven years Lowth's senior. Spence is best known as the compiler of his *Anecdotes,*[16] an indispensable source book to the age of Pope. In 1726, at the age of twenty-seven, he had unveiled his *Essay on Pope's Odyssey* (1726,27). Much admired by Samuel Johnson,[17] this critical essay met with the approval of Alexander Pope himself.

In a world of acrid criticism, Spence's gentle perceptiveness in his essay anticipated his charming *Polymetis* (1747), a work in which a long poem by Robert Lowth appeared. When Lowth was eighteen, Spence became, partly because of his *Essay on Pope's Odyssey,* Professor of Poetry at Oxford in 1728, the position which Lowth would occupy more spectacularly some thirteen years later. Among Spence's letters is one which refers to "Bob" Lowth, and another jokingly describes the younger man, well-built and stocky in his prime, as a guinea-pig.[18] It seems likely that the close friendship between the adolescent and the successful critic began in the atmosphere of Winchester schoolboy hero-worship. Nevertheless, whatever the sentimental admiration between the well-known and the aspiring writer, this friendship had the advantage of extreme usefulness to Lowth which several of his later relationships, such as those with Benjamin Hoadly (1676-1761) and with the Cavendishes, the Dukes of Devonshire, also possessed.

Spence exemplifies, at a date earlier than Lowth, the keen interest in "primitive" verse that became characteristic of the Wykehamist Romantics. He was, notably, the protector of the "Thresher Poet," Stephen Duck (1705-1756), who was an untutored man of the soil who received national attention in the early eighteenth century and who wrote such Biblical poems as *The Shunamite* (1736) with the explicitly stated intention of rejecting Greece and Rome and turning to Biblical sources. Duck is among the first in a long line of "Herdsman," "Dairy-maid," and "Ploughman" poets — the unsophisticated folk of the soil — which culminated in the apparently simple primitivism of William Blake (1757-1827), Robert Burns (1759-1796), and John Clare (1793-1864). However, Spence's primitivism is also evident in his *Essay on Pope's Odyssey* in which he on occasion compares Homeric techniques of poetry with those of the Old Testament. We have observed the significance of William Lowth's interest in the prophet Ezekiel. Spence's *Essay* specifically isolates a prophetic technique seen in Homer as "an *orientalism*" — a term Spence explicitly coins for the occasion — and he finds comparable examples in the Hebrew prophets, especially Ezekiel.

The two poems which Lowth wrote while he was a schoolboy at Winchester show a very shrewd sense of current modes. In *The Genealogy of Christ,* which he perhaps composed at fourteen, and which was published in 1729, he images the Old Testament figures on the stained glass of the Winchester College chapel. Clearly a prophecy, the poem fulfills the requirements of "an *orientalism*" as described by Joseph Spence in his book on Pope's *Odyssey,* although Lowth's composition apparently preceded that work. It is noteworthy that the young Lowth trod also in his father's footsteps, for the elder Lowth had worked extensively among the prophets and the small change of Jewish history. *The Genealogy of Christ* anticipates Lowth's lectures on Hebrew verse; and his other Winchester poem, *Katherine Hill* (1733), written in 1729 on the subject of the schoolboys' traditional recreation ground, anticipates his interest in English primitivism. Technically a "hill poem," it moved the reader's emotions by conjuring up not images of Oriental prophecy but of antique times in the Winchester locality.

It is doubtful that the "young bard," as Lowth calls himself in *Katherine Hill*, would have written these works if the Winchester program had not encouraged the writing of poetry. However, a thirst for new fashions is evident when we consider that the greater part of Lowth's day had been spent from the age of twelve in reading in Greek and Latin authors. These considerations suggest that, in the Age of Pope, vigorous young writers avoided the example of the established Augustan mode and that the primitivism both Oriental and Northern European which was to become so important a part of the Romantic movement, partially through the agency of Lowth and the Wykehamists, had its roots extremely early in the eighteenth century. It is important to observe that the "young bard" seemed conscious of current philosophy also and wove into his poetry some of the new ideas concerning perception which had been current in English thought since the publication of Bishop Berkeley's *A New Theory of Vision* (1709) and the *Principles of Human Knowledge* (1710); but we shall deal later with this aspect of primitivism.

Lowth went up to New College, the Oxford legacy of William of Wykeham, in 1729, already a published poet. His father was to die in 1732 at the age of seventy-two, and it was at this time that Robert began research for his *Life of William of Wykeham* (1758), his memorial to the Medieval father of the Wykehamist family. Two points might perhaps be made concerning this development. The first is that Lowth already seems to have been a rising star at Oxford as he had been at Winchester, for he was encouraged to make use of the archives concerning Wykeham both at Wykeham's two schools and at the Bishop's Palace in Winchester. The second point, one less certain but more intriguing, is that an interest in the sublimity of remote images of the past — one similar to that of Thomas Chatterton (1752-1770), writer of the supposed Medieval

"Rowley" poems — greatly stirred the young Lowth. A Medieval biography was an extremely ambitious project, then more so than now, for a twenty-year-old, even one as well placed as Lowth. Paternal figures seem to have played an important part in the young Lowth's attempts to make literature out of what were then regarded as the "first ages" of the world.

During the Cromwellian struggle between Parliament and Crown of the seventeenth century, Oxford had been a noted center of Royalist resistance. The Royalist and conservative taint of the past was a burden to Oxford in the first half of the eighteenth century, a time when the Stuart kings to whom Oxford had been loyal were replaced by the Hanoverian Georges, whose parliaments, mainly Whiggish, weakened the power of the monarchy. From the Restoration in 1660 to the advent of George I, Oxford had flowered in numerous ways. The momentum begun during these days continued, perhaps at levels unseen by the average undergraduate, with a remarkable driving force.

Oxford had received a definitive addition to her bricks and mortar which characterizes the city to this day. The Old Ashmolean Museum had been completed toward the end of the seventeenth century. The Sheldonian theater was the first work of Sir Christopher Wren (1632-1723). The nearby Radcliffe Library was built between 1737 and 1748. The Royal Society, the most influential intellectual institution in England's history, which was to change not only scientific thinking but the nature of ideas and literature during the century to come, had flourished first in Oxford. John Wilkins (1614-1672) of Wadham College had gathered around him the nucleus of the Royal Society in Oxford itself; and he had also attracted to Oxford the co-founder of the society, Robert Boyle (1627-1691), with his brilliant protégé, Robert Hooke (1635-1703), inventor of the famed wind pump.

Scientific activity fostered the travels of naturalists and anthropological observers to the lands of the East from which the Bible had come. One of the first names in Oxford Oriental studies is that of Christian Raue or Ravis (1613-1671), who had travelled extensively in Europe collecting Oriental manuscripts on behalf of the biblical chronologist Archbishop James Ussher (1581-1656). Author of an Oriental grammar himself, Ravis was influential in the development of a fount of Arabic print for the production of books in Arabic. We have mentioned above John Harris, council member of the Royal Society whose collection influenced William

Lowth's commentary on the prophets.

One of the most influential Oriental travellers who also belongs in the pantheon of great names of Oxford men was Edward Pococke (1604-1691). First Professor of Arabic in the university and, at the same time Professor of Hebrew, Pococke was a man of enormous pioneering influence. Early chaplain to the English merchants in Aleppo, Pococke visited Istanbul, spoke Arabic, founded the Bodleian library's Oriental collection with bequests of rare discernment, and produced, on the Oxford press's lately developed fount of Arabic characters, the *Specimen historiae Arabum* (1650), a collection of documents of inestimable importance in the study of the history of the Middle East.

The period which we are investigating is one during which the inherited structures of the past were demolished by scientific enquiry. The way in which practical enquiry whittled away the theological structure of scriptural mythology and replaced it with a cultural appreciation of the human milieu which had produced the Bible could not be suggested more succinctly than by one of Pococke's Biblical emendations. Micah 1:8 had read, "wailing like the dragons," but Pococke, having lived in the East, emended the phrase to read "howling like the jackals." It is indicative of the interrelation of academic Orientalism and literature that Joseph Trapp (1679-1747), first Professor of Poetry at Oxford (1708-18), quoted in his earliest lecture an ode on the death of Dr. Pococke by the poet Edmund Smith (1672-1710) as an example of the highest form of poetry, the Oriental ode.

In the Oxford to which Robert Lowth went in 1729 Orientalism based on supposed Biblical models had been the dominant new fashion for almost a quarter of a century. The Professorship of Poetry at Oxford, which was then as now a national platform from which literary policy was announced, had been founded in 1708, by a bequest made for that purpose by a Jesuit don of no other significance. From the start, this Professorship appears to have been influenced by current "scientific" notions of investigation into the origins of poetry, which it found to be in the earliest literature extant. The nature of man, it was assumed, lay hidden in his earliest beginnings: the nature of poetry similarly lay best preserved in the East, where apparently it had begun. Several of the ideas contained in Lowth's lectures in the middle of the century have at least their beginnings in the work of the early professors of poetry at Oxford. Joseph Trapp emphasized the superiority of Oriental poetry and its claim to first place in the development of literature. Thomas Warton the Elder followed Trapp in the Professorship; and, like Stephen Duck, Warton in his own poetry proclaimed the superiority of the Bible as a model for contemporary writers of feeling. Joseph Spence, whom we have mentioned as Lowth's close friend and Professor of Poetry from 1728 to 1738, made his name in a work of Classical criticism, *An Essay on Pope's Odyssey,* which incorporated concepts of Oriental literature in an examination of Classical epic.

Stepping outside the ranks of professors of poetry, we note that Lowth's fellow Wykehamist, Edward Young, a Fellow of All Souls College, Oxford until 1730, wrote Oriental plays, *Busiris, King of Egypt* (1719) and *The Revenge* (1721), and published an influential *Paraphrase on Part of the Book of Job* (1719) that incorporated Oriental concepts already propounded in *Guardian No. 86.* The explicit rejection of Classical in favor of Oriental models had begun to affect the foremost critics and writers of the day, and scholarship in national as well as Oriental beginnings was flourishing also at Oxford when Robert Lowth was an undergraduate. Thomas Hearne (1678-1735), an antiquarian and under librarian at the Bodleian library until his death, published early English manuscripts too numerous to list here; but they included *The Itinerary of John Leland* (1710-12), a history in Latin of the reign of Richard II by a monk of Evesham, and the histories of Edward I, II, and III by Walter Hemingford.

These works illuminated the period of Geoffrey Chaucer and of William of Wykeham, Lowth's benefactor, whose biography he began while at Oxford and published after the lectures on Hebrew poetry had made him famous. The study of Anglo-Saxon, familiarity with which is central to Lowth's *A Short Introduction to English Grammar* (1762), flourished also at Oxford. Elizabeth Elstob (1683-1756), niece of George Hickes (1642-1715) whose own Latin *Thesaurus of the Ancient Northern Languages* (1705) suggests the beginnings of the Gothic movement, not only edited Anglo-Saxon manuscripts in Oxford but published her own Anglo-Saxon grammar in Oxford in 1715.

From the beginning, eighteenth-century concepts of the primitive mind bore a close resemblance to modern philosophical theories of knowledge. In Shaftesbury's *Characteristics* (1711), to take but one example, there appear side by side an exposition of a highly influential theory of perception which influenced Romanticism and an account of the *flora* and *fauna* of North Africa which became a *locus classicus* of "sublime" writing. Among the many critics influenced by the epistemology of John Locke (1632-1704) was Joseph Addison (1672-1719). In 1712, Addison extensively praised Biblical personification in the Hebrew prophets; and he selected an example from Habakkuk, a minor Hebrew prophet, which was repeated by Lowth thirty years later.[19] Addison's admiration both for English primitivism and for Hebrew poetry in particular is well documented. As early as his Sheldonian Oration in 1693, the young Joseph Addison had suggested the application of the new scientific philosophy to theories of literature. The philosopher whose theories of knowledge seem to be most closely paralleled in the "Orientalism" of Spence, Trapp, Young, and, later, Lowth is George Berkeley, Bishop of Cloyne (1685-1753). Berkeley's epistemology posited a timeless world of matter, perceived creatively by the human mind in the same timeless, spaceless context as God. The Old Testament in its influence on English literature, most importantly here in the work of Robert Lowth, was similarly seen in purely mechanical, materialistic terms as an example of primitive cognition in early man, a prime example of the real psychology of knowledge drawn from humanity's best and earliest phase.

The death of Lowth's father in 1732 seems to have been followed by Robert's successful cultivation of Benjamin Hoadly, the Bishop of Winchester and the latest successor to the glories of Wykeham himself — and apparently Lowth's "father in God." The significance of Hoadly is clear when we compare the change in the church to what we might term the "disappearance of the unseen" that is noticeable in the literature of the period; for as W. E. H. Lecky, the nineteenth-century authority on the eighteenth, wrote in his *England in the Eighteenth Century,* "Appeals both to authority and to the stronger passions gradually ceased. The more doctrinal aspects of religion were softened down or suffered silently to recede, and, before the eighteenth century had much advanced, sermons had very generally become mere moral essays, characterised chiefly by a cold good sense, and appealing almost exclusively to prudential motives."[20] The demystification of religion was a movement parallel to the development of materialistic philosophy. In the weakening of theological authority, the Bishop of Winchester, Lowth's patron and present father of the Wykehamist family, led all the rest.

In 1714 on Queen Anne's death and the accession of George I,

Elector of Hanover, Hoadly had written a satirical preface to Richard Steele's (1672-1729) *Account of the Roman Catholic Religion* (1715) in which Hoadly ridiculed church authority, flattered the new king fulsomely, and earned the bishopric of Bangor in Wales, which he is said never to have visited during his six years of office, so intent was he on forwarding in London his Low Church principles. Around Hoadly sparked all the major factors in the battles between Tories and Whigs, High Church and Low Church. He was in the highest favor at court, and he was the Whigs' favorite churchman throughout their ascendancy as the "great Advocate of Civil and Religious Liberty" as Lowth would write — significantly placing "Civil" before "Religious" — in his Dedication to the *Life of William of Wykeham*.[21] Hoadly's pamphlet, the *Plain Account of the Nature and End of the Sacrament of the Lord's Supper* (1735), is instructive in this regard, for this work attempted to remove all mystery from the Last Supper and to present it as a mere commemorative ritual.

Hoadly had already confirmed Lowth in his first living at Overton, Hampshire, in 1735. This was the man who was the head of the Wykehamist family in 1741 when Lowth was elected, by a majority of the Masters of Arts of Oxford University, to the position of Professor of Poetry at Oxford. The Wykehamist support, according to Mark Pattison, secured the position for the brilliant young poet.[22] The emphasis of Lowth's lectures as Professor of Poetry — the non-theological nature of Hebrew poetry viewed only as primitive literature — not only corroborates the conclusion of Lowth's brief memorialists that Lowth was little interested in the religious truths of his profession,[23] but suggests the possibility that Hoadly supported Lowth, poet as well as churchman, in order to weaken at least partly the religious and spiritual impact of Holy Writ. Of Lowth's tenure as Professor of Poetry at Oxford, we have little contemporary evidence. Edward Gibbon (1737-1794) later wrote in his *Memoirs* (1796) that Lowth was a great teacher — one of the few, in Gibbon's jaundiced view, that Oxford could boast.[24] The lectures were published, in the Latin in which they were delivered, in a handsome quarto in 1753. The influence of the lectures may be suggested by the emergence, during their ten-year delivery, of Edward Young's *Night Thoughts* (1742-45), a prophetic Biblical "sublime" poem of sentiment which imitated the vision of Ezekiel; by the odes of Williams Collins (1747), Lowth's fellow Wykehamist, who also employed techniques of Biblical verse and of Ezekiel; and by the extreme praise of Christopher Smart (1722-1771) who later reviewed in his *Universal Visiter* (1756) the published lectures with special praise for Lowth's "sublime" translating of Hebrew poetry.

In 1747, Joseph Spence published his major work, *Polymetis* (1747), the result of years of visits to Italy. It is an interesting study of the personified figures of Classical art as they occurred in the plastic arts and in literature. Spence's book is indispensable to a grasp of theories of personification in the mid-eighteenth century; but it is especially significant to a study of Lowth since the Tenth Dialogue of the Fourth Book contains his long poem that is based on Xenophon's *Memorabilia* (*c.*400 B.C.) and that recounts Hercules' temptation by Virtue and Sloth. This poem is important to a study not only of personification in the mid-eighteenth century, but also of music because it was set to music by Lowth's contemporary, George Frederick Handel (1685-1759). Moreover Lowth's eminence in his mid-thirties suggests an interesting parallel with Hercules: he *was* a success and he must have seemed a tower of strength to his lesser acquaintances. Like Hercules, he too had rejected at an early date the wiles of Sloth and had opted for the more arcane seductions of Hard Work and Virtue.

In a time of Whig ascendancy, Lowth was allied closely with Bishop Hoadly, the most powerful Whig favorite in the church, and Lowth's rise to the third highest position in the Church of England, the bishopric of London, was due, partly, perhaps almost entirely, to his cultivation of ties with the most powerful Whig family in the land, the Cavendishes. Lowth's true political views are, nonetheless, difficult to ascertain. It is most likely that he was politically expedient. His family, while genteel, did not have impressive credentials at a time when rank was indispensable. He needed powerful friends, and he found them. He knew where power was, how to find it, and we surmise, used it for liberating ends.[25] Behind the politics of survival, we might discern in his own personality the mark of a radical conservative, not unlike the politician Charles James Fox (1749-1806).

In 1748, Lowth accompanied Henry Bilson-Legge (1708-1764) as chaplain on a mission to Berlin on behalf of the German interests of the English king. Bilson-Legge, a star in the Whig galaxy, had been a great favorite of the long-lived prime minister, Sir Robert Walpole (1676-1745), and also Lord Lieutenant of Ireland. Seldom out of office, Bilson-Legge, by his own admission, was the most

Whiggish of the Whigs' and, as such, he was intimate with Lowth's later and more generous patron, the Duke of Devonshire. Lowth's good fortune continued when, in 1749, he was chosen to accompany the young sons of the Duke of Devonshire, Lord George and Lord Frederick Cavendish on the Grand Tour of Europe. The Duke of Devonshire, one of the greatest landowners in the country and a leader of the ruling Whig party, had at his fingertips almost unlimited patronage not only because of his own activities but also those of his numerous sons and cousins. The Grand Tour was intended to finish the education of young noblemen who went with unlimited credit to visit the courts, great sites, and eccentrics of Europe before entering their usually political manhood. Spence's *Anecdotes* tell of Lowth discussing with a workman in St. Peter's Cathedral in Rome the size of Bernini's baffling pillars, with a basic thirst for knowledge and curiosity for details familiar to readers of Lowth, and of his translating inscriptions from Latin into English in Vicenza and Piacenza (or Placentia as it was then known).[26] Since Lowth's *Isaiah, A New Translation* (1778) refers to a hand-mirror from Herculaneum, the Roman town buried by volcanic ash then being excavated,[27] it seems likely that Lowth acquired this souvenir during his Italian tour with the youthful Cavendishes. We cannot help wondering with what well-judged permissiveness Lowth guided his charges, for Lowth's relationship with the Cavendishes never faltered.

Bishop Hoadly of Winchester apparently approved as strongly as Lowth's non-ecclesiastical protectors. Resigning his Fellowship at New College, and the Professorship of Poetry in 1750, on his return he was appointed Archdeacon of Winchester by Hoadly, a solid and influential rank in the Winchester hierarchy which for a less gifted or ambitious man — for example Lowth's father — might have seemed the peak of a career. When the older brother of Lowth's two charges on the Grand Tour, William Cavendish, Marquis of Hartington (1720-1764), became Lord Treasurer of Ireland in 1754, this "gilded youth" of thirty-four carried with him to Ireland an extensive train which included his brother Lord Frederick as an aide-de-camp. His family's one-time tutor, Archdeacon Lowth of Winchester was Hartington's chaplain. The following year Hartington became Lord Lieutenant of Ireland; and after the death of his father he succeeded to the dukedom of Devonshire in 1755 and to its princely estates and patronage. Not surprisingly, when a vacancy arose among the Irish bishops in 1755, the celebrated Archdeacon Lowth was offered the position.

The publication of Lowth's *De sacra poesi Hebraeorum praelectiones* in 1753 is an important publishing date in the eighteenth century. The lectures on the sacred poetry of the Hebrews earned their author not only a reputation as Europe's greatest authority on the earliest poetry written by man (as it was then thought) but also a doctorate of divinity from a grateful university. Writing in the middle of the nineteenth century, Mark Pattison (1813-1884) observed that the work symbolized the throwing off of the Jacobite sloth of the earlier part of the century at Oxford.[28] After Lowth, Oxford might vie with the achievements of the Hanoverian University of Göttingen, a university peculiarly competitive with Oxford since it was within the boundaries of King George's German possessions. The first edition of Lowth's lectures is in Latin; a beautiful book, it is a handsome, large quarto, generously spaced with quotations in Hebrew, Greek and Latin. It was one of the first works from the new Clarendon Press, which had been founded with the profits from the Earl of Clarendon's best-selling book on the history of the Cromwellian rebellion, *The History of the Rebellion* (1702-4). We might observe here two more of Pattison's observations on Lowth, — observations especially authoritative since Pattison was not only learned, but a knowledgeable Oxford man himself, don, professor and warden. Lowth's ability in Latin, Pattison had decided, made him the greatest English writer of Latin since Addison, that is, for some fifty years. He tells us, further, that Lowth's elegance of spoken and written style became not only proverbial, but also a catchword well into the nineteenth century.[29]

It seems apparent that in his middle years, Lowth saw himself as destined for high office. In 1752, at the age of forty-two, he married Mary Jackson of Christchurch in Hampshire, an alliance that tied him more closely to local Winchester interests but one that, if it gave the future Bishop of London a family (of seven children only two of whom survived their father), hardly became the center of his extremely creative life. The choice that Lowth made on being offered the bishopric of Limerick in 1755 by his patron, the young Duke of Devonshire, Lord Lieutenant of Ireland, might be interpreted as that of a man who saw himself as going far: he chose to wait in a less important status in a strategically sounder location, for he rejected the chance of an Irish bishopric for a canon's seat and a rectory at Durham in the North of England. The preferment to Durham was especially portentous; for it was here

that Lowth first came into open competition with a canon of very
different background with whom he would fight in a literary battle
of the giants, William Warburton (1698-1779), Alexander Pope's
literary executor. William Warburton, the clumsy and belligerent
author of *The Divine Legation of Moses* (1738-41), which was a
lumber room of largely Oriental learning, felt ignored in Lowth's
Praelectiones. He chose to fight Lowth on the national stage, and
each published appendices or pamphlets against the other. The
affair became so notorious that the king asked Samuel Johnson
(1709-1784) his opinion of the matter in the famous interview in the
royal library.[30] Apparently to block the younger Lowth's promotion to bishop, Warburton finally and damagingly accused Lowth
of treason — of preferring the Stuart Pretender to King George.
Lowth triumphed over Warburton with one of the most thrilling
and devastating rejoinders in English literature in his *Letter to the
Right Reverend Author of the Divine Legation* (1765).

In Lowth's battle with Warburton, we must note two things. One
is that Warburton had come to fame as the defender of Pope's
Essay on Man (1733-34) against the charge of Deism. In Warburton's fight, ostensibly about the date of Job and the pre-eminent
position in this field of learning, the true issues did not come to the
fore. As Mark Pattison points out, of the two contestants for a
bishopric, Warburton was the older, less privileged man from a
background poorer than Winchester and New College.[31] But, fundamentally, Warburton and Lowth represented in their opposition
the beginning and the middle of the eighteenth century. Warburton
belonged to the earlier tradition which perceived allegory in all
things and which defended the supernatural or mysterious nature
of the universe. In spite of occasional "Deism," Warburton alone
was *the* authority on God's unseen purpose. The whole tendency of
Lowth's life, on the other hand, was materialistic. His interest in
ancient phenomena was that of an Addison, a Burke, or a modern
linguist; for Lowth was fundamentally obsessed with psychological
phenomena and with the reality of words in the cognitive mechanism. Warburton did not know, as "they say," the league in which
he was playing. In addition, we may note that Lowth was a
humanistic Wykehamist, brought up on Grotius rather than on
theology, a follower of Hoadly, who saw religion apparently as
good manners rather than as eternal salvation. Warburton, far
from elegant, seems to have believed the Christian "truths."

Among the reactions to the publication of Lowth's *De sacra poesi Hebraeorum praelectiones* was that of Christopher Smart (1722-1771), who was already the poet of more than a dozen poems, including *On the Eternity of the Supreme Being* (1750). The two works on the basis of which he is now considered a great poet — *A Song to David* (1763) and his *Jubilate Agno,* first published as *Rejoice in the Lamb* (1939) in the present century — were still to come; and both of these poems — Hebraic in pattern, clearly Biblical in conception and essentially "Romantic" — owed much to Lowth's lectures. As for Lowth's translation in his lectures from the original Hebrew into Latin of Isaiah 14 (the ode on the downfall of the king of Babylon), Smart, like Joseph Warton[32] some years later, found it to be one of the most sublime literary performances for over a hundred years. We might observe that, while Smart's dependence on Lowth's analysis of Hebrew parallelism is now recognized, the extent of his borrowing has still to be determined. It seems highly likely that Smart benefited from a number of the poetic insights of Lowth, not just one. Furthermore, it is clear that Smart was especially interested in the theories of perception and in the linguistic connotations of Berkeley's philosophy. Smart's simultaneous use of ancient Biblical patterns and also his Berkeleyan epistemology that was derived from the science of his own century point to a similar combination in Lowth.

The opening paragraph of the Dedication to Lowth's *Life of William of Wykeham* (1758), a work for which he had begun research in earnest as an undergraduate almost thirty years earlier, reads: "The great and good man, of whose life I have given an authentic, however imperfect, account, in the most earnest and solemn manner recommended his two Colleges, that is, his Estate, his Family, his Children, his dearer Self, to the care and protection of his successors the Bishops of Winchester." Lowth's *Life of Wykeham* is essentially a Romantic work. In one of the earliest of Medieval biographies, a genre not possible before the work of the antiquarians of the seventeenth and eighteenth centuries, Lowth sets out to create a picture of the unique reality of the times of Wykeham — to deal with the "particulars" of life in the era of Chaucer in accordance with the views of Lowth's friend, Joseph Spence, in his *Essay on Pope's Odyssey,* and in Joseph Warton's *Essay on Pope.*[33] Since the "pre-Romantic" nucleus of Winchester College crystallized so much of the Romantic esthetic, it is especially interesting to observe in this Wykehamist essay in Gothic writing, the fashionable Medievalism which later surfaced in such works as Samuel Taylor Coleridge's *Christabel* (1798, 1800), John Keats' *Eve of St. Agnes* (1819), and Walter Scott's *Ivanhoe* (1820).

It is significant also to observe that Lowth's glowing words are addressed to Benjamin Hoadly, to whom the *Life of Wykeham* is dedicated. Hoadly, we have observed, had been Bishop of Winchester for the past thirty odd years and was to die in 1761. Fathers — first his natural father, in whose footsteps Lowth followed as writer and churchman; William of Wykeham, his Medieval benefactor; and Benjamin Hoadly, Bishop of Winchester, Wykeham's latest successor—played a large part in Lowth's life. Lowth, indeed, admits publicly the parental role of Hoadly in the Wykehamist family: "Your Lordship hath long executed the Trust ... devolved upon you in such a manner as demands the most grateful acknowledgements of those societies: You have treated them upon all occasions with all the tenderness of an indulgent parent."[34]

But another event occurs in this short dedication, one which is of intriguing significance to politically sensitive minds: Lowth makes public also his independence from Hoadly. Lowth had carefully become a canon of Durham, at the other end of the country from Winchester; and he had recently been made a chaplain to the king. He praises Hoadly sturdily for refusing to accept a decision of the Fellows of Winchester in an election for the wardenship — or headship — of Winchester College, a controversy in which he himself played a large part as a result of this very preface, and in which he showed himself to be capable of protecting the rules and regulations of Wykeham's legacy. To Hoadly he apologizes, publicly, for his removal from his patronage. After Lowth acknowledges his many obligations to the Bishop of Winchester he asserts that "These obligations he [Lowth] is now the more ready thus publickly to acknowledge, as he is removed out of the reach of further favours of the like kind. And tho' he hath relinquished the advantages so generously conferred upon him, yet he shall always esteem himself highly honoured in having once enjoyed the patronage of the great Advocate of Civil and Religious Liberty.[35]

In *William of Wykeham,* Lowth might be seen as laying to rest the ghosts of his several "father figures." He had, in a manner of speaking, paid his debt to William of Wykeham, whose Medieval creativeness and wealth had molded his own life in the mid-eighteenth century. At the same time he acknowledged and parted from Benjamin Hoadly, who had also faithfully nurtured Lowth's growth. The timing of these movements, like the publication of a book in his middle years, suggests some kind of deep process at work which settled ancient debts, renounced early models, and thus opened the way for the successes of his later years which equalled and even outdistanced the achievements of his mentors as well as those of his actual father.

Lowth is one of the few "pre-Romantic" figures in English literature to have earned a significant European reputation during his own lifetime. At the Hanoverian University of Göttingen flourished one of the greatest figures of the European Enlightenment, the Oriental scholar Johann David Michaelis (1717-1791). In 1758, Michaelis produced the first volume of his own edition of Lowth's *De sacra pöesi Hebraeorum;* in 1761, the second. Michaelis, the first great annotator of Lowth, disagreed with Lowth on a number of points; but his recognition of him is interesting for two major factors. First of all, Michaelis, a contemporary, saw Lowth, not as a churchman *or* even as a professor, but as a poet speaking about poetry.[36] Tying the poet Lowth firmly to the movement of sensibility of the eighteenth century, Michaelis observed secondly that Lowth made the reader understand beauty not through reason but through feeling. This contemporary corroboration that relates Lowth's Orientalism to the eighteenth-century poetry of feeling is crucial; for as Michaelis wrote we "admire him and follow him like some oriental Orpheus."

Lowth's major link with German theorists on the nature of the earliest societies, and hence on the nature of language and poetry, was in his influence on Johann von Herder. His limited but crucial contribution to that German philosopher's *Vom geist der Ebräischen poesie* or *Spirit of Hebrew Poetry* (1783) gives him an important place in the tributaries of European Romantic thought. The major image which the European Enlightenment bequeathed to the Romantic era proper was that of earliest (and hence latest) man as myth-maker in his own right — as an autonomous creator of simultaneous language, poetry, and gods. In spite of token references to "heaven" and "the Creator," Lowth's work is in the major movement towards the European concept of the *volksgeist,* the concept, fashionable not only in Germany, of the first imaginative formation of unique societies by unaided man in the world's first dawn.

The last work of Lowth's life, his *Isaiah, A New Translation* (1778) is of the greatest importance to eighteenth-century Orientalism. The long preface offers an additional exposition and corroboration of his theories of parallelism first aired thirty years before at Oxford. The importance of Oriental prophecy in the eighteenth century is suggested by the overwhelming success of George Frederick Handel, especially his oratorio *The Messiah* (1741), a work in which the prophets and Isaiah particularly figure prominently. In publishing his translation of Isaiah at the age of sixty-eight, Lowth, the major authority in the field, not only was returning to the scene of one of his greatest triumphs — for both Christopher Smart and Joseph Warton had written that Lowth's translation of Isaiah 14, the prophetic ode, was one of the sublimest achievements of the century — he also was producing what he might well have viewed as his final effort in the field which had brought him solid fame. Lowth translated and the printer set Isaiah solely and simply as a great poem. The impression the reader gathers is more like that of reading T.S. Eliot's *Waste Land* (1922) than of encountering Holy Writ. Lowth's very detailed notes, several times longer than the body of the prophetic book itself, are a mine of arcane images of the sensuality of an Oriental bazaar; but these notations also suggest the establishment of that broad tradition of interest in the Middle East in general which became so fertile an area of sensibility for English writers both during the Romantic era and afterwards. Such examples spring to mind as Walter Savage Landor's *Gebir* (1798), S. T. Coleridge's *Kubla Khan* (1816), and Percy Bysshe Shelley's *Ozymandias* (1818). In later years, the stream broadened to include such examples as Charles Doughty's *Arabia Deserta* (1888) and T. E. Lawrence's *Seven Pillars of Wisdom* (1922).

Eighteenth-century scholars did not make the distinction which late nineteenth-century and twentieth-century Christianity has made, between the Judaeo-Christian tradition on the one hand and the Arab and Moslem tradition on the other. The highly educated, frequently learned men of the Anglican Church in the eighteenth century, who were markedly different from the Nonconformist preachers of the nineteenth and twentieth centuries, assumed that the background of Judaism was shared by the neighboring civilizations. Furthermore, the enormously significant explorations of the eighteenth century, which were to an interesting degree spurred by the scientific movement and by the Royal Societies of Europe, indiscriminately found in Syria, Persia, Lebanon, and Egypt enlightening evidence for the illumination of the earliest writers. The especially imaginative area of "timeless" literature which was named "Orientalism" was a *mélange* of mental habits and fantasies of varying but not exclusive kinds. The shift from a religious acceptance of the Old Testament to a view of it as a secular mine of cultural exotica that illuminated the Middle East in general occurred in Lowth's own life-time and, perhaps, largely because of his influence. Over and over again, in the book *George Frederic Handel* (1966), the musicologist, Paul Henry Lang, remarks on the totally theatrical and operatic nature of all of Handel's oratorios, "Oriental" in just the same way as Lowth's primitive poetry. It is only *since* the eighteenth century that "adventitious sanctity"[37] has begun to adhere to Handel's works in which Lang finds no religious abstraction whatsoever. The same point must be made of Lowth's *Isaiah,* the culmination of a career, for as Michaelis had observed of the lectures, nowhere is there a religious abstraction. At every line *Isaiah* speaks of the eighteenth-century sensibility's interest in the clear outline of comprehensive every-day images which appeal to the senses alone.

One example suggests the total effect of Lowth's translation, a work extraordinarily distinct from, for example, his father's treatment of the prophets in his *Commentary* some three-quarters of a century before. To Isaiah 3:21, William Lowth had added, as we have seen, a single paragraph in which, prophetic of things to come, he had appended an allusion to the writings of St. Augustine, and to the *Travels* of John Harris of the Royal Society. To the same phrase, which he gives as "jewels of the nostril," Robert Lowth, the Grand Tourist who had seen Bernini's pillars in Rome and had picked up a hand mirror from Herculaneum, gives two pages of observation. Quoting Nicholas Schroeder (1721-1798), the German Biblical scholar, Lowth distinguishes between jewelry on the forehead which hung down to the nose and objects actually placed *in* or *on* the nose.[38] Lowth cites at considerable length the contemporary French traveler Paul Lucas (1664-1737) whose second *Voyage to the Levant* (1719) described at length Persian women of the Euphrates basin who bored holes in their noses for the insertion of rings.[39]

Leaving the Frenchman, Robert Lowth then turns to one of his favorite authorities, the Italian Pietro della Valle (1586-1652) who had married a Lebanese woman and who had recorded the following about his Arab wife's ornaments,

The ornaments of gold, and of jewels, for the head, for the neck, for the arms, for the legs, and for the feet, (for they wear rings even on their toes) are indeed, unlike those of the Turks, carried to great excess; but not of

great value: for in Baghdad jewels of high price either are not to be had, or
are not used; and they wear such only as are of little value; as turquoises,
small rubies, emeralds, carbuncles, garnets, pearls, and the like. My
spouse dresses herself with all of them according to their fashion; with
exception however of certain ugly rings of very large size, set with jewels,
which in truth very absurdly, it is the custom to wear fastened to one of
their nostrils, like buffalos.[40]

This long disquisition on the Persian and Lebanese fashions in
jewelry sounds infinitely more like the travel books written in the
next two hundred years by curious but genteel tourists than it does,
for example, like a Biblical commentary of an authority attempting
to sharpen men's belief in salvation. We need only compare the following remarks by Doreen Ingrams, a mid-twentieth-century
traveler among Arab women in Yemen, who observed precisely the
same fashions in jewelry and who drew precisely the same comparison between Arab women with rings in their noses and animals as
had Lowth in 1778: "Strangest of all was their custom of wearing
an ordinary finger ring of silver or gold with a stone in it through
one nostril, a most unattractive adornment without any of the
exotic charm of the gold stud worn by Indian women. Shfa [a
friend] was no exception and had a large ring jutting out of her nostril like an animal ready to be led to market."[41] Sensuality, not
spirit; human exotica, not divine; and anthropology, not theology
join the late eighteenth- and the twentieth-century interest in the
Orient; and they suggest to readers of, for example, Christopher
Smart exactly the kind of intensely sensual pleasure in rare material
things which characterizes eighteenth-century "Biblical" poetry.

The enthusiasm of John Wilkes (1727-1797) lends credence to
this view. In 1764 the enterprising editor of the Parisian *Gazette
Littéraire de L'Europe* had the idea of engaging Wilkes, the notorious libertine (not to say pornographer) and London demagogue,
to review the second Oxford edition of Lowth's lectures. While
escaping prosecution by Parliament in London, Wilkes, the popu-
lace's symbol of "Liberty," wrote of Lowth's secular analysis of
Oriental poetry as a liberating achievement that was apparently
after his own heart.

Lowth's English reputation was secured in 1765 by his election to
the Royal Society in London. The firmness of his European fame
was confirmed in the same year by simultaneous election to the
Royal Society of Göttingen, in Germany. In 1765 Lowth became
Fellow of the two Royal Societies, and finished off William War-

burton in his famous and, to Warburton, humiliating *Letter*. A less confident man than Lowth might have begun to worry about the retribution of the gods, for his political patrons formed in the same year the national government. The way was set for a bishopric for the most brilliant Wykehamist of his day when the first vacancy should occur.

Lowth's enthusiasm for primitive civilizations found yet another expression. It is noteworthy that the boys of Winchester College did not study English grammar in the eighteenth century. Robert Lowth, Professor of Poetry at Oxford University, wrote and lectured in Latin. The rise of the vernacular was a major event of the middle of the eighteenth century. It is interesting to observe that, in the introduction to his *Short Introduction to English Grammar* (1762), Robert Lowth emphasized that a study of the grammar of the English tongue was *not,* even at that late date, part of the education of English children. Lowth was concerned to stress — in terms John Locke had used about the nature of the English language in Book III, Chapter vii of the *Essay Concerning Human Understanding* (1690) — that English, far from following the Latinate constructions, of, for example, the prose of Samuel Johnson, depended almost exclusively on prepositions. In describing English as a Northern European, indeed, Teutonic language, Lowth's *Grammar,* by far his best-selling work and one of the most widely-used grammar books of all time in England and America, was part of the massive shift which accompanied the Romantic revolution that led away from Classical forms to native linguistic roots. As in Lowth's Oriental and Medieval work, we observe again that his *Grammar* was a significant contribution to the primitive movement. Quoting Chaucer and giving instance after instance of Anglo-Saxon and Medieval word forms, Lowth cites the great linguists of the Royal Society, such as John Wilkins, the co-founder of the Royal Society and an authority on Icelandic and the Lapland tongue, and George Hickes the author of the *Anglo-Saxon and Moeso-Gothic Grammar.*

"On the bench of bishops, as every where else, the first step is the hardest. From thence each other advance follows with comparative ease,"[42] observed *The Gentleman's Magazine* in its obituary of Lowth in 1787. In 1763, the prime minister was the Duke of Bedford, who ran the government with the aid of George Grenville. Ostensibly, the government was Whig; but as the great statesman William Pitt (1708-1778) observed, its policies made it essentially

Tory. George III at the age of twenty-seven had been on the throne
three years since 1760, and was highly inexperienced. This inexperience had no doubt led to his agreeing to the infamous Regency
bill by which his own mother was excluded from power should the
king's mental derangement re-appear. Bitter resentment at this
exclusion now drove George closer to madness. Widespread riots
heightened the peril; and the king, unable to gain the cooperation
of William Pitt, turned to the main body of the Whigs. William,
fourth Duke of Devonshire, who had taken Lowth to Ireland in
1754, died in 1764, the year before the fall of Bedford's government; and the king called for the aid of the Whigs under their new
leader, the young Lord Rockingham.

In a century punctuated by incapable statesmen, Rockingham's
aristocratic incompetence was remarkable. But, from Lowth's
point of view, Rockingham's talents were immaterial since he
brought with him the great Whig families which had dominated
English politics since almost the beginning of the century. In the
words of W. E. H. Lecky, "the great family connection of the
Cavendishes, and many other Whig nobles distinguished only for
their wealth and position, joined the ministry, which represented all
that remained unbroken and unchanged of the powerful party
which in the last two reigns had governed the country."[43] In the
new administration, Lord John Cavendish (1732-1796), a highly lit-
erate and cultivated brother of the Cavendishes whom Lowth had
taken to Europe on the Grand Tour, became one of the Lords of the
Treasury and a member of the Privy Council. As *The Gentleman's
Magazine* put it, "in the administration ... Lowth's friends par-
ticipating largely, he was the first bishop that they made."[44] With
Hoadly recently dead (1761) we may surmise that the members of
the new Whig government wished to strengthen its position in the
House of Lords, where the bishops voted, and saw in Lowth a new
"Advocate of Civil and Religious Liberty." The ministry lasted only
a year, but in that time Lowth became first, Bishop of St. David's
in Wales, and, second, after only a few months, he moved in 1766
to the more important bishopric at Oxford — to the university city
in which he had been Professor of Poetry fifteen years before.

In 1777 Lowth was appointed to the highest ecclesiastical office
in the land (after the archbishops of Canterbury and York), the
bishopric of London. He was privy to political decision-making at
the highest level during the years of the American War of Independence, not only as a member of His Majesty's Privy Council and

Dean of the Chapel Royal, but also as administrator in charge of the colonial churches, a traditional responsibility of the see of London. It seems highly probable that Lowth's reputation for insight and strength gained him the position precisely because of the American situation. Before 1777 Lowth had corresponded with Dr. Samuel Johnson (1696-1772), head of King's College, New York, later Columbia University, which was then a seminary for the training of clergymen. The few letters from Lowth to Johnson in Yale University library give few details, but they confirm a vital link.

In 1783, Lord Rockingham was again in power; and Lowth's old friend and patron, Lord John Cavendish, was appointed Chancellor of the Exchequer. Lowth, then seventy-three years of age and suffering from the stone, rejected an offer of the Archbishopric of Canterbury, the highest church office in the land. This final recognition speaks of a nearly perfect career in the church. Lowth was not the Bishop of Winchester like his mentors, but there is little doubt that he was the most accomplished Wykehamist of his day and could well think of himself as a parent to the Wykehamist family. Lowth, who is especially illuminating in his *Life of Wykeham* about the impeccable shrewdness of Wykeham's grasp of law, showed himself to be a typically Wykehamist administrator. Coolness, manipulatory skills of the highest order, and extraordinary aggressiveness mark Lowth's administration as clearly as they did Wykeham's.

During his tenure of the bishopric of London, a very famous case took place which Lowth won by a hairsbreadth. In 1783, Lowth discovered that a gentleman named Ffytche, owner of a village and a benefice named Woodham Walter, had accepted from the clergyman to whom Ffytche offered the living a bond for three thousand pounds. When Lowth decided to fight this ancient abuse of "resignation bonds," Ffytche accepted the challenge. The case went against Lowth twice — in the Court of Common Pleas and in the higher court, the Court of King's Bench — and it was only technically possible for Lowth to take the case to the supreme court of the land, the House of Lords itself, of which Lowth, as Bishop of London, was an influential member. Of the thirty-six normal votes involved, eighteen of them were from bishops; the others were landowners who might be expected to vote against church interests. But a thirty-seventh vote — that of the Lord Chancellor, who presided at sittings — could be cast. The Lord Chancellor, Edward

Thurlow (1731-1806) was whiggish and also sympathetic to literature through his friendship with the poet William Cowper (1731-
1800). In the very last time that bishops spoke and voted as judges
in the House of Lords, Lowth won his case by Thurlow's one vote,
abolishing forever an abuse going back to Wykeham's times. In
Letter to the Clergy of the Diocese in 1784, Lowth explained that he
had proceeded "with the utmost caution." He had ". . . consulted
certain persons of the highest authority, both in Civil and Ecclesiastical Law," a phrase which might well point to Thurlow.

It is sad to have to observe that Robert Lowth, whose literary
and public career had been so resoundingly successful, seems to
have ended his life bowed by family and physical burdens. Five of
his seven children died before him, although his wife Margaret survived him into the nineteenth century until 1803. In his later years
he was attacked by the gout and by a case of the stone so severe that
when he was opened up after his death, eleven stones, one of great
size, were removed, as the Reverend Peter Hall, his memorialist,
records. Lowth was buried with great honors, in a vault at Fulham
in 1787; and in this same year his *Lectures on the Sacred Poetry of
the Hebrews* was translated by George Gregory (1754-1808). The
greatest single work on the nature of eighteenth-century primitive
poetry then became available in the vernacular which Lowth had
worked hard to perfect.

CHAPTER 2

The Professors of Poetry and the Oriental Tradition to the Mid-Century

IN Thomas Hearne's memoirs for July 14, 1708, he noted that "on Friday last the Statutes were read in Convocation and approved of for a Professorship of Poetry founded by Mr. Birkhead of All Souls Coll. and this day was a Convocation at 9 o'clock for electing a Professor, when Mr. Trapp of Wadham Coll. a most ingenious honest gent. & every wasy deserving of the place (he being but in mean circumstances) was chosen without any opposition to the satisfaction of the whole University."[1] The first Professor of Poetry was perhaps, "ingenious," and his appointment was supported by the university's Vice-Chancellor Lancaster. In its broadest sense, "honest" is open to some doubt; for Hearne returned to his original entry within the year to add that "it must however be observed that this Mr. Trapp is somewhat given to cringing and is a great commender of the tricks of Lancaster."[2]

The Professorship of Poetry continues to attract some interesting minds to this day, for this position has been occupied by men like Lowth, John Keble, Matthew Arnold, and in modern times, Robert Graves. Hearne notes laconically that the first lecture ever given by a poetry professor at Oxford was on "Oct. 19 (tu.). This day at 3 o'clock Mr. Trapp of Wadham our Poëtical Lecturer read the first time in the Natural Philosophy Schole, ... the drift of his lecture was in praise of poetry, and he concluded with a very short but flattering compliment on our Vice-Chancellor, who without doubt was pleased with it."[3] The fact that the lectures were delivered in "the Schole of Natural Philosophy" perhaps suggests the nature of the new departure in literary criticism since "Natural Philosophy" was the term equivalent to the modern portmanteau word "science." In the last half-century, men like Robert Boyle, Isaac Newton, and William Harvey, not to mention Thomas Burnet and

47

scores of lesser enquirers, had changed the intellectual climate of England and the concept of "Truth." The "real" nature and origins of all natural phenomena were to be investigated, scientifically.

The following Renaissance account of the origins of poetry is not "true" in a modern sense. Julius Caesar Scaliger, the famous father of a more celebrated son, described in this fashion the history of the growth of poetry in his *Poetics:* "First, there was that pristine, crude, and uncultivated age, of which only a vague impression remains" and of which "no name survives, unless it be that of Apollo, as the originator of poetry." "Then there is the second and venerable period, when religion and the mysteries are first sung. Among the poets of this period are numbered Orpheus, Musaeus, and Linus; Plato includes Olympus also. Of the third period Homer is the founder and parent...."[4] Apart from their exclusively Greek character, these origins of poetry seem unlikely since Apollo is a doubtful contender as the first poet; Orpheus, Musaeus, and Linus are figures only a little less shadowy; and although Homer in the third period is recognizable, did no other person compose verse at an earlier time? The truth in Julius Caesar Scaliger's beginnings of literary history is, of course, "deductive"; for he patterns the past according to what he hopes to be true — that poetry is divine, mythic, and epic. Alexander Pope also notably claims Orpheus, Musaeus, and Linus as the originators of poetry in his *Homer.*[5]

Trapp's eighteenth-century aim is different; for, working in a scientific age and milieu, he wishes to discover the "real" beginnings of poetry. The "origin and nature" of poetry was a double concept which Trapp had inherited from his major European authority, Vossius,[6] and he used it as the title of his second lecture. Curiously the new perspective made enquirers identify the best with a localized spot in time, and the beginning of eighteenth-century scientific criticism foreshadowed not only a poetry which would tend increasingly toward particularity but also a kind of historical criticism that moved in the same direction.

Like his contemporaries, Trapp was absorbed by the awareness of a "real" world that was thought to be six thousand years old; and this belief influenced his dating the origin of the art of poetry to the time of the Creation: "Poetry is co-eval with the world itself." Furthermore, "the Creator may be said in working up and finishing his beautiful poem of the universe, to have performed the part of poet, no less than that of a geometrician."[7] Convinced, like the Wykehamists, of the superiority of the most antique verse, Trapp approached the conclusion which afforded later poets, for example Collins, their most characteristic passages — that all poetry is mysteriously akin to the imaginative act which God performed in creating the world on the first day; therefore the existence, Trapp implied, of even material nature depended, as in the philosophy of Bishop Berkeley, on its being (creatively) seen.

Although Julius Caesar Scaliger is one of Trapp's occasional authorities, he avoided the account of the three ages of poetry outlined by that polymath; but loyally following Vossius into the underworld of literary history, Trapp noted that Orpheus, Linus, and Musaeus were not true, mythic figures. "The *Greeks*," he states scathingly, "who to their own refined taste ascribe the origin of all learning and arts, laid claim, likewise, to this, and instanced in *Orpheus, Linus,* and *Musaeus,* as the first poets."[8] Modern etymology derived from Europe and specifically from Vossius' *De artis poeticae natura, ac constitutione* (1647), had shown that these three mythic poets (with the exception of Apollo and perhaps Cadmus and the Muses, the fountainheads of Classical and Renaissance literary history) not only did not exist but were derived, like all other literary culture, from a source more Eastern. "Vossius proves it very probable that this Triumvirate of Poetry never existed; and that they are not proper, but common names, derived from the old **Phoenician** language."[9] In Trapp's second and third closely follows the general outline of "the Sublime" in other writers such as Thomas Burnet, Edward Young, and Edmund Burke; for the **Israelites**, not only before the Trojan War, but before the coming of Cadmus into Boeotia, who first taught the *Greeks* the use of letters."[10]

It is exciting to see the scientific demolition of bodies of myth which had served men for centuries — indeed, Pope's reassertion of Orpheus, Linus, and Musaeus was not to be made for several more years — for the event indicates a seismological shift in the most profound strata of imagination at which men deal with the largest questions, such as that of the nature of the past. The rearrangement of poetical-historical images which Trapp's lectures suggested closely follows the general outline of "the Sublime" in other writers such as Thomas Burnet, Edward Young, and Edmund Burke; but the Biblical poets who were writing at the Dawn of Creation apprehended Eternity through Nature. Job and David the Psalmist, wrote sublime poetry. Professor Trapp exclaimed, "If in the poems of Job, and David, and other sacred authors, we observe the inexpressible Sublimity of their words and matter, their elegant and more than human descriptions; the happy boldness of their metaphors ... triumphing, as it were, by a royal authority, over the narrow rules of mortal writers, it is impossible but we must in transport own, that nothing is wanting in them, that might be expected from the strength of poetry heightened by the energy of inspiration."[11]

Joseph Trapp was aware of the need to point to Oriental, Hebrew poetry that was different from that composed by Greek and Roman writers and by their admirers in contemporary Europe. He seems to have detected that at the heart of the Oriental, primitive spirit, original poetry had little to do with Mnemosyne, the mother of the Greek-born Muses; original poetry was closer to the motions and to the freer form of music than it was to the rational activity of man's mind. Early in Trapp's exposition of the origin and nature of verse, he pointed to a musical tradition several thousand years older than the Graeco-Roman civilizations. "And tho' we were utterly ignorant of what is mentioned concerning the Hebrew poetry," he noted, "yet the antiquity of music would teach us that the original of verse must be owing to the oriental nations; for little doubt is to be made but singing began in the very infancy of the world."[12]

Poetry, singing, and the earliest man were later identified in a single reality by the greatest philosophers of the mature Romantic movement, such as Johann von Herder; for the view that "Man is an animal that sings" was to be one of the movement's most profound conclusions.[13] In Trapp's lectures delivered as early as 1708, he made the same claim the fulcrum of his historical innovation. Like Vossius, his real aim was to suggest that Adam was a poet; but farther back than Jubal, inventor of music, Trapp could not, however, go. Vossius had termed Jubal, *"ipsius Adami trinepos fuerit,"*[14] which had some sense of "grandson"; but Trapp's translators call him "the seventh from Adam,"[15] which hardly captures the excitement of propinquity, although the idea remains. "This is farther confirmed," Trapp explained, "from what we read of Jubal, the seventh from Adam, who is styled the father of such as handle the harp and organ. Anciently, then, musicians and poets were the same."[16]

Jubal's particular skill, and invention, had been the lyre. It is not surprising that, for Trapp, the kind of poetry most poetical, "as distinct, both in style and thought, from the rest" of poetry, "as poetry in general is from prose,"[17] is the lyric. Trapp claimed that the Hebrews taught the Greeks not only the pastoral form — much of Theocritus, Trapp says in his lecture on pastoral, is borrowed from "the Song of Solomon"[18] — but also the supreme lyrical form, the ode, which was to be extraordinarily popular during the Romantic movement. We might note here that the mid-century Pindaric ode as practiced, for example, by Collins and Gray gained a peculiar power in suggesting Oriental images and the "sublime" oneness of the Creation and the poet's creative imagination. The main characteristic of lyric poetry was a kind of musical liberty and wayward progression: "it abounds with a sort of liberty which consists in digressions and excursions."[19] Trapp reminded his Classically-oriented listeners that "Pindar set his successors this example, in so much that this style, when applied to odes, is generally called Pindaric." "Not that he is to be esteemed the inventory of it: for it is plain that he, and the rest of the *Grecians*, received their learning from the nations of the East, the *Jews* and the *Phoenicians*."[20]

Pope's neo-Classical verse, which "imitates" Classical writers, makes the reader experience as a major effect the time dividing the eighteenth century in England from, for example, Virgil in first-century Rome. While alluding, Pope always alludes *back* to some distant moment. The step by step progress of Pope's couplets gives a sense of rational advance through equal moments of perception, a technique which Coleridge called a "conjunction-disjunctive,"[21] and one which reinforces the reader's dependence on sequences of time. The writer of Oriental poetry in the eighteenth century, on the other hand, gave the reader the impression that time did not separate the contemporary world from, for example, Job or Ezekiel, who seemed to exist, like the poem, in a prophetic, original moment. Edward Young, Christopher Smart, and William Blake deliberately set out to avoid also, a sense of temporal progress in the form of their poetry. They depended on a kind of "parallelism" of thought, in which one idea did not "follow" another but appeared in a sublime structure of simultaneity. The major significance of Trapp's *Praelectiones poeticae,* apart from his inauguration of Orientalism in eighteenth-century English poetry, is that they make a forthright claim for a formal organization of Oriental poetry which anticipates the major principle which Robert Lowth was later to popularize as "parallelism."

As distinct from lesser forms of poetry as poetry is from prose, the lyric ode — created, Trapp assumed, in the dawn of Creation by poets like Jubal — reflected the fundamental *penetralia* of the mind of man in intercourse with Nature in a "sublime" state. "Odes, therefore, and poetry, date their original from the same era: and, in truth, if we consider the internal motions of the soul, it will seem very probable that poetry, which is so peculiarly adapted to express the several Emotions of Joy, or Praise, or Gratitude, owes its rise to Nature herself."[22] As an example of the organization of the ode, Trapp selected a contemporary ode composed in Latin by "Mr Edmund Smith of Christ Church, Oxon," about the death of Dr. Edward Pococke (1604-1691), the first professor of Arabic (1636) in the university. Samuel Johnson claimed in his "Life" of Edmund Smith to have known the Pococke ode by heart and Johnson concluded that this poem was unequalled among "modern writers."[23] Although out of the reach of most modern readers, *"Pococki"* may be supposed to have been a very good piece of Latin verse. Its peculiar interest, however, lies in its position at the heart of English Orientalism; in its approach to principles of parallel composition; and in Trapp's implication that contemporary English experience and men may, with a "sublime" disregard of Time, become one with the ancient East in the discursive, indirect form of the ode. A few lines from the English translation of Trapp's lectures suggest the ode's character:

> Now Ninus' walls you search with curious eye,
> Now Babel's Tower, the rival of the sky.
> In vain! the mad attempt new tongues confound,
> The toil eluded by discordant sound:
> To his own sire the son barbarian grown,
> Unletter'd, starts a language not his own.
> Hence various bounds to nations set by speech;
> But not to you, who, orator in each,
> His proper tongue th'admiring native teach.[24]

Trapp is particularly struck by the way in which Smith diverts "from his purpose, that he may bring in a beautiful description of *Babel*, and the Confusion of Tongues"; then, "with no less elegance, he returns to the praise of his venerable traveller, surprisingly skilled in most of them."[25] This parallelism of thought across the barriers of Time and the freedom with which rational and sequential ordering are avoided while Smith juxtaposes the creation of language and contemporary Oriental studies are to Trapp at the very heart of the most poetical of all forms of poetry. Reflecting the "internal motions of the soul" and owing their rise to Nature, odes "begin and end abruptly, and are carried on thro' a variety of matter with a sort of divine *Pathos*, above rules and laws, and without regard to the common forms of Grammar."[26]

In particular, Trapp finds, Oriental lyric poetry employs unexpected metaphors, hyperboles, and long digressions. "The digressions which I chiefly admire," he admits, "are such as take occasion from some adjunct or circumstance of the subject, to pass on to somewhat else not totally distinct from it...."[27] What is being broached, although embryonically, in this early analysis by Trapp is a kind of poetry that was the opposite of what Coleridge was to call a "conjunction disjunctive." This development would be of little interest in itself if it did not accompany and reflect an imaginative departure from prevailing notions about the role of Time in the process of reading a poem and in the kind of knowledge a poem contained. In place of the neo-Classical perspectives of Rome and Greece, always closely allied with the formal organization of an Augustan poem, the Oriental movement was to offer a union of the experience of the original poets and of eighteenth-century English writers in which the ruins of Time would dissolve in the eternal Imagination.

Trapp's contemporaries seem to have entertained little suspicion that he and the professorship he had inaugurated might earn a place of some importance in the annals of English literature. Preaching, as he perhaps lectured, without notes, Trapp appears as "Parson Dapper," the admiration of the churchwarden, in *Tatler No. 66*. Eternally searching for preferment, Edward Young wrote in *The Universal Passion* (which was Ambition) that Trapp had become a scribbler by his elevation and, without it, might have been more.[28] Uniformly saturnine at the new professor's expense, Jonathan Swift categorized him as "a sort of pretender to wit, a second-rate pamphleteer for the cause whom they pay by sending him to Ireland"[29] when Trapp appeared in Dublin as chaplain to the Tory Lord-Lieutenant in 1711. To Swift, his verses were "not half as good as Stella's."[30]

But Trapp's notices were mixed. Although condescending, Pope thought well of Trapp's translations, especially of his *Paraphrase of Psalm CIV* which was printed in the same *Miscellany* (1709) as

Pope's and Ambrose Philips' pastorals.[31] Henry Cromwell wrote
that Trapp's *Psalm CIV* was "excellent"[32] but Pope comparing
Psalm CIV to Trapp's *Phaeton* in the same volume, replied:
"as to the psalm, I think David is much more beholding to him
than Ovid; and as he treated the Roman like a Jew, so he has made
the Jew speak like a Roman."[33] This poem on the Creation, it
might be noted in passing, in its best moments is a sparkling piece
of psalmic expansion that is authentically prophetic of Smart's
verse. Notably Trapp creates a repetitive patterning or trope on the
word "ADORATION" which effectively makes the reader dwell
on God's mysterious invention of words, and anticipates Christopher Smart's similar device in stanzas fifty-one through seventy-
one in *A Song to David* (1763). The strengthening of the Professorship of Poetry by more recognizable talents at a later date seems to
have done Trapp's reputation little harm. Shortly after Lowth's
election to the Professorship, Samuel Johnson himself noted that
the art of poetry could best be learned from John Dryden's prefaces and essays, from Addison's *Spectators,* from Joseph Spence's
Essay on Pope's Odyssey (the work which earned Spence the Professorship thirteen years before Lowth) and from Trapp's *Praelectiones poeticae.*[34]

Thomas Warton the Elder was a pioneer who influenced at a crucial moment the nature of English poetry in the age of Pope. As
much an antiquary as a poet, Warton, the second Professor of
Poetry, had seen that the New Chronology suggested by the antiquarians offered a phenomenology of the past from which a kind
of poetry different from the neo-Classical might derive. His spiritual brotherhood is that of his contemporary at Oxford, Hearne,
and the *virtuosi* of the Royal Society, men like George Hickes,
author of the *Thesaurus of the Ancient Northern Languages,*
whose niece, Elizabeth Elstob, forerunner of Henry Sweet, published her own Anglo-Saxon *Grammar* in Oxford in 1715; or Richard Mead the antiquarian physician who treated Pope and the Prin-
cess of Wales and diagnosed the Biblical Job's illness as elephantiasis in his *Medica sacra,* and whose collection of books,
coins, and statuary was the largest of the age; or John Wallis, atom-
ist, the era's greatest mathematician excepting Newton who drew
his binomial theory from Wallis' *Arithmetica infinitorum.* Characteristically, Wallis, like other scholars who were later to influence
Lowth, wrote about the nature of the language and contributed to
Greenwood's celebrated *Grammar* of 1711 the historical account of

the development of English.[35]

Among the subscribers to Joseph Warton's edition of his father's *Poems on Several Occasions,* that circulated in manuscript as early as 1717 but was not published until 1748, appears the name of the "Rev. Dr. Young, of Wellyn in Hertfordshire." That "the Bard of Welwyn" subscribed to the elder Warton's recognition was fitting, partly because the volume began with *An Epistle to Dr. Young, upon his poem on 'The Last Day.'* This epistle praised the "primitive" poem which Young had written in 1713 concerning the approaching dissolution of the earth. In noting Young's novel achievement, Thomas Warton reiterated the Oriental-primitive note and signaled its importance in the collection of poems which followed. Young's account of the disintegration of material Nature on the Judgment Day not only anticipates his better-known *Night Thoughts* (1742-1745) but affords the same poetic advantages that Young had noted in Job, which was composed at Nature's beginning. Young is like Abraham, Thomas Warton claimed: "When guilty Sodom felt the burning rain, / And sulphur fell on the devoted plain; / The patriarch thus the fiery tempest passed, / With pious horror viewed the desert waste; / The restless smoke still waved its curls around, / For ever rising from the glowing ground."

There are three distinct groups in Warton's *Poems on Several Occasions,* but even the poems roughly Classical in subject show a shift from the usual Augustan manner. Johnson's complaint about Thomas Warton the Younger's "uncouth" poems of 1777, "ode, and elegy, and sonnet,"[36] could be applied also to the Elder Warton's sentimental treatment of Greece and Rome. Even his *From the Thirteenth Ode of the Second Book of Horace,* smacks, if distantly, of the "antique ruff and bonnet," while *A Chorus, translated from the Hecuba of Euripides,* — in five quatrains — suggests the appreciation of Classical poets as writers of sensibility and feeling characteristic of a later date. *A Paraphrase on the Holie Book entitled Leviticus Chap. XI Verse 13, &c. Fashioned after the Maniere of Maister Geoffrey Chaucer in his Assemblie of Foules,* a literary hybrid if ever there was one, mixes elements from the two remaining groups of poems and suggests the combining of strains from Oriental and British "primitive" ages which we shall note in Lowth.

Warton's most widely known piece, *Retirement, an Ode,* recalls the importance of the ode form to the new movement and reminds us that Warton was an important metrist who bequeathed successful experiments to later poets.[37] The line from Warton to Thomas Gray, the most accomplished poet of Oriental and Northern mythology in the mid-century, is direct. Warton's fashionable interest in Northern mythologies, deriving partly from the Latin of Olaus Wormius in the works of Sir William Temple, inspired his *Runic Odes* on the death of Regner Ladbrog who was "mortally stung by a Viper," which influenced Gray's *Descent of Odin*; and, like Gray's *Fatal Sisters* and *The Bard*, Warton suggests an application of Oriental technique to Northern myth. We should not overlook such poems as Warton's *Verses written after seeing Windsor Castle* (a castle rebuilt by William of Wykeham) and *Verses on Henry the Eighth's seizing the Abbey-Lands*; for these poems contain the sense of things, of fabric and phenomena that is so much a part of eighteenth-century English primitivism.

"Orientalism" was a comprehensive term. In Lowth's notes to *Isaiah, A New Translation* in 1778, he remarked that "the present Emperor of China, in his very ingenious and sensible poem, entitled, Eloge de Moukden, a translation of which in French was published at Paris, 1770, speaks of a tree in his country, which lives more than a hundred ages."[38] Even Warton's lines, "All human race from China to Peru, / Pleasure howe'er disguised by art, pursue" — one source of the opening lines of Samuel Johnson's "The Vanity of Human Wishes" — were part of the emphatic Oriental content of *Poems on Several Occasions*.[39] Warton's opening poem, the epistle to Young on his *"Last Day"* that is in effect a dedication, points to the Oriental-primitive bias of his output. In view of Lowth's masterpiece of translation, according to Smart, of the fourteenth chapter of Isaiah,[40] it is noteworthy that among the verses in Warton's *Poems* is *A paraphrase of the XIIIth Chapter of Isaiah*. There is also a bestiary of leopards, "estriches," and other Biblical and Oriental animals, which recalls Trapp's beautiful *Psalm CIV* and Shaftesbury and which points the way to Smart himself. We find also *The Song of Judith paraphrased from the Apocrypha*, *A Paraphrase on the 65th Psalm*, *Stanzas imitated from Psalm CXIX*, as well as Latin versions such as the *Carmen Paraphrasticum in Ecclesiastici Caput XLIII^um* or *Song paraphrasing Ecclesiasticus, Chapter 43*.

In case the reader of Thomas Warton the Elder's verse should be left in any doubt about his preference for the lyric model of the Ancient Hebrews, he explicitly announced in *Stanzas on the*

Psalms the preference that Stephen Duck also announced in verse some years later:

> Not the songs that nobly tell,
> How *Troy* was sacked, and *Rome* began,
> Not the numbers that reveal
> The wars of heaven to falling man,
>
> Can boast that true celestial fire,
> That equal strength and ease,
> Or with such various charms conspire,
> To move, to teach, to please.
>
> Those complaints how sadly sweet,
> Which weeping Seraphim repeat;
> Those prayers how happily preferred,
> Which God himself inspired and heard.

In the work of Joseph Spence, the third Professor of Poetry in the University of Oxford and Lowth's friend, we approach the mind of Lowth himself. In the catalogue of the 1823 auction of the Lowth library[41] there appears, as item number 911, "Thomson's Seasons. A present from Thomson to Spence, and from Spence to I. H. Lowth."[42] Ernest de Selincourt has reminded us that Thomson's geology like Young's was derived from the physicotheologian, Thomas Burnet;[43] and McKillop has observed that "it is hardly necessary to prove in detail that Thomson's lines are in the tradition illustrated by Young's *Paraphrase on Part of Job* (1719)."[44] That Thomson also reveals these influences adds considerably to our interest; for Spence's most distinguished critical work provided a crucial turning point in the new poetry which Burnet, who was Addison's mentor, Young, and Thomson helped to shape — and in which Lowth was to be a major authority.

Joseph Warton commented in his edition of Pope in 1797: "By the favour of Dr. Lowth ... I have seen a copy of this *Essay on the Odyssey*, with marginal observations written in Pope's own hand," "generally acknowledging ... Spence's observations"; moreover, "I know no critical treatise better calculated to form the taste of young men of genius, than this *Essay on the Odyssey*."[45] "Lest it should be thought that this opinion arises from my partiality to a friend with whom I lived so many years in the happiest intimacy," he went on as an old man of seventy-five who was remembering the beginnings of the movement then nearing its maturity, "I will add,

that this was also the opinion of three persons, from whose judgement there can be no appeal, Dr. Akenside, Bishop Lowth, and Mr.
James Harris."[46]

Spence's *Essay on the Odyssey* earned not only Lowth's but
Johnson's approbation. A very graceful and lucid discussion written as a Greek dialogue between two friends, this essay is as much
about the nature of Homer as about the merits of Pope's translation. Antiphaus, "who has a very clear head, and has given much
into a strict way of thinking,"[47] is "prejudiced for the Ancients,
from the purity and justness, which we find in most of their
works."[48] The occasional apostasy to the side of the new "Sublime" by Antiphaus, the traditional neo-Classical critic, is one of
the attractions of this quietly humorous work. His companion,
Philypsus, represents everything that is new in criticism. Enjoying
an "inlarged genius," as Spence puts it, which "always led him to
dwell upon the most beautified parts of a poem with the greatest
pleasure,"[49] Philypsus prefers "the flourish and colouring of the
Moderns."[50] In effect, Philypsus is the early man of sensibility.

In the five "Evenings" of discussion, which range over many
aspects of Homer, several significant events occur. The most illuminating is the introduction during the fourth "Evening" of discussion of an entirely new literary term, "an *orientalism*." "From
the invocation of the Muse in the entrance to his poem, the poet has
a right of prophesying," Philypsus comments, "and it might be
partly from this, that the name of *prophet* and *poet* has, in some
languages, been used in common."[51] "Some of the strongest
speeches in Homer and Virgil are delivered after this manner, by
men of prophetic character," he continues; and he points to the
prophecy by Theoclymenus of the downfall of the suitors. At the
heart of Theoclymenus' speech occurs the line (in Pope's *Odyssey*
Bk. XX, line 429) "Nor gives the sun his golden orb to roll." Antiphaus takes up the thread.

I beg pardon (says Antiphaus) but the speech of Theoclymenus is a particular favourite of mine: and now you repeat it in *English,* I seem to want
something of the strong pleasure it used to afford me, where the *Greek*
speaks *'Of the sun being perished out of Heaven, and of darkness rushing
over the Earth!'* I cannot express the fulness of the words — But you know
the original; and, I fear, will never see a translation equal to it. This whole
prophetical vision of the fall of the suitors, is the *True Sublime;* and in particular, gives us an higher *Orientalism* than we meet with in any other part
of Homer's writings. You will pardon me a new word, where we have no

old one to my purpose: You know what I mean, that *Eastern way of expressing Revolutions in Government, by a confusion or extinction of light in the Heavens.*[52]

Homer's use of this *"orientalism"* — a term introduced by Spence to suggest a technique of "sublime" poetry common in Romantic poetry such as Young's *Night Thoughts,* Blake's *America, a Prophecy,* and Keats' *Hyperion* and *The Fall of Hyperion* — is compared with the prophecies of Amos, Joel, and Ezekiel. Homer, who has stepped down from the Popean pedestal to which neo-Classical writers elevated him, mingles with the Oriental poets of the Mediterranean perimeter. Behind Spence's comments is the work not only of Anne Dacier,[53] who had shown Homer to a Europe largely ignorant of him as a real person in a simple tribe in a primitive epoch, but also of Giambattista Vico, "a pioneer in what is sometimes called the philosophy of history," who had concluded in 1725 that Homer was "the mirror of a simple age" and whose *Scienza nuova* in the edition of 1730 announced the "discovery of the true Homer."[54] In England, the trend was to be consolidated by Thomas Blackwell's *Enquiry into the Life and Writings of Homer* (1735), "a fine though sometimes fanciful effort of genius," Gibbon observed,[55] and by Robert Wood in unmistakably Romantic terms in his *Essay on the Original Genius of Homer* (1769).

Taking the shorter view, we may conclude that the primitive, Oriental movement had so permeated literary criticism by 1726 as to have become an effective criterion by which Pope is measured. "I have often wondered, *Philypsus,*" concludes even Spence's traditional Antiphaus, "at some particular persons, who are ever ravished with any thing of the Sublime in common authors, and yet seem to have no taste for the finest touches of this kind, those which are so frequent in our sacred writings"; and he specifically cites — by footnote — Anthony Blackwall's *The Sacred Classics Defended* of 1725.[56]

"The Sublime" and "the true Sublime" are terms often on the lips of Antiphaus and Philypsus. The second most significant event in Spence's *Essay on the Odyssey* is the identification of this "Sublime" with the contemporary enthusiast's ideas of Nature as expressed in one of the most important chapters in eighteenth-century Orientalism — Shaftesbury's hymn to the "original wilds" of North Africa. When Antiphaus and Philypsus are discussing the shipwreck of Ulysses off the coast of Phaeacia, they agree with

contemporary writers on "the Sublime" that "greatness" or vastness is a major source of the response; and they find that some of
Homer's most considerable effects arise from this cause. They
remark that motion added to vastness is strangely effective in
arousing emotion: greatness is "more vigorous and affecting ...
when some more moving considerations are annexed."[57]

Then responding sensitively to the scene of "rough sea, terminating in craggy shores, and rocks, and a tempestuous sky" (highly
reminiscent of "Romantic" painters such as Salvator Rosa) and
etching a scene in which "every object has an additional terror
from ... Ulysses painted in the midst of these dangers,"[58] Philypsus turns for illustration to contemporary Orientalism, and a well-
known passage in Shaftesbury's *Characteristics*. "I remember a
passage of this kind," he says, "in a writer of a very strong imagination";[59] and he then quotes the evocation of Mt. Atlas. It is, says
Philypsus, "delivered in this bold poetical kind of prose."[60] *"See,
with what trembling steps poor Mankind tread the narrow brink of
the deep precipices!"* Spence begins the familiar words, suitably
italicized, *"from whence with giddy horror they look down,
mistrusting even the ground which bears them; whilst they hear the
hollow sound of torrents underneath, and see the ruin of the
impending rock, with falling trees, which hang with their roots up-
wards, and seem to draw more ruin after them...."*[61]

Joseph Warton's opinion of Spence's *Essay on Pope's Odyssey*
has been remarked upon; but as Professor MacClintock has indicated in his study of the background of Warton's *Essay on Pope,* it
was the insistence by Spence on the primary importance of "particulars" which strengthened Warton's own dislike for the Nature
of general categories or species drawn by the neo-Classical writers.
"One particular passage in this essay influenced Warton greatly,"
wrote MacClintock.[62] "Spence says 'with poets and in history *there
may be some fraud in saying only the bare truth.* In either 'tis not
sufficient to tell us, that *such a city,* for instance, *was taken and
ravaged with a great deal of inhumanity.* There is a *poetical falsity*
if a strong idea of each particular be not imprinted on the mind;
and an *historical,* if some things are passed over only with a general
mark of infamy or dislike.'"[63] Spence insists that a translator
should emphasize the particulars peculiar to the original's environment and Lowth was to do so as the Oxford Professor of Poetry.[64]

Even when Spence considers the entire Classical epic, he uses the
Oriental model for the basis of his criticism. The criticism of even

Pope's *Homer* took place in 1726 in an aura of comparative enquiry influenced by the New Chronology and by the principle of Universal History which placed the Hebrews at the center of the history of man. Antiphaus, for example, notes that "custom and prejudice" have now rendered it impolite for a man to commend himself, an illuminating commentary on Augustan *mores;* but, as he also notes, "it was not thus anciently ... Homer therefore acts with propriety in making Ulysses say, that *Nestor and himself were the wisest of all the Grecians.*"[65] For us he concludes most significantly, that "what puts this beyond dispute ... is to be found in the sacred writings, in which Moses says of himself, that he was the *Meekest Man upon the Earth.*"[66]

The simple identification of Hebrew as "Oriental" was, of course, to be found everywhere. "'He swalloweth the ground' is an expression for prodigious swiftness, in use among the Arabians, Job's countrymen, at this day,"[67] "John Lizard," probably Edward Young, had observed in *Guardian No. 86.* John Wallis, in the second section of his Preface to Greenwood's *Grammar* (1711), comments on the similarity of Welsh and Hebrew and states that "It hath great Affinity with the *Eastern* languages."[68] Addison noted in *Spectator No. 405* "a certain coldness and indifference in the phrases of our *European* languages, when they are compared with the Oriental forms of speech,"[69] and he then observed that "it happens very luckily, that the *Hebrew* idioms run into the *English* tongue with a particular grace and beauty."[70] Lowth advised his audience to become acquainted with a certain way of thinking about the Biblical writers because of the numberless difficulties in the verse of "the Orientals above all foreigners, they being the farthest removed from our customs and manners; and of all the Orientals more especially in the Hebrews."[71] Later, Hugh Blair, looking back with helpful hindsight over the eighteenth century, observed that "the style of the Old Testament, which is carried on by constant allusions to sensible objects ... we have been accustomed to call ... the oriental style."[72]

A study of the early eighteenth century reveals several essential elements of Orientalism discernible in literary thought, perhaps especially in Oxford, long before Robert Lowth. Joseph Trapp is pedestrian and crude, but he seems to have started some of the hares Lowth saw home in triumph. Trapp insisted on the primacy of Oriental poetry in time and quality. His interest in materialist psychology anticipates the non-religious view Lowth took of Old

Testament verse. Trapp's parallel between the Creation of the universe and the creativity of the poet's mind — a metaphor at the heart of Orientalism — predates William Collins' and William Blake's similar claims. Trapp sees the poetic strength of the Oriental confusion of time, and elevates to a principle of Orientalism a wandering disjointedness which suggests irrational forces at work in the shaping of a poem. Thomas Warton, poet more than critic, made into a fashionable part of the new movement of feeling the simple, emotional, Biblical and Medieval verse which related new directions in "sentimental" poetry to the antiquarianism of the Royal Society. Lowth's close friend, Joseph Spence, was especially important because he applied the new sensationalist "sublime" and Oriental criteria to the traditional Classicism of Pope and isolated a poetic technique — to which he gave the name *"orientalism"* — in which the sun and hence time stood still and the images of poetry embodied an infinite stasis. This perception, suggesting in "original" poetry contemporary concerns of eighteenth-century philosophy, seems never to have been far from Robert Lowth's mind when composing his own poetry or when analyzing the techniques of ancient Hebrew verse.

CHAPTER 3

Lowth's Poetry

I "The Young Bard": Schoolboy Poetry

ROBERT Aubin has noted that Lowth's poem, *Katherine Hill,* first published in 1733 but written while he was a scholar of the school, probably in 1729, was a "hill poem" like Sir John Denham's *Cooper's Hill* or *Windsor Forest.*[1] In the most influential hill poem in the language, *Cooper's Hill* (1642), which shaped many topographical verses, notably Pope's *Windosr Forest,* Denham had dwelt on the sights, such as St. Paul's Cathedral, which could be viewed from his hill; and he had paid graceful compliments to Charles I who, at that time, was not far from his tragic fate. In the most famous couplets in English for over a hundred years, Denham addresses the River Thames,

> O could I flow like thee, and make thy stream
> My great example, as it is my theme:
> Though deep yet clear, though gentle yet not dull,
> Strong without rage, without o'erflowing full.

Lowth's poem, which appeared in *The London Magazine,* was a precocious project for a schoolboy. Addressing the hill on which Winchester boys walked, hunted badger, and played cricket without supervision, he wrote,

> O! could with thee my rival fancy vie,
> As sweet, as awful, as secure, as high!
> Could I, like thee, so regularly climb,
> Pleasant though steep, and sportful, 'tho sublime;
> Then Cooper's hill to thee should yield in fame,
> Nor my muse shrink at Denham's awful name.   (ll. 9–14)

63

In terms recalling *Windsor Forest* and also George Berkeley's observations on the ambiguity of distance in *A New Theory of Vision* (1709), Lowth enlarges on the view of his friends who are walking below,

> Where the wild path, one little plain commands,
> And a small spot contains a length of lands.
> See! how they labour in the folded race,
> And measure all the comprehensive space;
> Through all the regular confusion run,
> And seem to end, where they the course begun:
> Close join'd the barriers and the goal appear;
> (Delusive sight!) how distant, and how near!   (ll. 23-30)

This poem of feeling not only images the delusions of Space but the relationship of feeling to Time as represented in the ruined architecture of the distant and the recent past ages. Coins of the Emperor Constantine had been found in excavations, and an ancient fortification stood on Katherine Hill. With a mixture of "the Sublime" of history and of architecture, which Addison had said in *Spectator No. 415* was the most likely to produce "the pleasures of the Imagination," Lowth exclaims,

> But what vast rising bulwark's mighty row,
> War's dire remains, frowns horrid on thy brow?
> Here, deep and wide, down sinks a trench profound:
> There, huge, and high up-heav'd, a tow'ring mound
> Swells formidable; and begirts thy crown
> With dreadful pomp, and terrors not thine own.   (ll. 31–36)

With some stretching of poetic license, the hill is compared to Achilles' shield. "Fields, woods, and countries," may be seen from the hill; and, mixing "horror and delight," she shows us the contrary states of life so that "we seem to see / All the vast world's epitome in thee." As well as the Classical allusion more reminiscent of Warton than of Pope, Lowth offers a prophetic image of the Nile. The "peaceful Itchin," which runs past Hampton Court and into the Thames, is a "thrice happy stream!": "...bounteous as the Nile, his blessings sends; / But those no monster as the Nile attends" (ll. 59–60).

The architectural sublime of the earlier half of the poem is a prologue to the devastation that occurs in the latter portion. Lowth ingeniously turns to the sack of Winchester, a Cavalier stronghold, by Oliver Cromwell some eighty years before. Loyal to William of Wykeham, Lowth applauds the Roundhead Wykehamist who prevented the sack of the college when every other part of the city was ransacked:

> In ruin then had Wickham's house been spread,
> (Fate hover'd o'er her undeserving head)
> But her false son, relenting, sav'd her wall,
> When Winton's stately tow'rs were doom'd to fall;
> He that so many oaths had broke before,
> For one oath's sake this horrid crime forbore. (ll. 76–81)

Charles' son, King Charles II, had begun a vast palace there of grandiose design in 1683; and it too was now an object of ruin, for its shell only was complete. A cupola had been planned which would have been visible far out to sea, which itself was distant from Winchester. The remnants were an object of regret for an enthusiast of the city which had previously been the capital in King Alfred's day. Lowth complains,

> See there ascends the hapless orphan dome,
> Old in her youth, and with'ring in her bloom.
> At grateful Charles's will this blessing rose,
> To balance all a plunder'd city's woes.
> But ah! when most she thought her hopes secure,
> Charles fell, nor left her infant wall mature.
> That cloud did all our dawn of day dispel:
> In him that pile, in him this city fell. (ll. 92–99)

There were hopes that King George would now repair the loss of the plundered marble and complete the building; and Lowth's youthful hill poem ends on this tentative note.

Katherine Hill is an authentic work of art. The bold esthetic of the ruin and of "the Sublime," joined with Denham's topographical tradition, suggests a broad awareness of past and current fashions in the "young bard," as he calls himself, and an ability to make something new of them. As William Cowper wrote of these poems much later, "Had I been present when he spoke them, I should have trembled for the boy, lest the man should disappoint the hopes such early genius had given birth to."[2] We find in the emotional range of *Katherine Hill* a forecast of the fine sensibility which would thrill to the great national issues of the Hebrews in, for example, Lowth's appreciation of Isaiah.

More than a hundred lines long, the poem is composed in heroic couplets. Although we immediately refer, of course, to Pope and to contemporary Augustan versification, these couplets are soft and resonant; there is an underlying melancholy in them; and a sense of reverberating tragedy is present. Lowth's inexperience is evident in his inability entirely to channel and control the emotions which he suggests, but his ability to arouse feeling from these materials indicates a career of great achievement in some branch of sublime poetry related to history.

Robert Lowth's father had noted in his *Commentary upon the Prophets* that "one great use of the writings of the prophets, is to instruct us in the *signs of the times*; and tho' the warnings they give had a particular aspect upon their own age, yet they were likewise *written for our admonition, upon whom the ends of the world are come.*"[3] The closeness of the poetry and the images of the Old Testament to the eighteenth-century mind was related to a widespread belief in the approaching end of Nature. In the son, Robert, we eventually see this cultural phenomenon develop an esthetic rather than a religious bias, yet we may imagine the ease with which the heir to this expert on prophecy might write *The Genealogy of Christ as it is represented on the East Window in Winchester Chapel* (1729).

The awareness of the Berkeleyan revolution, a conviction that the *locus* of reality was the mind of each individual man, is present in both of Lowth's juvenile poems. In his depiction of the House of David on the windows of the Medieval school chapel, the contemporary mind and imagination of the spectator are one with the illuminated figures of the ancient East:

> Who views the sacred forms, in thought aspires,
> Catches pure zeal, and as he gazes, fires,
> Feels the same ardor to his breast convey'd,
> Is what he sees, and emulates the shade.   (ll. 7–10)

There is a close parallel between the window and the poem; for Lowth hopes that the work of the designer will impart to his muse "some emanation from her sister art, / To animate the verse, and bid it shine / In colours easy, bright, and strong, as thine." When Lowth describes the "awful figure" of Jesse, "the Founder of

Messiah's line," he anticipates the combination of prophecy and poetry, a major theme of his adult writing that had already been touched on by Spence, in this stanza:

> In DAVID all exprest, the good, the great.
> The King, the hero, and the man complete.
> Serene he sits, and sweeps the golden lyre,
> And blends the Prophet's, with the Poet's fire. (ll. 37–40)

The East as an entirety is also present in this poem. With a use of an allusion later found in Young's *Night Thoughts,* Akenside's *Pleasures of the Imagination,* and Keats' *Hyperion,* and with one that images the capacity of poetry to surmount the limitations of material Nature, Lowth alludes to the statue of Memnon in Egypt that was reputed to emit sounds when struck by the first light of dawn. Lowth imagines the awakening of David in Wykeham's chapel and the sound of David's lyre wafted from the humming glass:

> Could the warm sun, as erst when Memnon play'd,
> Wake with his rising beam the vocal shade:
> Then might he draw the attentive angels down,
> Bending to hear the lay, so sweet, so like their own. (ll. 47–50)

The schoolboy poet dramatizes each of the characters, and among them are Ammon, "proud, incestuous lord!'"; Absalom, "base usurper youth!'"; and Nathan, whose "looks the emotion of his soul disclose." In Solomon's hand,

> In miniature the glorious temple stands.
> Effulgent frame! Stupendous to behold!
> . . . .
>
> The wand'ring Ark in that bright dome enshrin'd,
> Spreads the strong light, eternal, unconfin'd!
> Above, th'unutterable Glory plays,
> Presence Divine! and the full streaming rays
> Pour through reluctant clouds intolerable blaze. (ll. 84–85; 87–91)

Lowth's manipulation of the images of Time, as in *Katherine Hill,* is an important source of the poem's effect. Lowth accomplishes to an extent his promise to make the ancient figures now move and live, but he wishes them to do so not only in the window but also in the reader's mind. As the poem moves laterally through the line of descendants of David and the forebears of Christ, its scope and speed also give the effect of eternal stasis. Centrally, Lowth dwells on the relativity of Time. When Hezekiah's life is miraculously renewed, and the sun and the shadow on the sun dial are turned back (Isaiah 38), Lowth writes,

> Ev'n now the soul maintains her latest strife,
> And Death's chill grasp congeals the font of life.
> Yet see, kind heav'n renews thy brittle thread,
> And rolls full fifteen summers o'er thy head;
> Lo! the receding sun repeats his way,
> And, like thy life, prolongs the falling day.
> Tho' Nature her inverted course forego,
> The day forget to rest, the time to flow. (ll. 172-79)

Lines 176 and 179 about the sun's repeating his way and Time's stopping copy the stationary sun of Homer's Theoclymenus — "Nor gives the sun his golden orb to roll" (in Pope's *Odyssey,* Bk. XX, l. 429) — on which Joseph Spence had based his definition of the poetical technique of prophecy which he termed — in his *Essay* — "an *orientalism.*"

After the coming of Christ, "the pleasing burden" of the Holy Mother, the climax of the poem prophesies the end of the world in terms which recall both Lowth's father and Young's *The Last Day* (1713). The "satiate jaws" of "thou O Tomb" open to "give up all thy prey," while

> . . . the proud dissolving mountains glow,
> And yielding rocks in fiery rivers flow;
> The molten deluge round the globe shall roar,
> And all man's arts and labour be no more.
> Then shall the splendours of th'enliven'd glass
> Sink undistinguished in the burning mass.   (ll. 253-58)

The "young bard" concludes by hoping that until that final day, this "fair creation" may "All the vain rage of wasting Time repel, / And his tribunal see, whose cross they paint so well."

The Genealogy of Christ is an accomplished poem. It belongs to a "window" genre later used by Thomas Warton the Younger in his poem about Sir Joshua Reynold's window in New College. Lowth's basic motif and running image are found in the light which Lowth says in his opening lines makes the viewer become "what he sees."

By means of this illumination, the images on the Winchester College window absorb those of the Bible and are then projected both into the mind of the reader and into the future. Lowth's concept of the nature of Hebrew verse is already partially evident and hints at his future achievements. How close the esthetic theories in the poem are to later Romantic verse may be seen by glancing at Coleridge's *Christabel* in which the "figures strange and sweet" inside the heroine's chamber are "all made out of the carver's brain" (ll. 179–80) in a not dissimilar context of historicity and timelessness.

The heroic couplets are weighty and sonorous, but they are not at all like those of Pope. If there is one weakness in the poem, it is that the light of the sun that illuminates the figures is of this world and time but is called upon to stand for eternal light throughout. However, since the uniting of the temporal and eternal is a respectable function of poetry, perhaps this criticism is inadmissible. Indeed, of particular interest in Lowth's poem, which first appeared when he was nineteen in 1729 and then in Dodsley's *Collection* in 1770, is the explicit use of what Spence had termed "an *orientalism*" in his *Essay* in 1726 as "that *Eastern way of expressing Revolutions in Government, by a confusion or extinction of light in the Heavens.*"[4] These verses of Lowth's boyhood prove that the interest in the manipulation of Time central to Lowth's lectures on Hebrew poetry at Oxford was a lifelong preoccupation that perhaps speaks of something deep in his personality. The interest in the imaging of timelessness — and spacelessness — suggests also a sophisticated awareness of the direction of contemporary philosophy which maintained, for example in Bishop Berkeley's *Principles of Human Knowledge* (1710), that man's native true perception was, technically speaking, infinite.

II The Choice of Hercules

Lowth's era had practical experience of the primitivism about which it theorized. In 1745 the Scottish clans, still organized on timeless social patterns, invaded England as far as Derby, some seventy miles from London, under "Bonnie Prince Charlie," the Young Pretender. About the event Lowth's Horatian *Ode* was suitably conservative, for it chastized the English, and their morals, as a punishment for which the invasion, Lowth fictionalized, had been ordained. Of more lasting interest is Lowth's long poem *The Choice of Hercules* published in 1747 but written before 1741, because it establishes a link with the greatest English composer of the era, George Frederick Handel (1685-1759), who used *Hercules* in one of his compositions. The link between Lowth's poetic ability and Handel suggests a further parallel between the greatest eighteenth-century authority on Oriental, Hebrew poetry, and the greatest European composer of operas and oratorios on Biblical themes.

Lowth's *Choice of Hercules,* in large part completed before his taking up of the Professorship of Poetry at Oxford, is also of peculiar interest to us, because it indicates his thinking on a crucial image in "primitive" poetry: personifications of moral qualities. Personifications play a crucial part in eighteenth-century poetry at large. Lowth devoted an entire lecture to them in his lectures on Hebrew poetry and returned to them frequently. In Lecture XIII he observed that the Hebrews "greatly excel the most sublime [poets] in force and majesty" when they "assign character and action to an abstract or general idea, and introduce it in a manner acting, and even speaking as upon the stage."[5] Much of Lowth's lecture on personification is given over to the famous chapter fourteen of Isaiah, and Lowth's translation of it which won the praise of Joseph Warton and Christopher Smart. Personification *was* felt to be peculiarly sublime, and Lowth thought himself an authority on personifying.

Perhaps it was for this reason that Joseph Spence asked him to contribute a poem on a famous iconographic theme to Spence's major work of his middle years, *Polymetis* (1747). Having spent many years in Europe studying Classical remains, Spence had added to the laurels of his *Essay* by projecting a large work which would place side by side for the reader — and spectator — etchings of famous groups of abstractions, including gods and goddesses of the ancient world, and the literature of the ancient world in which they appeared.

Why, we might ask, did Lowth compose a poem which was a translation of part of the historian Xenophon's (?430 B.C.-?355 B.C.) memoirs of *Memorabilia* concerning Socrates, in which that ancient philosopher narrated the fable about Virtue and Sloth and their wooing of the youthful Hercules, which had its source, Xenophon reported, in the shadowy and little-known figure of the philosopher Prodicus? Since fables were part of the curriculum at Winchester, Lowth must have felt on home ground; but another answer lies in the writing of Joseph Addison.

In *Spectator No. 183,* Addison had devoted himself to the subject of fables. "Fables were the first pieces of wit that made their appearance in the world,"[6] Addison began his essay in 1711. Addison found two kinds of ancient fable: in one of these "the Actors are Passions, Virtues, Vices, and other imaginary Persons of the like Nature."[7] Touching on his interest in the mechanics of literary response, which he would raise again a year later in an interesting, related discussion of personification, he noted that even the Classical epic is a kind of fable of this sort and that "the several names of Gods and Heroes are nothing else but the affections of the mind in a visible shape and character."[8] In researching this most ancient of kinds of poetry, Addison discovered that "the first of this sort that made any considerable figure in the world was that of *Hercules* meeting with Pleasure and Virtue, which was invented by *Prodicus,* who lived before *Socrates,* and in the first dawnings of Philosophy."[9] It is clear that, in composing a poem on the ancient theme of Hercules' meeting with Pleasure (or Sloth) and Virtue (or Hard Work), Lowth, following Addison's lead, thought of himself as dealing with literature of the very first ages of man: primitive Greece in "the first dawnings of Philosophy" provided the story. The verse form which Lowth adopted, like the one William Shenstone also used in his version of the poem in 1741, *The Judgement of Hercules* (which appeared probably after Lowth's was written), was similar to Edmund Spenser's verse form in the *Fairie Queene* (1590). But Lowth's form is slightly different: it has ten lines to Spenser's nine; its rhyme scheme also differs somewhat. But Lowth's poem has the same sense of stately progress, or lack of progress; it sets up complex inner harmonies; and, although basically iambic pentameter, it also ends with a single Alexandrian, or line of six feet, like the Spenserian stanza. The description of Pleasure (or Sloth) in the fifth stanza suggests Lowth's effects at their best:

> The other dame seem'd ev'n of fairer hue;
> But bold her mien; unguarded rov'd her eye:
> And her flush'd cheeks confess'd at nearer view
> The borrow'd blushes of an artful dye.
> All soft and delicate, with airy swim
> Lightly she danc'd along; her robe betray'd
> Thro' the clear texture ev'ry tender limb,
> Height'ning the charms it only seem'd to shade:
> And as it flow'd adown, so loose and thin,
> Her stature shew'd more tall; more snowy-white, her skin. (ll. 41–50)

In using a stanza similar to Spenser's and archaic diction, Lowth, we must add, was again following Addison. In keeping with the eighteenth-century habit of viewing Spenser as a "primitive" poet — as it were, an English counterpart to Ezekiel — Addison noted in regard to the ancient fables, "Spenser's *Fairy-Queen* is one continued Series of them [fables] from the beginning to the end of that admirable work."[10]

We meet Lowth's hero, young Hercules, walking in an allegorical countryside, "Far in a lonely vale, with solitude / Conversing; while intent his mind survey'd / The dubious path of life: before him lay / Here Virtue's rough ascent, there Pleasure's flow'ry way" (ll. 17–20). It is interesting to note that the allegory does not work in the eighteenth century as it did for Spenser. Although the countryside offers two roads, one apparently belonging to Pleasure and the other to Virtue, when these figures appear they have no real relationship to the country they are said to own. The contrast with Spenser is instructive; for in the Renaissance allegory the allegorical figures owned nearby castles or caves, and the details of the "fable" are carried out in every respect. Both figures appear at the same time before Hercules, to address him. At the heart of Xenophon's version is the notion that the delight to be derived from hard work and exercise (in a word, pain) is greater than that to be derived from hedonism. Xenophon cites the hard work of an athlete which is followed by the delight of victory, and the pain of spiritual exercise which is followed by the enlarged pleasures of the soul. The eighteenth-century "Sublime" suggested, as we see in Edmund Burke's *Sublime and Beautiful* (1757), that delight resulted from its apparent opposite, pain. The Marquis de Sade (1740-1814) was only the culminating theorist of this "sublime" assumption. In *Spectator No. 183,* Addison had made up his own fable on the theme. *"If Pain comes into an heart he is quickly followed by Pleasure; and if Pleasure enters, you may be sure Pain is not far Off,"*[11] Addison concluded, with a happy ending to his psychological fable in which Pleasure and Pain actually marry each other in a ceremony and, of course, live happily ever after.

In Lowth, Sloth (or Pleasure) offers the young Hercules a bower of bliss — "Rich odours, breathing choicest sweets around; / The fragrant bow'r, cool fountain, shady grove: / Fresh flowers, to strew thy couch, and crown thy head; / Joy shall attend thy steps, and Ease shall smooth thy bed" (ll. 77–80) — that the reader knows full well will quickly pall. Sloth goes on,

These will I freely, constantly supply;
Pleasures, nor earn'd with toil, nor mix'd with woe;
Far from thy rest repining want shall fly;
Nor labour bathe in sweat thy careful brow.
Mature the copious harvest shall be thine;
Let the laborious hind subdue the soil:
Leave the rash soldier spoils of war to win;
Won by the soldier thou shalt share the spoil:
These softer cares my blest allies employ,
New pleasures to invent; to wish, and to enjoy.   (ll. 81–90)

Virtue's abrupt and dramatic challenge to the sensuous Sloth's speech, which she rudely interrupts, accepts in theory the close relationship of Pleasure and Pain to each other; but, like a contemporary philosopher, for example David Hume (1711-1776), Virtue casts doubt on cause and effect. Human beings must not avoid travail. Only if we choose difficulty, does Pleasure — we should read Burke's term "delight" here — follow. "The sparkling nectar, cool'd with summer snows; / The dainty board, with choicest viands spread; / To thee are tasteless all! Sincere repose / Flies from thy flow'ry couch, and downy bed" (ll. 161–164), Virtue tells Sloth. Such luxuries lead only to "A youth, of follies; an old-age, of cares!" (l. 192).

Virtue offers other delights.

First conquer thou thyself. To ease, to rest,
To each soft thought of pleasure, bid farewell.
The night alternate, due to sweet repose,
In watches waste; in painful march the day:
Congeal'd, amidst the rigorous winter's snows;
Scorch'd, by the summer's thirst-inflaming ray.
Harden'd by toil, thy limbs shall boast new might:
Vigour shall brace thine arm, resistless in the fight. (ll. 133-140)

Hindsight tells us that Hercules, the greatest and strongest of all the ancient heroes, took Virtue's painful advice. The moral is plain. If we wish to gain the success and reputation of Hercules, we too shall choose hard work, and discipline — pain! The plainest food will seem delightful to us; we shall sleep sweetly; and, "by a soft descent, / At length to age all gently sinking down, [we shall] Look back with transport on a life well spent," a life during which, we might add, with Lowth in mind, we shall have created works which will keep our names alive for centuries after our deaths.

It is interesting to contrast Lowth's poem with Shenstone's *Judgement of Hercules*. Where Shenstone is lax, Lowth is taut. Where Shenstone is smooth, Lowth is dramatic and direct. As a piece of Spenserian verse Lowth's *Hercules* is remarkably accomplished. But, the extraordinary thing about it is that, while a dramatic confrontation takes place among Vice, Virtue, and Hercules, and an import choice is made, what is achieved is a rich sense of timeless stasis. The countryside, clothes, sensual delights and painful disciplines are vividly described, but the action is only apparent; the poem accumulates detail; surface activity is belied by a static centre. Lowth was attempting to write primitive poetry, and the timeless tapestry of the country of the mind forms the milieu of the poem. We recall that this is a mid-eighteenth-century poem, set in the style of a late sixteenth-century English poet, of a well-known story from Xenophon (4th century B.C.), who is recalling the fifth-century Socrates who, in turn, is recalling the more ancient Prodicus. Layer upon layer of historical time lie within the story negating each other, and the timeless values of "Sloth" and "Virtue," the only images the reader knows firsthand, are thrown into high relief and hence appear to be infinite and "Sublime." In sum, *Hercules* is an example of the kind of poetry Lowth spoke of in his lectures.

The confusion in the poem is the problem of the era: in *Spectator No. 183,* Addison, influenced by John Locke, had spoken of the figures in ancient fables and in Homer himself as being mere "affections of the mind": that is, shapes and forms which the mind mechanically produces and enjoys but ones which bear no or little relationship to anything outside of the mind such as true moral values. In the case of Lowth's *The Choice of Hercules,* we enjoy the poem because we like seeing abstractions on the page, as poetic figures. We do not enjoy it because we are believers in an unseen moral world in which "Virtue" and "Vice" are important realities. Addison and eighteenth-century philosophers lived in a world where concepts were relative. Pain and pleasure seemed interestingly to mingle. Lowth's poem glories in this mechanistic interest. He does not convince us, as Spenser does over and over again, that there is a moral landscape in Nature and an unseen scheme of things sanctioned by God; for where man himself is timeless there is no other divinity. The poem is *not* an allegory; it is a piece of iconographic manipulation, and an extremely accomplished one.

Personifications were naturally "sublime," and Lowth was centrally concerned with sublime poetry. Another connection between Addison and Lowth reminds us that even the personifications in the Bible were to be seen as psychological data. Saying in *Spectator No. 357*, in 1712 that no other critic had treated the subject, Addison turned from dealing with the personifications of Sin and Death in John Milton's *Paradise Lost* as "improper agents" (since they became "principal actors, and engaged in a series of adventures"[12]), to praise, as an alternative, "one of the prophets, who describing God as descending from Heaven, and visiting the sins of mankind, adds that dreadful circumstance; *before him went the Pestilence.*"[13] "It is certain," he went on about this phrase from Habakkuk 3, that "this imaginary person might have been described in all her purple spots. The *Fever* might have marched before her, *Pain* might have stood at her right hand, *Frenzy* on her left. . ." but "the mentioning of her as it is done in Scripture has something in it more just, as well as great, than all that the most fanciful poet could have bestowed upon her."[14] The reason points directly to Addison's interest in practical esthetics. Such sublime figures "are not designed to be taken in the literal sense, but only to convey particular circumstances to the reader after an unusual and entertaining manner."[15]

The line from Addison to Robert Lowth is direct. In Lecture XIII, on personification, Lowth repeats the very example Addison had praised at length in *Spectator 357:* "Exquisitely imagined, and, from the boldness of the fiction, extremely forcible," is the personification "in Habakkuk, of the Pestilence marching before JEHOVAH when he comes to vengeance."[16]

Like his lectures on the sacred poetry of the Hebrews, Lowth's *Choice of Hercules* reveals the paradoxical stance of the eighteenth-century "primitive" writer. He wished to imitate the "original," earliest writers of the world, but he did not believe in the unseen powers which those men had taken for granted. Literature was a pleasurable, humane activity, which reflected the laws of man's perception. Lowth's exercise in a Spenserian, Greek, fable reminds us, as do his lectures on Hebrew poetry, that the time when the literary techniques of the first ages entered the mainstream of English literature was the era when men least believed in unseen truth and when John Locke, George Berkeley, and David Hume made personified abstractions a purely psychological or physiological phenomenon.

We must observe one other salient fact about the poem's structure. This is related to the choosing of Lowth's poem by Handel as the basis for his serenata, *The Choice of Hercules* (1749). The mark of mid-eighteenth-century poetic form is the break-up of a sense of purposeful progression down the page. The association of ideas, the repetitions, and the statuesque, frequently Spenserian primitivism in *Hercules* offer a vivid, undramatic, texture in which echoes are felt across and over the apparent development of the story-line. This lack of sequential, rational, progress is reminiscent of the core of Handel's music. Echoing tableaux made Lowth's poem suitable for musical expression. Clearly Lowth's sensibility was working in his *Choice of Hercules* on a form of poetry similar to the parallelism he would analyze memorably in Hebrew poetry at the high point of his lectures. The simultaneous appreciation by Lowth and Handel of these characteristics of primitive poetry is further corroborated by Handel's many "Oriental" compositions such as *Deborah* (1733), *Judas Maccabeus* (1748), and *The Messiah* (1741) — a prophecy, given first in the first year of Lowth's lectures and depending heavily on a kind of antiphonal repetition, or parallelism, similar to that which Lowth popularized.

CHAPTER 4

The Lectures on Oriental Poetry

I   The Substance of Lowth's Lectures

L OWTH is best known for his *De sacra poesi Hebraeorum praelectiones* or *Lectures on the Sacred Poetry of the Hebrews* which first appeared as a series of thirty-four lectures spoken in Latin between 1741 and 1750.[1]

As Pattison indicates, "In the year 1753 the Clarendon Press at Oxford brought out, in a splendid quarto with all the honors of typography, the series of Lectures which Lowth had delivered during his ten years' occupancy of the chair of poetry in that University." To Pattison, "It was not the externals only of the volume of which the University was proud," for "it was no less remarkable for its matter. It was the first sign of the awakening of Oxford from that torpor under which two generations had now lain, under the besotting influence of Jacobite and high-church politics. The Lectures *De Sacra Poesi Hebraeorum* seemed to combine the polish of a past generation, long gone, with the learning of a new period to come."[2]

In Lowth's first lecture, the author strikes three chords: the propriety of the academic study of poetry, the source of the art of verse solely in Nature, and the simultaneity of its creation with that of the very first man from whose "new-created mind" lyric poetry flowed "almost involuntarily" "in sentences pointed, earnest, rapid, and tremulous." In Lecture II, which introduces the subject of prophetic poetry, Lowth observes that prophecy has always been metrical; for the style must be consistent with images "so infinitely surpassing all human conception" as "the prediction of future events." He makes clear, however, that his lectures are to be literary and critical and that "theological disquisitions will be avoided." He notes that all critics have hitherto evaded a truth cen-

tral to poetry, that poetry is an art which "has been conceded to
man by favour of his Creator" at the Creation, and that it is necessary for that reason to study "the only specimens of the primeval
and genuine poetry" that exist.

Probing the beginnings of form in Hebrew poetry, Lowth notes
in Lecture III that there were certain Psalms in which the initial letters of each line were placed in an alphabetical pattern and in series
repeated in succeeding stanzas. Furthermore, the metrical line in
these Psalms generally was one with the syntactical construction, a
characteristic — as the obscure later commentator "Mr. Henley"
observes in a footnote — of "some of our earliest writers, particularly Piers Plowman." To Lowth, the Hebrew poets treat "one subject in many different ways, and dwell upon the same sentiment";
they express "the same thing in different words, or different things
in a similar form of words"; their images echo images and "opposites, opposites." The word they gave to this form of composition,
mizmor (Psalm), was related to the pruning of trees.

While Greek poetry is complex and wordy, Lowth observes, the
Hebrews' simplicity, their radical uniformity, their small number of
inflections, and their uncomplicated meter made their Oriental
verse grave and temperate — and also aided one in accurate
translations. At the same time, he notes in Lecture IV, an antira-
tional "mode of thinking" is peculiar to this Oriental poetry. The
"secret avenues" of the imagination opened, and the "inmost con-
ceptions" rushed together "in one turbid stream, without order or
connection." From earliest antiquity, this enthusiastic mode,
related to music and dance, was found extremely memorable by the
primitive mind; it was therefore used for public records in Arabic
and Persian, as well as in Hebrew. Aside from this style, which he
terms *parabolic,* Hebrews employed the less important *didactic*
style which, unlike the parabolic, was used for the expression of
moral wisdom. The parabolic style builds up in lines expressing
similar or even contradictory sentiments in the same form of
words. The entire poem is frequently divided into distichs, or couplets, in patterns of amplification, accumulation, or antithesis, in a
"perpetual splendour" of "accurate recurrence." The expression
and form were, hence, highly wrought in a concise complexity
which made even prosaic notions poetical.

In Lecture V, "The Figurative Style, and its Divisions," Lowth
notes that *Mashal,* the Hebrew term for "Parable," denotes
"resemblance." The figures used are metaphor, allegory, simile,

and personification (a bolder metaphor). Because such Oriental poets are the farthest from us both in Place and Time — far away in distance and of extreme antiquity — Lowth exhorts his listeners to copy Comparative Astronomers and to shift their position in the cosmos; they are to assume the very habits and shapes of the thoughts of the people, "hearing or delivering the same words, at the same time, and in the same country." This adaptation is especially important in appreciating Hebrew verse which "abounds most in those images which are furnished by the senses" and in which the highest topics are represented by the lowliest images "in order to depict the obscure by the more manifest, the subtle by the more substantial."

From Lecture VI to and through Lecture IX, Lowth explored the four kinds of metaphor used in parabolic verse. The first and principal kind is that derived from Nature. Verse of "uncommon grandeur and sublimity" employed daring, often extended, images from Nature that were "borrowed from the most obvious and familiar objects." Calamity was a deluge; the favor of God, light; Job's friends were as desert streams after the rain had swiftly disappeared into the sand. From this practice came the uncommon clarity of Hebrew verse. The barn, the threshing floor, and the winepress supplied the metaphors for some of the most dramatic of poems, he notes in Lecture VII; for the king and the peasant shared one experience. In 2 Kings, xxi, 13, God threatens to destroy Jerusalem in an image of drying dishes, "as a man wipeth a dish." If we are to grasp the richness of Isaiah xiv, in which the dead kings of many nations rise from their dusty beds to greet sardonically the King of Babylon, "Art thou also come down to us?" etc., we should know about the tiered royal burial caves as described by the contemporary travelers, Henry Maundrell, Edward Pococke, and others. The same achievement of sublimity through the use of commonplace images gives Ezekiel his characteristic "terrific" or terrible power.

Other sources of imagery, Lowth points out in Lecture VIII, are, for example, the regulations concerning cleanness in food and person, the vestments of the priests, and the design of the tabernacle. To Lowth, it was easy to mistake in poetry "of so old a date" this kind of imagery as "vulgar, mean, or obscure" when it had been "accounted among the most perspicuous and sublime by the people to whom it was addressed." In Lecture IX, Lowth dealt with imagery from the history of the Jewish people that was used in poetry to illuminate the future by allusion to the past — the Chaos, the Creation, the Flood, the Exodus, the destruction of Sodom; for example, in Joel iii, 15, "The sun and the moon are darkened, / And the stars withdraw their shining," or in Psalm xi "He shall rain live coals upon the ungodly." "There is nothing . . . more forcible and elevated" in prophetic poetry, for this kind of image suggests the approaching event but avoids details; as a result, the imagery gives a decent obscurity to the pronouncement, and it allows amplification without commitment.

In Lecture X, Lowth deals with the extended metaphor; and he observes that the parable as an admonitory fable with a hidden meaning is a very restrictive use of the term. The parabolic style denotes an effect of striking the listener's mind "more forcibly." "Judah is a lion's whelp," Genesis xlix reads. "From the prey, my son, thou art gone up," the passage continues with a change of person. And it continues, "He stoopeth down, he coucheth, as a lion." Lowth describes a species of "mystical allegory" not uncommon in prophecy where a poem connects David, or Jerusalem, with far-distant phenomena. The "unusual fervour of language" and "brilliancy of metaphor" of Psalm ii in which David's inauguration also alludes to the coming of Christ gives the poem, as it were, two applications and affords a higher degree of expression and perspicuity than it would have had. The earthbound yet sublime effect of the parabolic style is especially adapted to express human and divine concepts, for it retains an essential degree of ambiguity without vagueness. Time, the eleventh lecture concludes, "which darkens every other composition, elucidates" the poetry of prophecy for those living after the event.

There are two contrary operations of the mind, Lowth observes in Lecture XII on comparison. Judgment, which is a protective faculty, reveals disagreements between things which were thought to be similar. Imagination, on the other hand, draws to our attention the similarities between things which judgment had told us were distinctly different; and Lowth cites Virgil's comparison of an agitated mind to boiling water as an example of an imaginative comparison. The "principal excellence" of comparison is in bringing together images distinct in kind but "correspondent in some particular circumstances." In Isaiah vii, for example, the hearts of men are said to be moved "as the trees of the wood are moved with the wind." The Hebrews used metaphor more than other poets, and their comparisons frequently depend upon a single word. They frequently accumulated several together, like Moses in Deuteronomy xxxii, who compared God's doctrine to dew, to light rain, and to thick drops. Comparisons used for illumination are frequent; for example, the Assyrian king's triumphs are compared to a boy's bird-nesting. Unlike the Greeks and Romans, the Hebrews did not have a store of fables; and they therefore resorted to such images from Nature as cedars and palms, that stood for prosperity and opulence; Mt. Lebanon indicated majesty; Mt. Carmel stood for beauty.

Like other primitive races, the Hebrews did not present religion as unseen abstraction, Lowth observes in Lecture XIII. Their poetry was full of sense images of which "by far the boldest and most daring" was the personified abstraction. He cites again the example which Addison in *Spectator No. 357* had found especially "sublime" in Habakkuk iii, 5, "Pestilence marching before JEHOVAH when he comes to vengeance." We find also the personifying of nations as sons and daughters and the magnificent images of manufactured articles such as "The Sword of Jehovah." Lowth's translation of Isaiah xiv, which Smart was to praise in the highest terms, was an entire lyric drama of personified objects: cedars, nations, mountains, kings of fallen nations; and, as such, it formed a version of the greatest extant lyric ode.

The fourteenth through seventeenth lectures constitute a single essay about the nature of the Hebrew "Sublime"; and Lowth deals with it first in general, then in expression, in sentiment, and in passion. By "sublime," Lowth means simply "that force of composition, whatever it be, which strikes and overpowers the mind." The Hebrews had such "force of composition" to an extreme degree; and Lowth finds, unlike Addison, that the basis of "the Sublime" is not in reference to great *things* but in an entire method of composition which is forceful and overpowering. In Job iii, 3., "Let the day perish wherein I was born, and the night in which it was said, There is a man child conceived," is characterized — like the *mashal* of Balaam in Numbers xxiii, — by "exalted sentiments"; and that "spirit of sublimity . . . energy and enthusiasm," an overpowering attack on the senses, is achieved by a concrete brevity of images.

Lowth returns thematically to the Hebrews' attitude to Time: they express "future events by the past tense, or rather by the perfect present, as if they had actually taken place; and, on the contrary, past events by the future, as if immediately or speedily to happen." Such disregard for temporality was part of the passionate language of poetry, and Lowth suggests that the "mental emotion" characteristic of such verse is not produced by the imitation of external Nature alone but of the mind in action. We are aware, in the language of *reason* or judgment, of the "accuracy of the description" of whatever is delineated "by the aid and through the uncertain medium, as it were, of the memory." But in *sublime poetry,* memory is of small significance; for the object that appears in the verse is "clear and distinct at once" and "the mind is immediately conscious of itself and its own emotions," a description which recalls Lowth's own *Choice of Hercules.*

Most interesting is a technique of what might appear to be an inappropriate response. The most sublime effect was produced says Lowth by the lowliest images such as "And the Lord awaked . . . Like a strong man shouting because of wine," (in Psalm lxxviii) and as "Jehovah from on high shall roar . . . A shout like that of the vintagers shall he give" (Jeremiah xxv). "From ideas, which in themselves appear coarse, unsuitable, and totally unworthy of so great an object, the mind naturally recedes, and passes suddenly to the contemplation of the object itself, and of its inherent magnitude and importance." Lowth illustrates his notion of "the Sublime" with a description of the sensations attached to sublimity that is more memorable than any in eighteenth-century criticism; and, characteristically, it is redolent of the contemporary and paradoxical sense of endless space. The astonished intellect, leaving the suburbs of Creation, "imperceptibly glides into the void of Infinity: whose vast and formless extent, when displayed to the mind of man . . . impresses it with the sublimest and most awful sensations, and fills it with a mixture of admiration and terror."

These lectures are succeeded by another group of four about prophecy. Next to the lyric, or ode, prophecy was the most important genre; and it was both sublime and parabolic. "Prophet," "poet," and "musician" were all designated by one word in Hebrew; and prophesying was usually "accompanied with a very violent agitation of the mind." The sacred hymns were frequently designed for memorizing, and were parabolic rather than didactic. Indeed, colleges of apprentice prophets existed where composing to music was a special discipline. Prophetic poetry was ordered in repeated patterns that agreed with the number of syllables in the line; a special poetic language was employed; each metrical ending coincided with a syntactical conclusion; the meter and the meaning were closely identified with each other. Since the poems were chanted by two groups, patterns of parallelism and distichs developed such as "Saul hath smote his thousands," and "And David his ten thousands" in 1 Samuel xviii, 7ff. The practice became Christianized in the responsive singing of Psalms. These prophetic patterns coincided with the echoing structure of the earlier poems meant for memorizing. The nature of the language also supported these developments which, flowing together, influenced other kinds of poetry even when the original purposes were left behind.

Almost every Hebrew poem, Lowth finds, "possesses a sort of responsive form"; and, while such form is more adapted to lyric than to prophetic poetry, it nevertheless occurs equally in the latter. This parallelism, for which discovery Lowth became famous as a scriptural scholar, "consists chiefly in a certain equality, resemblance, or parallelism between the members of each period; so that in two lines . . . things for the most part shall answer to things, and words to words, as if fitted to each other by a rule or measure." In *synonymous* parallelism, the sentiment is repeated in different terms in the same pattern, as in Psalm cxiv: "When Israel went out from Egypt; / The house of Jacob from a strange people: / Judah was as his sacred heritage; / Israel his dominion." Among the variations may be found a repetition of the first phrase in the couplet such as "With the jaw-bone of an ass, heaps upon heaps; / With the jaw-bone of an ass, a thousand men have I smitten" (Judges xv, 16); triplet parallelisms; and stanzaic forms of five lines — two distichs divided by a central line.

In *antithetic* parallelism, an image is, as the name implies, illustrated by its contrary in an exactly repeated pattern; for "sentiments are opposed to sentiments, words to words, singulars to singulars, plurals to plurals" as in Proverbs xxvii, 6 and 7: "The blows of a friend are faithful; / But the kisses of an enemy are treacherous. / The cloyed will trample upon an honey-comb; / But to the hungry every bitter thing is sweet." The more sublime poetry does not use the antithetic parallelism as a rule, but passages in Isaiah characteristically impart sweetness and dignity to it: "In a little anger have I forsaken thee; / But with great mercies will I receive thee again" (liv, 7ff).

The last kind of parallelism, *synthetic* or constructive, does not parallel by repetition like the first kind, or by antithesis, but by only the echoing of construction. Characteristic of this last category is the use of exact numbers to denote inexact quantities: "For three transgressions of Damascus, / And for four, I will not restore it" (Amos i, 3). Triplets are common in constructive parallelism, as is also a detailed balancing of syllable by syllable as in "My-doctrine shall-drop, as-the-rain;/My-word shall-distil, as-the-dew" (Deuteronomy xxxii, 2).

In Lecture XX, Lowth turned to the general characteristics of prophecy. The *aim* of prophecy, he found, was to excite the "fears and apprehensions" of, or to afford consolation to, "those generations that precede the events predicted." The *means* to fulfill such objectives were, he found, amplifications of the subject. The usual method was a descent into particulars in one or two instances and the use of a "general propriety in the imagery" throughout. Comprehensive or general ideas which were common in prophecy reveal the infinite in widely scattered events. Emotion, feeling, the passions, were the "peculiar province" of all prophecy. Other characteristics were a brilliance of imagery, a clarity of diction, and a use of metaphor from Nature and sacred history. The central place also of this overall form was demonstrated in Isaiah xxxiv and xxxv in which images of victory, stinking corpses, mountains melting with blood, goats, rams, cormorants, and courts of owls depict the devastation of Armageddon in chapter thirty-four, while images in the next chapter of the blind, deaf, and crippled who are cured and of the desert blossoming imaged the Second Coming that would follow this great battle between nations before the Day of Judgment. These vivid images of Nature and of the past victories of Jehovah, such as the razing of Sodom, refer to the distant restoration of the church and offer an excellent example of the power of parabolic particulars to suggest new and distant prophetic ends.

Isaiah was the Homer; Ezekiel, the Aeschylus; and Jeremiah the Simonides of the Hebrews, Lowth declares in Lecture XXI which is about the characteristics of individual prophets. Isaiah's "Uncommon elevation and majesty" in his emotions, elegance, sensitivity, and broad allusiveness of his imagery, as well as the uncommon delicacy in the formal arrangement of his poem, are noted and praised. "Deep, vehement, tragical ... full of fire, indignant," Ezekiel's imagery is "crowded, magnificent, terrific, sometimes almost to disgust"; and his language is "pompous, solemn, austere, rough." "From the vehemence of passion and indignation," Ezekiel produces frequent repetition and sentences "so rude and incompact, that I am often at a loss." Jeremiah's sentiments are not always as elevated as Isaiah's, and his periods are less well-formed on occasion. Otherwise, he is in no way inferior. Hosea's style is "of very remote antiquity"; Joel is "elegant ... and fluent"; Amos in the sheep-fold was actuated by the same spirit as Isaiah and Daniel in the court; Nahum, "bold and highly luminous," is outstanding among the minor prophets; Micah is forcible; Habakkuk and Zephaniah are striking but without distinct characteristics; and Jonah and Daniel are somewhat more historical than poetical. Of the remaining prophets, Haggai and Zachariah tend to be prosaic; but Malachi's dates and middle style indicate that, after the Babylonian captivity, the Jewish muse suffered a marked decline. Lowth concludes his lecture with reference to Virgil's Fourth Eclogue, that is similar in prophetic kind, and the mystery of which he says he is utterly at a loss to explain.

Every poetic tradition produced the elegy, a form which, unlike the lyric, as he notes in Lecture XXII, deals with only one emotion — grief. "O my son Absalom! O Absalom, my son, my son!" (2 Samuel xix, 4) reminds us that the Hebrew elegy was simple and unaffected. Elaborate patterns were, however, constructed and reproduced artificially after the manner of professional mourners. "Whatever the instant sentiment of sorrow dictated" appears to have accumulated naturally as in, for example, the Lamentations of Jeremiah in which five parts, each of twenty-two lines, are divided into stanzas. This natural accumulation is the form of elegy; and, like other Hebrew poetic structures, it combines apparent impulsiveness and flow of emotion with elaborate patterning. No poem but the Lamentations displays such a "splendid selection of imagery in so concentrated a state." Lowth asks his audience to consider the personification of the abandoned capital as a widow, "Is it nothing to you, all ye that pass by?" (Lamentations i, 12). Nine chapters of Job are elegiac, Lowth notes, as are many Psalms. "Grief is of a timid and suspicious temper," he observes, "sullen and querulous, wayward and peevish." These characteristics add diversity, for example, to David's lamentation over Saul and Jonathan: "Declare it not in Gath, / Publish it not in the streets of Ascalon" (2 Samuel i, 17–27).

Lowth, who had earlier divided Hebrew poetry into the *parabolic* and the *didactic,* now turns, in Lecture XXIV, to Proverbs — the major book of didactic poetry. Poetry was originally pedagogic, he notes; for it contained moral lessons in memorable form. This style of "remote antiquity," abandoned by other cultures, remained with the Hebrews until very late. "Apples of gold in a network of silver / Is a word seasonably spoken" (Proverbs xxv, 11), Solomon observed, stressing the necessity of profundity and smoothness. Brevity is also of the essence of a proverb, for a saying of more than twelve words is a harangue. Elegance is also necessary, as is a degree of obscurity designed to give the reader a sense of discovery. He alludes briefly to Ecclesiastes, also the work of Solomon, and to the book of Wisdom and to the Wisdom of the Son of Sirach as inferior as poetry and as wisdom.

With Lecture XXV, Lowth returns to a major theme — the ode. We must image, he notes, "man on his first creation ... in perfect possession of reason and speech ... not an unobservant spectator of the beautiful fabric of the universe," who poured out in that first dawn his spontaneous admiration and joy. Since we must assign a lyric ability to original man, Milton was quite right to put into the mouth of Adam the praise for Creation of Psalm cxlviii. In ode, a form which Lowth surmised was "coeval with ... the Creation of Man," he found "sentiments rising delicately and artfully from each other, yet without any appearance of art." For this apparently loose and wayward form was responsive to the spontaneous demands of a changing topic and emotion, "finishing by a gentle turn of the sentiment in a part where it is least expected, and sometimes as it were by chance."

Among Hebrew odes, Lowth found three kinds: the sweet, the sublime, and the middle kind. The first, the sweet kind, tended toward pensiveness and hope — "The Lord is my shepherd"; and other Psalms excited tender passion with delightful imagery and spare diction. There were no poems more perfect anywhere. Among the sublime odes, to which he moves in Lecture XXVII, Lowth finds two kinds: those sublime by reason of their form; others by reason of their topic. The fiftieth psalm, which is theological in content, observes that God prefers piety to sacrifices; but the manner in which it is organized in two parts creates the most sublime effect: with the summoning of the whole earth before God, which sublime image is dramatically succeeded by the introduction of God Himself "pronouncing his sentence."

The second kind of sublime ode is exemplified by Exodus xv, the "thanksgiving ode of Moses" that was "composed after crossing the Red Sea," an ode on a great event. With its image of drowning Egyptians that is expressed in a variety of ways — "the horse and the rider he hath o'erwhelmed in the sea," "the depths have covered them; / They went down into the abyss as a stone" — the ode has the effect of "passions struggling for vent, labouring with a copiousness of thought and a poverty of expression, and on that very account the more expressly displayed." In Lecture XXVIII, he examines odes of the sublime kind which achieve their effect from a combination of diction, sentiments, and the poem's progress; and he cites the prophecy of Moses in Deuteronomy xxxii as both prophetic and lyric. Its magnificent exordium, "Give ear, O ye heavens, and I will speak; and hear O earth, the words of my mouth...''; the display of God's love and of the people's ingratitude; and the magnificent personification, "He is the Rock..." and the final promise of hope combine the energy and the boldness of the ode with the variety and the grandeur of prophecy.

In Lecture XXVI, he had observed that the middle style of ode which is both sweet *and* sublime was more perfect than the ode of Pindar because it had a notable ease and grace of digression. In dealing with the triumphal ode of Deborah — Judges v, 28–30, another sublime ode of triumph that is pregnant with allusions to sacred history — he notes that it "breathes the free and fervid spirit of the Lyric Muse" in "the most eccentric excursions of the imagination" without leaving its main design.

The Hebrew hymns or idylls, Lowth observes in Lecture XXIX, are similar but superior to the idylls of Callimachus, Homer, or Theocritus; for these types are lighter poems on humbler topics which evaded other classification. They are of moderate length, like the ode of the middle style, sublime but elegant, sweet and clear. "Among the most elegant monuments of antiquity" is Psalm cvii, which is divided into five parts which outline God's concern for desert wanderers, the starving, the imprisoned, the sick, and the people at sea. The sentiment of the epode, applicable throughout, is repeated in a variety of forms. The hymn of David on "the creation of this infinite All" of Psalm civ — which, as we recall, was translated by Trapp, the first Professor of Poetry — has for Lowth also the very first place in poetry; there is nothing more perfect.

Dramatic poetry occupies the rest of Lowth's *Lectures,* from the thirtieth up to and including the thirty-fourth lecture. He distinguishes two kinds of dramatic poems: the first, with dialogue only; and the second, complete with an entire action or plot. Psalm xxiv, a poem celebrating the induction of the Ark on Mt. Sion, contains dialogue and celebrates a theatrical event; but since it has no sustained and varied action, it belongs in the first and inferior category. In the second and more finished category there are only two possible entries, the Song of Solomon and Job. Jacques Bossuet (1627-1704) had shown, Lowth remarks, that it is likely that the seven definable sections of the Song of Solomon correspond to the seven days of the marriage feast. Among the speakers in the song, Lowth finds Solomon, his bride, and a chorus. But "the whole was one even tenor of joy and festivity," and there is no "change of fortune." Therefore, while somewhat dramatic, the Song, he reluctantly finds, is not a finished drama.

Eighteenth-century writers were fascinated by Job, the poet of "the most ancient poem in the world" as "John Lizard" (probably Edward Young) had written in *Guardian 86* (1713). It is perhaps fitting that the greatest *critique* of Oriental poetry should end with a lengthy and detailed analysis of Job, "the most ancient of all the sacred books," a poem that runs the gamut of all the passions, that displays varied character, that has the greatest sublimity, that is far superior to the greatest Greek dramas, and that was composed "so many ages before."

This poem is possibly the least Hebrew of the sacred writings, Lowth notes, for it has closer affinities with Arabia than with the Israelites. Job tells of a virtuous man, suddenly precipitated from the summit of prosperity, who is consoled by friends who add to his afflictions by becoming reproachers. The first friend questions his integrity; the second advises wise humility; the third upbraids him with vanity and lying. These accusations commence the action in which several stages of accusation, recrimination, and response lead to God's review of Creation and His demonstration of Job's weakness. The principal object of the whole appears to be this climax says Lowth, the aim of which is to teach men "an unwavering and unsullied faith." Lowth observes, however, that the disputes, while necessary, are separate from the work as an esthetic whole and that "the end of the poetical part is different from the design ... at large."

After referring to Aristotle's *Poetics* and after comparing Sophocles' *Oedipus,* the Professor of Poetry found that Job's conversion, which completes the intervention of the Almighty, is not a true action; for it is merely a continuation of what has gone before. Though not a true drama, the poem is, nevertheless, a very great work of sentiment and feeling, especially "in the more vehement passions, grief and indignation and violent contention." Lowth finds the sublimity of terror central to it; and, like Edward Young the probable author of *Guardian No. 86*, and like Edmund Burke who later (1757) expanded Lowth's observations in his *Sublime and Beautiful* (Part II, Section v), Lowth comments upon "the ardour and alacrity of the warhorse, and his eagerness for battle" that are depicted in the lines, "He swalloweth the ground with fierceness and rage: neither believeth he that it is the sound of the trumpet. He saith among the trumpets Ha, ha; and he smelleth the battle afar off, the thunder of the captains and the shouting" (Job xxxix, 24, 25).

Lowth concluded his nine-year series of lectures by congratulating his auditors on having Professor Thomas Hunt, professor of Arabic and Hebrew, to unfold for them "the inexhaustible treasures of Oriental literature"; and he hoped that he himself had been able to open "a few of the more delightful retreats of this paradise" to them. The published work concludes with a "brief confutation" of a contemporary bishop's system of Hebrew meter on the grounds that our ignorance of Ancient Hebrew prevents our knowing the quantities of the syllables, a point which he had touched upon in Lecture III.

II *The Significance of Lowth's* Praelectiones

The single over-riding image of Lowth's literary theories is that of the nature of the first man. "It is worthy observation," he told his audience in his first lecture, "that as some of these writings exceed in antiquity the fabulous ages of Greece, in sublimity they are superior to the most finished productions of that polished people" (I, 37). The shift to Orientalism, in a word, was a shift not only to "the best" but to the most ancient or primitive. In picturing a kind of Adam who reveled in his sudden unexpected life, who exercised an art "derived from nature alone," and who "only at an advanced period of society" conformed to "rule and methods," Lowth dwelt on "man on his first creation" as "in perfect possession of reason and speech" and as "...not an unobservant spectator of the beautiful fabric of the universe" (XXV, 190). Moreover, Lowth most significantly asked his audience to project themselves into that "new-created mind (undepraved by habit or opinion)" (I, 37-38).

The function of this art was not imitation of external nature; it was the impression of the self-contemplating mind observing itself in the act of knowing. "Since the human intellect is naturally delighted with every species of imitation, that species in particular, which exhibits its own image, which displays and depicts those impulses, inflexions, perturbations, and secret emotions, which it perceives and knows in itself, can scarcely fail to astonish and to delight above every other" (XVII, 367-68). Lowth's perception at this point is most crucial to an understanding of the significance of Orientalism in English poetry in the mid-eighteenth century, for he formally states the passing of the Classical notion of poetry as an art dominated by Memory. He posits instead an ideal central to the Romantic movement — the concept of art as a continual experience of developing knowledge. Many characteristics of mid- and late-eighteenth-century verse are related to this shift; and among them are the sense of curious, even mystical oneness of the reader with the poem, the weakening of the personality or self of the poet in the poem, and the exploration of words as mysterious objects in Nature whose important function is not referential but creative.

In this poetry of passion, "the mind is immediately conscious of itself and its own emotions," and "it feels and suffers in itself a sensation either the same or similar to that which is described" (XVII, 368). This lyric poetry, irrational and sublime, was distinct from the poetry of reason — and we might add of Pope — in which "the understanding slowly perceives the accuracy of the description in all other subjects ... being obliged to compare them by the aid and through the uncertain medium, as it were, of the memory" (XVII, 368). Mnemosyne, the ancient Greek goddess of memory, is no longer the mother of the Muses; nor, even in the work of Lowth, a prominent cleric, was a distinct God the object of enquiry; for, in poetic creation, "this ecstatic impulse became the God of the moment" (XVII, 367).

In the modern world, we relate emotion to vagueness and reason to clarity; but Lowth did not. Those images "explored by reason and argument" are to him "the least clear and evident" (V, 117). Those provided by the impact of external objects on the senses in a state of excitement are "more evident and distinct" (V, 117). In this state of excitement, the mind does not move from the word to a memory of whatever the word indicates: instead, it responds parabolically while in a state of sublime shock, *away from* the word as from an intruder; and, the more lowly the image, the greater the degree of elevation or sublimity experienced by the reader. This interesting theory accounts for Lowth's lectures on the nature of everyday imagery in Hebrew poetry (Lectures VI and VII), and for the apparent paradox that the Ancient Hebrews wrote the most sublime poetry and that it was almost entirely composed of images of the senses taken from their own everyday peculiar surroundings. Lowth cites verses in which God himself is imaged as a shouting, drunken man (Psalm lxxviii, 65) and as a villager noisily tramping out the grapes (Jeremiah xxv, 30); and he affirms: "from ideas, which in themselves appear coarse, unsuitable, and totally unworthy of so great an object, the mind naturally recedes, and passes suddenly to the contemplation of the object itself, and of its inherent magnitude and importance" (XVI, 364).

Lowth's emphasis on parallelism is directly related to his concept of imagery, for it posits a form of composition in which things are not subordinated to the complex syntactical patterns which in themselves reinforce the function of memory in reading. Echoing lines, in which object answers object, and adjective adjective, as if overwhelming an imagination tyrannized into reiterated patterning, suggest an absence of logic and a combination of temporal and spatial phenomena within an infinite stasis. This lack of the sequential aspect of ordinary cognition is reinforced by Lowth's sense of the Orient for, like Smart and Blake, he appears to confuse, deliberately, the Middle East of thousands of years ago with that of the present time. John Chardin, Thomas Harmer, Edward Pococke, George Sandys,[3] the "modern" and contemporary travelers, supply the vast underpinning of timeless "reality" on which Lowth's empathy ambivalently rests. "He who would perceive and feel the peculiar and interior elegancies of the Hebrew poetry," Lowth advised his listeners, "must imagine himself exactly situated as the persons for whom it was written, or even as the writers themselves ... hearing or delivering the same words, at the same time, and in the same country" (V, 114). But the time, like the place, is neither now nor then; it is the springboard for the experience of the infinite.

The tradition to which Lowth's Orientalism belongs begins with Thomas Burnet's *The Theory of the Earth* (1684,90) which was translated by his own pen from his Latin original. Burnet, who claimed that the cosmos was some five thousand years old, denied the existence of any Garden of Eden or Paradise. There *was* an early perfection, he noted, but it was the perfection of a material globe which was perfectly smooth all over and which was known in Oriental legend as "the Mundane Egg." At the Creation, which occurred at the same time as the Flood, the "inner sea" and the "inner fire" burst the shell of the Mundane Egg and left the extra-

ordinary ruin which we now behold, a globe where four-fifths of
the earth's surface is ocean, and where "ghastly" mountain ranges
— the broken shell of the Mundane Egg — crisscross the once
smooth sphere. Burnet, a "physico-theologian," attempted, in the
face of the materialism of the Royal Society to wed religion, especially as seen in the Bible, and the new physics — and geology.

The importance of Burnet is that he imaged God's total skill and
perfection as involved in the making of material things. The
*super*natural unseen did not exist, and there *was* no truth distinct
from that which our senses gave us of Nature. Burnet's great and
representative works mark the disappearance of allegory from
interpretations of the Bible; for Burnet regarded the writers of the
Old Testament, especially Ezekiel, Moses, and St. John, as depend-
able witnesses of what had physically occurred in the earliest years
of the globe, as it was thought, about five thousand years before.
These original prophets seemed to be naturalists rather than inspired visionaries; meticulous geologists rather than authorities
about unseen mysteries. We note almost as a side issue Burnet's
founding of what we may term "the eighteenth-century Sublime."
Burnet wrote,

The greatest objects of Nature are, methinks, the most pleasing to behold;
and next to the great concave of the Heavens, and those boundless regions
where the stars inhabit, there is nothing that I look upon with more pleasure than the wide Sea and the Mountains of the Earth. There is something
august and stately in the air of these things, that inspires the mind with
great thoughts and passions; We do naturally, upon such occasions, think
of God and his greatness: and whatsoever hath but the shadow and
appearance of INFINITE, as all things have that are too big for our com-
prehension, they fill and over-bear the mind with their Excess, and cast it
into a pleasing kind of stupor and admiration.[4]

Burnet's eighteenth-century "Sublime" became influential. His
concept is distinctive in that it relies on our senses alone, positing no
"superior" or noble portion of man's faculties. It simply describes
a subjective, psychological response. It images a world without
hieratic form. It depends on material objects only. In combination
with George Berkeley's philosophy, it cast radical doubt on the
reality of external Nature. Most importantly, it allowed man, in his
irrational, awe-inspired response to great or huge objects, to experience directly as an esthetic, non-religious phenomenon the infinite
or eternal, as a result of his natural perceptive mechanism. In a

sense, all that had been a traditionally religious, could now be thought of as a secular, response to Nature. The fundamental importance of Burnet's "Sublime" not only to Old Testament studies, themselves "sublime," but to Romanticism at large may be observed in the work of Samuel Taylor Coleridge in whom Burnet is singularly important, especially in Coleridge's poem *The Ancient Mariner.*

At an early date, Joseph Addison's notion of "the Sublime," which is unveiled in his *Spectator Nos. 411-421,* was influenced by Burnet, who had been his schoolmaster at The Charterhouse. As we have suggested, however, Addison related literary theory and current philosophy; and it is this mixture of literary theory, Burnet's "Sublime," and eighteenth-century philosophy, first explicit in Addison, that we may detect especially in the work of Robert Lowth. We have noted Addison's influence in Lowth's concept of personification. Far from representing moral qualities truly "outside" of a work of poetry, as for example, in the prophet Habakkuk, moral abstractions came to be seen only as mechanical contrivances which worked in a poem for a number of reasons which had to do only with the psychology of cognition.

At an early moment in the eighteenth century in the history of poetry imitative of the Old Testament, the philosophy of George Berkeley became important. We may see his effect in Edward Young's poem *The Last Day* written in 1713. Berkeley had posited in *A New Theory of Vision* (1709) a world where externality did not really exist; it was merely a subjective creation of the mind. The same subjectivity, we may observe, adhered to the notion of Time in Berkeley. We have noted in Lowth's youthful, prophetic poetry strong evidence that, as a young man at Winchester, Lowth was already well acquainted with the poetic possibilities of Berkeley's philosophy in which all material objects may be thought of as pressing, without duration (Time), spatial qualities — or extension — on man's perceptive creativity. In Young's *Last Day,* which, like most primitive poetry of the eighteenth century, was located at the end of the time spectrum, either at the Creation or at the end of the world, the world of material things is gathered around God's throne, as all finite measurement disappears; and "Time, and Place, / Matter, and Form, and Fortune, Life, and Grace, / Wait humbly at the footstool of their God, / And move obedient at His awful nod" (ll. 215–18).

The poetic imaging of a timeless and spaceless world is pursued

in *Guardian No. 86* where "John Lizard" suggests that the extraordinary sublimity of Job derives from the poet's seeing all things
as "in the eye of the Creator," that is, like God. This view recurs in
a famous passage in "Night VI" of Young's *Night Thoughts* where
the prophet, Young, sees man's senses as "half-creating" everything he sees. In a passage which suggests the theory of imagination
not only of Romantic poets — William Wordsworth (1770–1850)
took the term "half create" from this passage for his *Tintern
Abbey* (1798) — but also perhaps the concept of imagination even
of Wallace Stevens (1879–1955), Young saw man as significantly
creating what he saw by and in seeing it. In George Berkeley's terms
in the *Principles of Human Knowledge* (ʾ3), the *"esse"* (being) of
"unthinking things" coincides with their *"percipi"* (being perceived). In "Night VI" of *Night Thoughts,* Young observed that
man's senses, as opposed, we note, to spirit or soul,

> . . . inherit earth and heavens;
> Enjoy the various riches Nature yields;
> Far nobler! give the riches they enjoy;
> Give taste to fruits, and harmony to groves,
> Their radiant beams to gold, and gold's bright sire;
> Take-in, at once, the landscape of the world,
> At a small inlet, which a grain might close,
> And half-create the wondrous world they see. (*Night VI,* ll. 420–27)

We should, of course, remind ourselves that Young's *Night
Thoughts* was an explicit prophecy consciously modeled on Ezekiel. Again in Wykehamist "primitivism," "Orientalism" and
eighteenth-century philosophy of perception meet.

Lowth's Old Testament is that of Burnet; it is a material phenomenon, not a spiritual manifestation. It is — in spite of occasional references to heaven that are not remarkable in a man who
had his career to make in the church — based on current
eighteenth-century theories of perception. It embodies a "Sublime" — an experience of the infinite — which is not a vision of a
veiled God; it is an exploitation of man's native imaginative
resources.

The connection between Lowth's lectures and his earlier poetry
lies in the exploitation at length of the notion of an *"orientalism"*
suggested in Spence's *Essay on Pope's Odyssey.* As we have seen,
Spence's suggestion that the cessation of Time — as, for instance,
in the stopping of the sun prophesied in the *Odyssey* — was the

heart of Oriental prophecy; and this concept was given direct application in Robert Lowth's *Genealogy of Christ* (ll. 174-9) where the
sun repeats his course and Time forgets to flow.

Lowth's major interest is prophetic poetry. It is when he is discussing prophecy that he advances the theory of parallelism which
made him famous as a Biblical scholar. What interested Lowth in
primitive poetry was precisely the topic that fascinated eighteenth-
century philosophers, man's imaging of Time. Prophecy for Lowth
— as for his father — was the one artifact in which man escaped
from the control of Time; he forecast what was going to happen;
and he created, as it were, by imagining. It is interesting to observe
not only that Lowth's "parallelism" itself is a way of ordering
experience within a poem (since the reader experiences a kind of on-
the-spot repetition which is incantatory and destructive of the
rhythms of Time in the reader's mind) but also that prophecy itself
suggests a view of the reality and function of words reminiscent of
George Berkeley and Edmund Burke. The major activity of poetry
in Lowth was the contemplation of the mind without the uncertain
aid of Memory in a state of heightened emotion; Lowth observed
that the syntactical patterns of ordinary language were weakened or
destroyed; the words formed new relations, a vision of the future
rather than the associations of the past; the prophet, as it were,
drew the reader or listener into a shared creation in which words,
devoid of individual memory content, and thereby only weakly
recalling what they "stood" for, had an immediate, particular,
"sublime"—an infinite, effect. This use of words, devoid of memory and intellectual meaning, derives from George Berkeley, perhaps the greatest English philosopher. In *Principles of Human
Knowledge* (1710) he wrote:

Besides, the communicating of ideas marked by words is not the chief and
only end of language, as is commonly supposed. There are other ends, as
the raising of some passion, the exciting to, or deterring from an action,
the putting the mind in some particular disposition; to which the former is
in many cases barely subservient, and sometimes entirely omitted, when
these can be obtained without it, as I think doth not infrequently happen in
the familiar use of language. I entreat the reader to reflect with himself,
and see if it doth not often happen either in hearing or reading a discourse,
that the passions of fear, love, hatred, admiration, disdain, and the like
arise, immediately in his mind upon the perception of certain words, without any ideas coming between. At first, indeed, the words might have
occasioned ideas that were fit to produce those emotions; but, if I mistake

not, it will be found that when language is once grown familiar, the hearing of the sounds or sight of the characters is oft immediately attended with those passions, which at first were wont to be produced by the intervention of ideas, that are now quite omitted.

(Introduction, 20)

In Edmund Burke's *Sublime and Beautiful* (1757), as in Lowth's earlier lectures, Biblical poetry was a major example of "the Sublime." Burke's lines on Job in his section on "Power" (Part II, Section v) seem to be derivative of Lowth and, farther back, of "John Lizard." In spite of the differences of emphasis, we find a very explicit echo of Lowth's notions of "sublime" poetry in Burke's fascinating theories about how words actually produce their effects. Burke describes words functioning in "the Sublime" as essentially "noumenal," a word coined by the great German philosopher Immanuel Kant (1724-1804) to describe intuitive, creative, and non-referential moments — ones that might be conceived in the early linguistic development of children or in Nature's children, primitive peoples. Reflecting the core of Lowth's insights when describing the parabolic effect of Hebrew poetry in the Hebrew *Mashal,* and with a significant emphasis on abstractions, Burke wrote in Section iv, Part V of the *Sublime and Beautiful,* "The Effect of Words":

If words have all their possible extent of power, three effects arise in the mind of the hearer. The first is the *sound;* the second, the *picture,* or representation of the thing signified by the sound; the third is, the *affection* of the soul produced by one or by both of the foregoing. *Compounded abstract* words, of which we have been speaking, (honour, justice, liberty, and the like), produce the first and the last of these effects, but not the second. *Simple abstracts,* are used to signify some one simple idea without much adverting to others which may chance to attend it, as blue, green, hot, cold, and the like; these are capable of affecting all three of the purposes of words; as the *aggregate* words, man, castle, horse, &c. are in a yet higher degree. But I am of opinion, that the most general effect even of these words, does not arise from their forming pictures of the several things they would represent in the imagination ... I do not find that once in twenty times any such picture is formed, and when it is, there is most commonly a particular effort of the imagination for that purpose. But the aggregate words operate as I said of the compound abstracts, not by presenting any image to the mind, but by having from use the same effect on being mentioned, that their original has when it is seen.

The final emphasis that Burke makes here — that the "sublime" effect of a word is that of the thing possibly as seen *for the very first time,* — suggests the reason why Lowth continually spoke in his lectures about the newly created mind of the very first man. At the heart of the mid-eighteenth-century "Sublime," and in the midst of theories about Biblical poetry, we discover the true importance of "primitive" Oriental theories, which was that all men, everywhere, continually experience the sublimity of newly created man, and that the significant use of language in poetry — devoid of memory of what words stood for (in the past) — is one in which we are all primitives continually creating the new world (hence the importance of the "New World" in the Romantic sensibility). This assumption is at the heart of Lowth's influence on Christopher Smart, and this highly significant aspect of Romanticism was perhaps first isolated in any form nearing explicitness in Lowth's analysis of poetry. What is especially clear here is that eighteenth-century notions of perception are at the heart of so-called "primitivism," and that "Orientalism" is an application of concepts of perception which were abroad in the most advanced thinking of the time.

The "Sublime" of Edmund Burke, outlined in his *Sublime and Beautiful* four years after the publication of Lowth's lectures, offers emphases distinct from "the Sublime" of Lowth. For one thing, Burke is almost exclusively interested in terror as a source of "the Sublime," whereas Lowth is by and large interested in the psychological response to language. Burke seems to psychologize in general about "the Sublime," whereas Lowth is concerned with linguistic response in poetry. Burke, moreover, does little to pin down the effect of the direct experience of the infinite, which is in essence the significance of "sublimity," whereas Lowth etches in a kind of self-induced spatial voyage to the edge of Creation in which the high and the low are commingled in a way which suggests *The Marriage of Heaven and Hell* of William Blake (1757–1827).

In poetry, for Lowth, "low," "coarse" words induce a sense of immediate sublime shock, and the highest kind of parabolic flight of the mind. Lowth also carried forward the doctrine of "particulars" which we noted in Joseph Spence and in Joseph Warton. The mind, in not referring back in memory to the ideas or "meaning" of words but in responding sublimely to words in a state of heightened emotional shock, naturally is left with an experience of single, particular, isolated images towards which it, like a prophet, continually moves forward in an experience of futurity.

What is especially interesting in this regard is the sense of Nature that we see in Lowth. For the neo-Classical mind, Nature was an external reality structured on Time and Space. In the mid-eighteenth century, Nature became a mass of isolated particulars, ones that always called forth from the mind its imaginative resources. But, in the mid-century, for example in Burke, there was *some* ambiguity. In a sense "Nature" remained stubbornly external, and yet it produced a subjective, individual response which was not shared by others. In Lowth, however, the significant emphasis is upon the prophetic ability of the mind, that is on the creative capacity of the human mind *in poetry,* to ignore, or mold, Time (and Space), and to make new infinite worlds of its own. For this reason, Lowth is a humanistic theorist, not a Christian. Nature in him, we might conclude, is not fallen and guilt-ridden; instead, it is an ever-extending reality, one continually created by man's perception. Man himself becomes the *Deus Creator,* the creating God. This imaginative activity of Oriental prophecy suggests strongly the matrix in the mid-eighteenth-century of a faculty very much akin to the creative imagination which we find in Christopher Smart and William Blake, almost all of whose poetry illuminates these characteristics of Oriental verse. As for S. T. Coleridge, such imaginative activity of Oriental prophecy suggests strong reasons why, among the most memorable poems in that great Romantic's output, was the Oriental poem, *Kubla Khan.*

CHAPTER 5

Lowth after the Professorship of Poetry: Warburton and The Life of Wykeham

I The Battle with Warburton

O NE of the few well-documented events in Lowth's life, his battle with William Warburton, is useful in underlining the distinction between the two views which existed of the first ages. William Warburton (1698–1779) had defended Pope against the attacks of the Swiss theologian Jean Pierre de Crousaz, about the Deism of the *Essay on Man,* a defense which gives the clue to Warburton's essentially spiritual instinct. As a result of his championing, Warburton had become a close friend of the poet, had visited him often at Twickenham, and had become assured of the position as Pope's literary executor. The most famous of Warburton's works was an incomplete but ever growing collection, *The Divine Legation,* which Francis Jeffrey considered in the *Edinburgh Review* to be "the most learned, the most arrogant, and most absurd work, which has been produced in England for a century."[1]

Unlike Lowth, Warburton stressed theology, the inability of the senses to arrive at truth, the importance of revealed religion as opposed to Deism, and the value of interpretation of the Bible by geniuses like himself. He also claimed paradoxically that "In revealed religion, besides those interior marks of truth ... which require the delicate operation of a great Genius," there were "more univocal marks of truth ... which require no great qualities, but humility." The demonstration of supernatural truth he had come upon was "so strong and beautiful," "so easy and simple," that he could not decide "whether the pleasure of the discovery, or the

99

wonder that it is now to make, be greater."[2]

He was, he said, concerned about the spread of the notion that a person could be a Christian and disregard Jewish history. Such a belief was "the same with the *Socinian, that Christianity is only the republication of the religion of Nature.*" To the confusion of Deists and Socinians alike, he would prove "that the doctrine of a future state of reward and punishments is not to be found in, nor did make part of, the Mosaic dispensation" and "that therefore the Law of Moses is of divine origin." Repetition was characteristic of Warburton, and his syllogism bears repeating: "whatsoever religion and society have no future state for their support, must be supported by an extraordinary Providence." "The Jewish religion and society had no future state for their support": "therefore, the Jewish religion and society were supported by an extraordinary Providence."[3]

Edward Gibbon's *Memoirs* make clear the ubiquitousness of Warburton's oracular obsession. In the *Divine Legation,* Warburton had also argued that the descent of Aeneas into the Underworld in the sixth book of the *Aeneid* represented "the initiation of Aeneas, in the character of a lawgiver, to the Eleusinian mysteries."[4] "This hypothesis," opined the author of *The Decline and Fall of the Roman Empire,* "a singular chapter in the Divine Legation of Moses, had been admitted by many as true; it was praised by all as ingenious; nor had it been exposed . . . to a fair and critical discussion."[5] Gibbon then noted about Lowth's fight with Warburton, which began in 1753 with the publication of Lowth's lectures, that "whatsoever might be the merits of an insignificant controversy, his victory was clearly established by the silent confusion of Warburton and his slaves";[6] but Gibbon admitted that "*I* too, without any private offence, was ambitious of breaking a lance against the giant's shield."[7] Warburton's "most learned," "arrogant," and "absurd" work of a century had appeared first in 1738–1741, and, before Lowth's *Praelectiones*, his book was the major account of the primitive Oriental world published in the century, and many shared Warburton's high opinion of its author's importance.

Mark Pattison, by far the most sympathetic nineteenth-century commentator, tells the story in his study of Warburton. Considering the fight with Lowth to have been Warburton's "most desperate battle, and his last,"[8] Pattison begins with the publication of Lowth's *De sacra pöesi Hebraeorum* in 1753, "the first sign of the awakening of Oxford from that torpor under which two generations had now lain, under the besotting influence of Jacobite and high-church politics."⁹ "The 'classic elegance of Lowth,' became a standard phrase," he notes, "and continued to be so till into the present century."¹⁰ In 1755, five years after resigning his professorship of poetry, Lowth collided with Warburton "on the same stage of the ladder of Church preferment, each of them obtaining in that year a stall at Durham."¹¹ Both were prebends of the cathedral church, both were heading for a bishopric; but Warburton was fifty-seven; Lowth, forty-five.

Lowth's *Praelectiones* had been published in 1753; and Warburton decided two years later that his inviolate opinion of the date of Job had been dismissed in Lowth's final lectures. He sent Joseph Spence and a Dr. Chapman to see Lowth at Winchester and to "demand satisfaction for this constructive treason."¹² Pattison writes, "what must have been Warburton's surprise and rage when, instead of the apologetic submission to which he had been accustomed, he was met with the easy courtesy of an equal, aware of his strength, and yet disguising it under a thin veil of polished indifference."¹³ Warburton, who then tried patronizing, offered to help Lowth to a royal chaplainship, a position that the younger man was capable of acquiring for himself. Then, in 1763, Lowth "brought out a second edition of the *Praelectiones,* in which he not only did not modify the objectionable opinion on Job, but strengthened its point by additions which seemed unmistakably to aim at the view patronized in the *Divine Legation.*"¹⁴

In the Appendix to the inevitable next edition of the *Divine Legation,* Warburton observed "The learned professor has been hardily brought up in the keen atmosphere of *wholesome severities,* and early taught to distinguish between *de facto* and *de jure.*"¹⁵ The reader of Warburton's Appendix was to infer that Lowth had been "hardily brought up" to appreciate the *"wholesome severities"* once inflicted by Catholics on Nonconformists, and the claims of the *de jure* Stuart kings (rulers "by right") against those of *de facto* Hanoverians (rulers "in fact") both at Oxford and Winchester. This charge was, in effect, one of treason. "Malignant"¹⁶ is the word Pattison uses for Warburton's clumsy attempt to put a halt to Lowth's career by attributing to him Stuart sympathies by the use of these loaded traditional terms. It is of interest, perhaps, to note that John Wesley rated Warburton only lower than Richard Bentley in the scale of eighteenth-century unpleasantness.

Praising Bentley's learning, Wesley noted in his sermon entitled *On Pleasing All Men,* "yet how few were less beloved! unless one who was ... equally distant from humility: the author of the 'divine legation of Moses.'"[17]

At the close of the long vacation in 1765, the Clarendon Press printed Lowth's *A Letter to the Right Reverend Author of the Divine Legation,* a pamphlet which went into four editions within eighteen months. Of Lowth's rebuttal of Warburton, Pattison's judgment is interesting: "In polished dexterity of argument, tinged, and not more than tinged, with the raillery of one who knows exactly what is due both to himself and his antagonist, this short piece has perhaps never been surpassed in literary warfare."[18]

"Pray, my lord," Lowth asked the Bishop of Gloucester, Warburton, "what is it to the purpose where I have been brought up? You charge me with principles of intolerance and disaffection to the present royal family and government. You infer these principles, it seems, from the place of my education. Is this a necessary consequence? Is it even a fair conclusion? May not one have had the good sense or the good fortune to have avoided or to have gotten the better of the ordinary prejudices of education? ... Had I not your lordship's example to justify me, I should think it a piece of extreme impertinence to enquire where *you* were bred."[19]

Appearing in the interval between the court action against John Wilkes and the excitement of the Stamp Act, Lowth's *Letter* attracted public attention as no *riposte* in any literary squabble ever had. Pattison comments: "The town hailed, with the Monthly Reviewers, the fall of 'the haughty and overbearing Colossus,' and the 'ample vengeance that had been taken upon the imperious aggressor'"; moreover, "the newspapers teemed with squibs, parodies, and *jeux d'esprit.*"[20] Pattison suggests that Lowth's *Letter* might be equated with Burke's *Speech to the Electors of Bristol* and with Johnson's *Preface to Shakespeare.*[21]

"It is commonly said your lordship's education was of that particular kind," Lowth went on, "concerning which it is a remark of that great judge of men and manners, Lord Clarendon, that it particularly disposes them to be proud, insolent, and pragmatical."[22] In Clarendon's *History of the Rebellion,* Colonel Harrison, a prominent regicide, was executed in 1660. He was, says Lowth, "the son of a butcher, and had been bred up in the place of a clerk ... which kind of education introduces men into the language and practice of business."[23] It went without saying, Lowth declared ironically, that Warburton, once a law clerk, had eluded the fate of such an upbringing: "Now, my lord, as you have in your whole behaviour, and in all your writings, remarkably distinguished yourself by your humility, lenity, meekness, forbearance, candour, humanity, civility, decency, good manners, good temper, moderation with regard to the opinion of others, and a modest diffidence of your own, this unpromising circumstance of your education is so far from being a disgrace to you, that it highly redounds to your fame."[24]

As for Lowth's own education at Winchester and New College, Lowth, tongue in cheek, pleads deprivation and lack of advantage, and asks for Warburton's understanding:

For myself, on the contrary, it is well if I can acquit myself of the burden of being responsible for the great advantages which I enjoyed. For, my lord, I was educated in the University of Oxford; I enjoyed all the advantages, both public and private, which that famous seat of learning so largely affords. I spent many years in that illustrious society, in a well-regulated course of useful discipline and studies, and in the agreeable and improving commerce of gentlemen and scholars; in a society where emulation without envy, ambition without jealousy, contention without animosity, incited industry and awakened genius; where a liberal pursuit of knowledge, and a generous freedom of thought, was raised, encouraged, and put forward by example, by commendation, and by authority.[25]

And then Lowth finally thunders, "And do you reproach me with my education in this place, and this most respectable body, which I shall always esteem my greatest advantage and my highest honour?"[26] When D'Israeli compared Lowth's "Attic style" with the "tasteless and fierce invective"[27] of his opponent, he asked "Was ever weapon more polished and keen?" "Lowth's victory was complete," Pattison concludes; "it was, too, as public a triumph as the most ambitious man could have desired."[28]

The clash between Lowth and Warburton is important because it polarized the scientific and the Deist view of the Orient and the traditional, theological view. As Peter Hall observed, "Lowth was by no means a spiritual divine"; and, remarks Hall, "of the fundamental doctrine of Christian faith, — the glory of God manifested in the salvation of his people by the blood of Christ, — we hear but too little." Literary "veneration for the sublimity of the word of God, especially the mysterious and solemn language of prophecy, may be sometimes found to exalt the capacities of the mind without purifying the corruptness of human will, or softening the asperities of human temper."[29]

Lowth was a scholar interested in language and in primitive societies. In Warburton's *Divine Legation,* there was a continuing attempt to discover "revealed Religion," those "univocal marks of truth, which God has been pleased to impress upon his dispensations." Warburton *was* a spiritual though muddled divine; and, unlike the early anthropologist Lowth, who suggested that scholars should cultivate relativity "passing through, and surveying the whole universe, migrating from one planet to another, and becoming for a short time inhabitants of each,"[30] Warburton perceived the Old Testament only as a body of arcane Holy Writ. In fact, Warburton was old-fashioned; he had indeed missed the benefits of the post-scientific age.

Furthermore, the peculiar nature of the primitive mind to Lowth, the less egocentric enquirer, was that it was peculiarly concrete. Not only was Hebrew poetry, for example, full of everyday things, but such primitive poets — as Smart was to corroborate so happily — were primarily interested in things and in sense experience to such an extent that they changed whatever was unseen into the seen — not the seen into the unseen. Perhaps the clearest expression of this deeply held eighteenth-century view of primitivism is expressed by Hugh Blair, fittingly the champion of Ossian, in his *Lectures on Rhetoric and Belles Lettres.* "The style of the Old Testament," Blair wrote, "is carried on by constant allusions to sensible objects. Iniquity, or guilt, is expressed by a 'spotted garment'; misery by 'drinking the cup of astonishment'; vain pursuits by 'feeding on ashes'; a sinful life by 'a crooked path'; prosperity by 'the candle of the Lord shining on our head.'" "Hence," Blair observed most revealingly, "we have been accustomed to call this sort of style the oriental style."[31] The Oriental, primitive style was then, notably materialistic, for it changed even abstractions into material objects. After Blair had noted that the American Indian also used abstractions in this manner he added that "it plainly appears not to have been peculiar to any one region or climate; but to have been common to all nations, in certain periods of society."[32] Nothing could have been more misleading, therefore, than the heavy-handed posturing of the ever-interpretative Warburton.

The greatest literary battle of the century did not escape the notice of Dr. Johnson. In his famous interview with George III, we find him awarding the match to Lowth on points. "His Majesty having observed to him that he supposed he must have read a great deal, Johnson answered, that he thought more than he read," Boswell reported, "that he had read a great deal in the early part of his life, but ... he had not read much compared with others; for instance," referring to the current *cause célèbre,* "he said he had not read much, compared with Dr. Warburton."[33] The king graciously picked up the lead. He had heard "Dr. Warburton was a man of much general knowledge, that you could scarce talk with him on any subject on which he was not qualified to speak; and that his learning resembled Garrick's acting in its universality. His Majesty then talked of the controversy ... which he seemed to have read, and asked Johnson what he thought of it. Johnson answered, 'Warburton has most general, most scholastic learning: Lowth is the more correct scholar. I do not know which of them calls names best.' The King was pleased to say he was of the same opinion."[34]

Johnson's distinction was, as usual, acute. Warburton's scholarship *is* pedantic, massive, and indiscriminately applied. About Lowth's learning there is a sense of accuracy and relevance — what the age would have called "perspicuousness" or perhaps "elegance." This sense of a complete grasp of objective information used to convey a complex, other reality of distinct places and times, had been used by Lowth to great advantage in the *Praelectiones.* Retired Professor of Poetry Lowth now turned his attention to another "primitive" age, the Middle Ages; and he offered his "correctness" in the service of his greatest benefactor, William of Wykeham.

II *Lowth's* Life of William of Wykeham

It is conceivable that Robert Lowth felt that he owed everything to the founder of the two educational institutions which had nurtured him. In the case of his Winchester school fellows, we might imagine a sentimental loyalty to the Medieval churchman, William of Wykeham, who had established Winchester College and New College, Oxford, in the late fourteenth century, by providing not only buildings and a society, but even endowments which would meet many of the students' financial needs as they acquired the skills of their future careers. Lowth not only owed his education to this distant Medieval bishop, but probably the good fortune of his fame as Professor of Poetry at Oxford. Without the support of the present head of the Wykehamist family, Benjamin Hoadly, Wykeham's latest successor as Bishop of Winchester, Visitor or chief overseer of the schools, Lowth would be unlikely to have been elected Professor of Poetry by the Masters of Arts of Oxford, which body included a high proportion of Wykehamists.

As we have seen in Robert Lowth's early poetry, Lowth had an interest in and a natural talent for a new kind of literature which emerged in the early eighteenth century, the poem of emotion or sentiment which dwelt on local images of the past. It is important to make a distinction between this sentimental literature and the work of, for example, Alexander Pope, whose verse imaged the Classical past, but was poetry of reason that distanced and judged. Pope's past, moreover, was that of Greece and Italy, countries which he had never visited. The new poetry of feeling dealt with local, English, images of the Medieval period which had initially produced "the Romance." Glancing at an ancient fortification in his poem *Katherine Hill*, the self-styled "young bard," Lowth had exclaimed,

> But what vast rising bulwark's mighty row,
> War's dire remains, frowns horrid on thy brow?
> Here, deep and wide, down sinks a trench profound:
> There, huge, and high up-heav'd, a tow'ring mound
> Swells formidable; and begirts thy crown
> With dreadful pomp, and terrors not thine own. (ll. 31–36)

It is no less emotion which informs the dedication to Lowth's *Life of William of Wykeham*. Addressing in his dedication "My Lord" Benjamin Hoadly, Bishop of Winchester, Lowth thus begins his Medieval biography: "The great and good man, of whose life I have given an authentic, however imperfect, account, in the most earnest and solemn manner recommended his two colleges, that is, his estate, his family, his children, his dearer self, to the care and protection of his successors the Bishops of Winchester."[35] Hoadly himself, Lowth writes, has treated Wykeham's schools "upon all occasions with all the tenderness of an indulgent parent"; where he had to be stern he was stern, but his was always disinterested action "in every respect as [Wykeham] would have acted himself."[36]

The emotion is compounded in Lowth's Medieval biography by controversial concerns which bring the subject directly into contemporary life. First, there was the dispute between the Fellows of New College and Bishop Hoadly over the new Warden of Winchester College. The Fellows of the Oxford college had put forward their own Warden as a candidate for the school's headship. Hoadly, strongly supported by Lowth, who composed a pamphlet on the subject, saw the transference of the head of New College to the helm of Winchester as a violation of the Founder's regulations.[37] It is interesting to note that, by the middle of the eighteenth century, the Winchester post had become much more valuable than the Oxford position; and it was therefore felt that abuses and corruption could quickly spread if both wardenships were open to one and the same man. Second, Lowth was concerned about the eighteenth-century image of William of Wykeham; for two authorities had dwelt on the apparent weaknesses in Wykeham's career as a wealthy and adroit statesman and as a prince of the church under three extraordinary kings. Thomas Hearne had published between 1710 and 1712 *The Itinerary of John Leland the Antiquary* in nine volumes, and his books had reappeared between 1744 and 1745. In the fourth volume of Leland's *Itinerary* appeared a commonplace book which contained an attack on Wykeham's reputation by one John London, a disaffected Wykehamist who had died in 1543. The reappearance of this sixteenth-century assault on Wykeham was corroborated by an unknown annotator of a recent *Complete History of England* who had scurrilously not only repeated London's charges but added his own embellishments. Finally, a Mr. William Bohun — a lawyer of the Middle Temple — had added to his disputes with his fellow Wykehamists at New College by attacking in the *Institutio legalis* (1732) the memory of the founder of the society with a virulence which Lowth found outrageous. Bohun had "conceived a violent resentment against the Society of New College," Lowth wrote in Section IX of *Wykeham,* and had "set himself to collect everything he could meet with that was capable of being represented to ... [Wykeham's] discredit, and to improve it with new and horrible calumnies of his own invention."[38]

We observe that, if poetry is, as Lowth had commented frequently in his lectures on the poetry of the Hebrews, the product of passion, then Lowth's *William of Wykeham,* written by a loyal son in the spirit of committed controversy which marks much of his output, was likely to be a work with some claim to poetic distinction. For a creative writer of a Medieval biography in the mid-eighteenth century, there were few models. But there were in plenty, and especially among the Wykehamist early Romantics who were Lowth's contemporaries, deeply held novel theories concerning the way in which history, and poetry, should be written. In 1726, Robert Lowth's close friend and older guide, Joseph Spence had written: "Both with poets and in History, *there may be some fraud, in saying only the bare truth*. In either, 'tis not sufficient to tell us, that such and *such a city,* for instance, *was taken and ravag'd with a great deal of inhumanity*. There is a *poetical falsity,* if a strong idea of each particular be not imprinted on the mind; and an *historical*, if some things are passed over only with a general mark of infamy or dislike."[39]

Similarly, Spence observed that in poetry "When all the *circumstances* are laid out in their proper colours, and make a complete piece; its images strike us with greater energy, than when the *Whole* of the thing is only mention'd in general." Spence then spoke of the overpowering effect of particulars viewed in what, in the twentieth century, we might call a "close up." Making a distinction between a general "diffused style" which "makes a larger and more continued impression" and his preference for "a just and emphatical *conciseness*" which "may be more collected, and pierce the deeper," Spence noted that "it fills us with a noble and enlarg'd pleasure to consider the heavenly bodies, their courses, and their immense distances," but, on the other hand, if we view the planets "close up," in all their naked particularity (in the mechanical planetary model which the eighteenth century called an "orrery") "we are struck with a very particular admiration."[40] Admiration, we recall, was a word especially used in relation to "the Sublime."

The principle, we note, was to give the reader an overwhelming "close up" of objects viewed without perspective, so that he would be shocked into a heightened esthetic awareness and not be lulled by a constant sense of an overview or by a sense of the whole work. By and large, this principle enunciated by Wykehamist critics of the early eighteenth century is similar to that of Gothic architecture, in which the many, individual details, crowding in on the viewer's attention, constantly disturb his desire to place details within a larger view or within the formal organization of the entire work, the "Whole" of Classical theory.

Criticizing Pope's *Pastorals* (1709) for the generality of images shared by Theocritus and Virgil in differing climatic circumstances, Joseph Warton, yet another Wykehamist, in his *Essay on Pope* (the first part of which appeared in 1756 almost at the same time as

Wykeham) praised James Thomson (1700–1748), the poet of *The Seasons* (1726–30). Influenced by Spence's remarks, Warton listed examples from Thomson's poetry in which a single leaf in the Fall "slowly circles through the waving air" and startles the lonely walker in the woods or in which cattle stand in the stream and bend to sip the circling water, or flick the flies from their bodies with their tails. Such particulars had never before been observed by poets, said Warton, praising the "innumerable" "little circumstances" in Thomson's descriptions as hitherto "totally unobserved by all his predecessors."[41] These were the stuff of the "Sublime" and the "Pathetic" Warton assumes in an appreciation of Thomson which occurs not far in his text from his appreciation of Lowth's translation of Isaiah 14, which had appeared in the *Praelectiones* in 1753.

In Lowth's Medievalism, or Gothicism, we may observe the same insistence on particulars and the same neglect of an overview of "the Whole." Lowth clearly admits that not a great deal is known about Wykeham, lost as he was in the mists of time; but Lowth observes, nevertheless, that "the peculiar and distinguishing characters of men are much better conceived, and more accurately marked, from little circumstances and incidents in private life, than from a long series of actions in a public station: these may raise in us a high idea of a great and good man, and strike us with a distant admiration of his abilities and his virtues." Like Spence's viewing the planets close up in the orrery, Lowth does not find distancing conducive to biography. It is by the little circumstances and minute details of Wykeham's private life that we "are introduced to his acquaintance, that we learn his particular turn, his temper, his humour, his failings, as well as his amiable qualities, and become in a manner intimate and familiar with him."[42]

The execution of a kind of art which dwelt on minute particulars was made possible by the prodigious supply of information about England's "primitive" period, the Middle Ages, which became available in the seventeenth and early eighteenth centuries. The imaginative "Romantic" literature of the Romantic movement of the early nineteenth century — and the late eighteenth century — was built on generations of painstaking, scholarly work in the "primitive" eras of English history. The great minds of the late seventeenth and early eighteenth centuries bent their intellects to discovering the truth about their own race in their own locality, especially in its apparent beginnings. In fact, the amount of original research into the reality of life in the Middle Ages which occurred in the late seventeenth and early eighteenth centuries under the general and frequently particular influence of the Royal Society is little short of astounding. Lowth would not have been able to write his biography of Wykeham a hundred years earlier for the simple reason that the majority of works upon which he relied for his information about the fourteenth century had been published in the late seventeenth century and the early eighteenth century.

Lowth's footnotes alone indicate a wealth of material, of which the following is a representative but not complete selection. For royal and state affairs, Lowth relied on Elias Ashmole (1617–1692), the founder of the Ashmolean Museum in Oxford and author of *The Institution of the Order of the Garter* (1672); Arthur Collins' (1690–1760) *The Life and Glorious Actions of Edward Prince of Wales (the Black Prince)* (1740); and the work of Thomas Hearne (1678–1735), the foremost antiquarian of the day. In particular, Lowth was indebted to Hearne's work on William Camden (1551–1623), teacher of Ben Jonson and author of *Remains of a Greater Work Concerning Britain* (1605). Camden's *Annales rerum Anglicarum et Hibernicarum regnante Elizabetha* appeared in Oxford in 1717. Hearne's industry had also furnished Lowth with "the Monk of Evesham's account of Richard II," the *Historia vitae et regni Ricardi II* (1729) and with Walter Hemingford's *Historia de rebus gestis Edvardi I, Edvardi II & Edvardi III* (1731), a chronicle of England under the three King Edwards.

It is also interesting to observe that the eighteenth-century discovery of Shakespeare was preceded by a marked interest in the chronicles, upon which some of the historical plays were based. Perhaps the best known of the chroniclers, Raphael Holinshed — first published in 1577 — made a fragmentary reappearance in 1722–23, when portions of his *The Firste (Laste) Volume of the Chronicles of England* were reprinted. They were reprinted again twice before the end of 1728. It is important to observe that Lowth had a full acquaintance with the other chroniclers, such as John Stow (?1525–1602), whose *Survey* had been edited by John Strype (1643–1737) in 1720 and re-issued in 1754; Jean Froissart (?1333–?1400); and Polydore Vergil (c1470–c1555). For the *minutiae* of state and parliamentary business, Lowth had several impressive sources, for Sir Robert Cotton (1571–1631), founder of one of the world's most renowned libraries, had been responsible for the collection and publication of *An Exact Abridgement of the Records in the Tower* (1657?). We should not overlook, in addition, the contemporary and perhaps unexpected giant among Medievalists, Thomas Rymer (1641–1713), the rigid Classical denigrator of Shakespeare, who is best known for his *A Short View of Tragedy* (1693) which holds up *Othello* in particular to ridicule. The Herculean researcher who well illustrated the moral of Lowth's *Choice of Hercules,* Rymer toiled to produce not only "Rymer's *Foedera*" (1704–35), the twenty volumes of English state papers from the Middle Ages down to 1654, which became an indispensable landmark in historical studies, but also *fifty-nine* large unpublished volumes, that were neglected, as Lowth says in his preface, but, "with regard to personal history and incidental matters ... [were] perhaps ... of equal use with the printed volumes."[43] Lowth's near contemporary Thomas Tanner (1674–1735), Bishop of St. Asaph, had worked especially on those Patent Rolls in the Tower which recorded grants to William of Wykeham; and, although unpublished, these records had been "communicated in the year 1732, to Dr. Coxed then Warden of New College"[44] while Lowth was a student in the college.

Tanner's work on church history was also of great importance to Lowth, especially his *Notitia monastica: or an account of all the abbies, priories and house of friars, heretofore in England and Wales, and also of all the colleges and hospitals founded before A.D. 1540,* which was published in 1744. A remarkably exhaustive account of the ecclesiastical legislation of William of Wykeham's era is to be found in *Concilia Magnae Britanniae et Hiberniae,* edited by David Wilkins and published in four volumes in London in 1737. To Wilkins, Lowth was able to add the work of William Wake (1657–1737) whose *State of the Church and Clergy in England* had appeared in 1703 and also that of Henry Wharton (1664–1695) whose *Anglia sacra* or history of the church up to 1540 appeared in 1691. Local church history was augmented by Richard Newcourt's *Ecclesiasticum parochiale Londinense,* or parochial history of the diocese of London, which came out in 1708–10.

Lowth's *Life of Wykeham* represents among other things an interesting contribution to our knowledge of the Gothic movement in the eighteenth century. At one point, Lowth's description of Wykeham's rebuilt Winchester Cathedral furnishes a definition of Gothicism valuable in the history of esthetics and ideas. Wykeham's service to several kings was firmly based on his remarkable talent as a surveyor and architect. He rebuilt Windsor Castle, and he crowned his career not only with the building of his colleges but a lasting reconstruction of Winchester Cathedral. Among the architectural authorities to whom Lowth turns is the greatest architect of his day and perhaps of many centuries, Sir Christopher Wren (1632–1723), whose *Historical Account of Westminster Abbey* was augmented by his *Parentalia, or Memoirs of the Family of the Wrens* (1750). Richard Widmore's *Enquiry into the first foundation of Westminster Abbey* (1743) supplied information which Lowth could not obtain from the magisterial *A Survey of Cathedrals* which came from the hand of Browne Willis (1682–1760) between 1727 and 1730. Anthony Á. Wood (1632–1695) supplied additional information concerning the founding of New College in his *Historia et antiquitates Universitatis Oxonienis* of 1674.

It is interesting to observe that, for example, in Samuel Johnson's *Lives of the Poets* (1779–81), an outstanding example of accounts of men's lives in the eighteenth century, we get the impression that there are certain patterns into which acceptable human behavior falls. Johnson generalizes about the usual domestic tyranny of men who always speak of liberty in his *Life of Milton,* about the idiocy of waiting until the mood for writing strikes one in *Gray,* about Pope's unnatural miserliness in his *Life of Pope.* These general standards of acceptable behavior that have been acknowledged since Classical times persuade us. Typically neo-Classical, Johnson, a writer, generalizes constantly about other writers from his own experience, but Lowth's *William of Wykeham* is a totally different kind of work. Biography was one great achievement of the Romantic mind because Romanticism faced the "sublime" possibility that each man was not a variation on a general theme: a man was a wholly unique particular phenomenon, and an understanding of him called for a novel departure of the reader's and writer's imagination.

A strange departure into unknown areas (to an eighteenth-century reader perhaps one not unlike the eerie feeling that science-fiction produces today) is suggested by Lowth's account in Section I of how a boy so obscure that he needed to be named after the village from which he came became secretary to Nicholas Uvedale, Governor of Winchester Castle, and was then rapidly introduced to the then Bishop of Winchester and, through both of these men, to King Edward III. Characteristically, Lowth warns about Wykeham's lack of a family name, "we must have a care, lest, being prepossessed with notions taken from our own usages, we should be led into error in our reasonings upon those of former times."[45] This esthetic principle parallels precisely his warning in his lectures on Hebrew poetry: that, like comparative astronomers, we must visit without any home base, one planet after another "becoming for a short time inhabitants of each"; and, in reading of earlier times, we must imagine ourselves "exactly situated as the persons for whom it was written, or even as the writers themselves."[46]

The three strands which go into weaving *The Life of Wykeham* are ecclesiastical matters, national affairs, and the role of Wykeham in the local schools, charities, and buildings of Winchester. Lowth never departs in his treatment of these subjects from the principle of accumulation of an overwhelming number of details, which suggests the greatness of Wykeham, who was able, through rare personal qualities, to succeed in battling the obscure forces of destruction around him to the happy creative conclusion of Winchester and New College. Sections I, IV, and V tell of William's political elevation. In Section I, he meets and begins work for Edward III; in Section IV, he survives John of Gaunt's rise to power as Edward declined; in Sections V and VII, we see Wykeham in the reign of Richard II. Lowth is perhaps best at conjuring up the sense of "sublime" instability which readers of William Shakespeare's *Richard II* will recognize. "The King was wholly possessed by a set of favourites and flatterers intent upon their own views of avarice and ambition," Lowth observes; "the King himself was of that easy and complying temper, which laid him open to the practices of insinuation and flattery, and rendered him wholly subservient to the will of those who gained his affections."

Surrounding the king with vignettes of courtiers — such as "Michael de la Pole . . . a man of excellent parts and fine natural endowments . . . who had not either by nobility of birth or dignity of character sufficient credit and authority for the station to which he was raised," and "Robert de Vere, Earl of Oxford . . . a young man of no abilities, nor any other merit than that of a graceful person, and an unlimited compliance with the King's humour" — Lowth continues by painting a picture filled out with details of food, textures, and personalities of the fourteenth century. "As he had no great inclination, so neither was he encouraged or suffered by his favourites to apply himself to public affairs: he pursued nothing but his pleasures; he loved feasting and jollity, the company of the sprightliest young men and the gayest ladies of his court," Lowth narrates of Richard; and he adds, "his court was the most splendid and magnificent of all of that time, and the standing expense of his household far exceeded what it had ever been in any preceding reign." Every day retainers to the number of ten thousand flocked to eat at court, and three hundred servants manned the kitchens.

Quoting from Richard Grafton's edition (1543) of John Hardyng's fifteenth-century *Chronicle,* which was composed in verse, Lowth characteristically gives the reader the actual names of kinds of cloth and the transient details of Medieval fashion which cannot but communicate the insecurity of Richard's position. The unnatural and unstable excess of distant and disturbed times is emphasized by typography. Gothic black letter is used for the metrical description of Richard's hedonistic court: "Women and gromes in cloth of silk arayed, / Sattyn and damaske, in doublettes and gounes, / In cloth of grene, and scarlet for unpayed; / Cut werke was great, bothe in court and tounes, / Bothe in mens hoddes, and also in their gounes; / Broudur and furres, and goldsmith werke ay new, / In many a wyse, eche day that did renewe."[47]

While alternate sections deal with the national scene and Wykeham's varying fortunes under three kings — Edward III, Richard II, and Henry IV — the sections in between indicate the progress of Wykeham's church career in and around Winchester. For the Winchester background, Lowth had two main sources: one was a collection of papers peculiarly available only to Wykehamists, and, as it were, in the family; the other was his own knowledge of Winchester, especially his schoolboy experience in Wykeham's charitable foundations, which, absorbing all of Wykeham's wealth, were, as it were, the extension of his life into eternity, a sublime notion indeed! Lowth especially made use of "Wykeham's Register," "which is still preserved at Winchester in the office of the register of the chancellor of the diocese." This unpublished work turned out to be "a diary of thirty seven years" which "would not only itself supply many important facts, but would serve moreover as a test to which other facts and circumstances might be brought, to be tried by a continued series of sure and infallible dates, and by such trial to be most evidently disproved or verified." On this foundation, Lowth, using an architectural image peculiarly appropriate to a master builder, writes that "a more firm and more ample structure might be raised, than had hitherto been attempted."[48]

It is from such intimate sources that we learn in Section III that, as Bishop of Winchester, Wykeham inherited at his installation, "127 draughthorses, 1,556 head of black cattle, 3,876 weathers, 4,777 ewes, 3,521 lambs" (67); that, an architect by vocation, he re-opened an abandoned quarry on the Isle of Wight and set about repairing all the buildings of the diocese. From such a source, too, we observe William of Wykeham straightening out abuses in charitable institutions in the environs of Winchester. It is here that we note Lowth's history is especially subjective. The schools founded by Wykeham at Winchester and at Oxford were, of course, charitable foundations in their beginnings, even if they later became islands of privilege. It was because of Lowth's own experience of these, and of their Medieval regimens, that he could describe with such telling detail the *minutiae* of the affair of St. Cross.

Founded by Henry de Blois, the brother of King Stephen, in 1136, the alms house or Hospital of St. Cross, still situated today on the road from Winchester to nearby Southampton, enjoyed an income of three hundred pounds from nineteen rectories. Provision was made from this sum for the total support of thirteen poor and incapable pensioners until their deaths or recoveries and for dinner each day for a hundred others, including thirteen poor grammar school boys from the school which preceded Wykeham's College of St. Mary. As Section III relates, "one loaf of good wheat bread, of five marks weight ... one gallon and a half of good small beer; a sufficient quantity of pottage; three messes at dinner, namely, one mess called *Mortrell,* made of milk and *Wastelbred,* one mess of flesh or fish ... and one mess for Supper" were provided for each boarder at the cost of threepence a week in Wykeham's day. The hundred poor who did not "live in" fared slightly less well with their twelfth-century benefactor; the Hospital varied their solitary dinner with "one herring, or two pilchards, or two eggs, or one farthing's worth of cheese."[49]

It is interesting in this regard to note that the eating experience of the boys at Winchester College was much like that of the poor men and the hundred poor at St. Cross down the road. A. K. Cook, in his *About Winchester College,* records in his translation of the poem by Wykehamist Robert Matthew that, having been up since five-thirty, the students had a break at nine. When "the bell rings," writes Matthew, we go into Hall, where the beer-butler gives us beer, and the bread-butler bread; and when we have done, 'Down' cries Prefect of Hall, and down we go. — Back again to school at eleven, after working for a time by ourselves. About twelve to Hall for dinner. A prefect, standing up with his nine companions, asks a blessing on the meal; another (hence called Bible-Clerk) reads aloud a chapter from the Old Testament; he has the week of his course for private study. Prefect of Tub sends a Mess of beef to Prefect of Hall; he walks round the tables as we dine, and takes his own meal with the servants afterwards. He distributes the messes among the children; a junior divides them in to equal 'dispers' [portions] and fills up 'jorums' [large bowls] from a 'jack.' When we have satisfied our 'barking stomachs,' Bible-Clerk steps out to what is known as the Round Table (the table where the servants afterwards dine), and bows respectfully to the Master. The Master nods; Bible-Clerk puts the table-linen into its chest; grace and a psalm are sung; we go back to work once more. The broken meats are poured into the laps of a crowd of old women; the quiristers [choristers] and the servants dine.[50]

In Wykeham's school, as at St. Cross, Medieval generosity made provision for bodily needs for all time. At both institutions, the legacy gave opportunity for crooked dealing. Interestingly, Wykeham's strategy was the same as Lowth's and Hoadly's was in the election of the Winchester Warden; he clearly defined the intentions of the benefactor and Founder, and he insisted on exact distinctions. Wykeham insisted that the Mastership of the St. Cross foundation had been looked upon, wrongly, as a church appointment and hence a position with tenure. He began clearing up the abuses by which the poor were robbed by sequestering all the goods of the Hospital. The incumbent Master then exchanged his position with an even more obdurate wrongdoer, one Roger de Cloune, who boldly asserted that the Master of St. Cross had "free administration of all possessions and goods," and de Cloune sent an appeal for support to the Pope in Rome. Wykeham, however, had already put his side of the case to Rome, and when the Pope appointed the Bishop of London as a referee in the affair, Roger de Cloune "had the impudence to" seize all the goods of the Hospital, building supplies, food, and all. As a consequence, the roof of the Great Hall literally fell in, and the poor old folk retreated from their lodgings. De Cloune tried to protract the case when the Bishop of London found against him; but, after extraordinary subterfuges and exhibitions of barefaced nerve, he was forced to submit. Wykeham brought the Hospital back to its former constitution, and "so far restored this charity to its original design," Lowth concludes in Section III, that when his successor in Winchester, Beaufort, wished to found his own hospital, he decided to reendow St. Cross, "which," in 1758 "still subsists upon the remains of both endowments."[51] With this kind of experience behind him, Wykeham planned his two colleges. The regulations, we surmise, which Lowth and Hoadly were so insistent on maintaining, were a fence against incursions that were ever threatening in an imperfect world.

It is fitting, of course, that Lowth's work on his Medieval parent-figure, as he himself described him, should be especially concerned with the founding of the two schools, Winchester College and New College, Oxford; for they were the nurseries of a nucleus of mid-eighteenth-century Romanticism and where Edward Young, Joseph Spence, Joseph Warton, William Collins, and Lowth himself were educated. As a priest and celibate, Wykeham — keenly aware of his own problematic rise from anonymous beginnings to Chancellor of England; of the needs of the country for trained civil servants, or ecclesiastical servants; and of the tumultuous times through which he was living — sought a way of leaving his enormous wealth, in today's terms that of a millionaire many times over, in a secure form for the good of the church and nation and for the health of his soul in the hereafter. He therefore began in the late fourteenth century a grammar school in Winchester and a college in Oxford, both named "The College of St. Mary," after his favorite saint; but these institutions later became renowned as Winchester College and New College, Oxford. Winchester, especially, became one of the famous "public" schools of England, which trained for centuries the public servants for the empire and for public life at home.

In the history of Oxford, Wykeham is one with Walter of Merton, founder of Merton College (1280) and with Walter de Stapeldon, founder of Exeter College (1314) — two Medieval benefactors who played a central part in the building of Oxford University. Wykeham's concepts were revolutionary. Since he regarded education as a continuous process from early boyhood to young manhood, he founded a grammar school to provide secondary education and a university college which would absorb the best of the stream, themselves to be educated by those further along, the "Fellows" of the college, who would form a reservoir for the undergraduate teaching. The extreme novelty of this scheme was enhanced by Wykeham's buildings. He had begun life, and indeed, in Winchester Cathedral ended it, as an architect of large buildings.

His New College, situated close to the ancient wall of Oxford for the sake of added siege protection in troubled times, assembled around a central quadrangle all that was necessary for communal academic life — a dining hall and chapel, a tower or "Muniments" for records, apartments for scholars, all giving onto the same small campus. The present Oxford arrangement of central quadrangles was introduced by William at New College and was thereafter adopted by all colleges. The tutorial system, Wykeham's educational innovation, and his architectural scheme, equally important developments for colleges in the Renaissance, set the patterns for Oxford colleges for centuries to come.

Section VI deals with the founding of the two institutions. In both cases, before building, Wykeham first founded a nucleus; before Winchester College was erected, a Grammar School began; and before New College arose "he formed his Society, appointed them a governor, allowing them a liberal maintenance, provided them with lodgings, and gave them rules and directions for their behaviour." The reason for this was "that his beneficence might not seem to lie fruitless and ineffectual while it was only employed in making his purchases of lands, and raising his building, which would take up a considerable time"; and "that he might bestow his earliest attention, and his greatest care in forming and perfecting the principal part of his design, and that the life and soul, as it were, might be ready to inform and animate the body of his College as soon as it could be finished."[52] This preparatory establishment at Oxford was founded in 1373, at about the same time as that at Winchester.

The Rolls of Accompts of New College, which Lowth records with graphic verisimilitude, give for the year 1376 "a Warden and seventy Fellows, called Pauperes Scholares Venerabilis ... Domini Wilhelmi de Wykeham Wynton Episcopi; and that it had been established; probably to the same number, at least as early as September 1375." The first Warden was Richard Toneworth, Fellow of Merton College, at a salary of twenty pounds a year. "The Fellows were lodged in Blakehall, Herthal, Shulehall, Maydenhall, and Hamerhall: the expense of their lodging amounted to 10 l. 13 s. 4 d. per annum [ten pounds, thirteen shillings and four pence]. They were allowed each of them 1 s. 6 d. per week for their commons: and they had proper servants to attend them, who had suitable stipends."[53]

Wykeham completed his purchases of land in Oxford in 1379. He obtained the King's Patent, dated June 30, 1379. He also procured a Papal Bull to the same effect. "He published his Charter of Foundation November 26th following; by which he entitled his College, *Seinte Marie College of Wynchestre in Oxenford.*" The title is given in Gothic black letter. "On the 5th of March following, at 8 o'clock in the morning, the foundation stone was laid: the building was finished in six years, and the Society made their publick entrance into it with much solemnity and devotion, singing Litanies, and marching in procession, with the Cross borne before them, at nine o'clock in the morning, on the 14th of April, 1386."[54] Thus was founded, in the late fourteenth century, the college which, in the annals of English literature became famous, as has been noted, as the nursery of Spence, Joseph Warton, Collins, and other Romantic writers.

When the school at Winchester was founded in 1382, "A natural affection and prejudice for the very place which he had frequented in his early days, seems to have had its weight in determining the situation of it." The school, Lowth records, actually stands on the site where Wykeham himself went to school as a boy. The first stone was laid on March 26, 1387, at nine o'clock in the morning. After six years of building, the Warden and Society from Oxford made their official entrance into it "chanting in procession, at nine o'clock in the morning on March the 28th, 1393." We note that the Duke of Lancaster, John of Gaunt, visited New College in 1392 with four knights and with a large train of attendants. They were entertained, "according to the constant usage of that time, with comfits, spices, and wine." Henry VI, Founder of Eton, visited Winchester five times in order to copy Wykeham's design in his own two colleges, Eton and King's College, Cambridge. He was always received with much honor, Lowth records, and he adds: "At one time he made them a present of one hundred nobles to adorn the high altar, with which was purchased a pair of large basons of silver gilt: at another he gave his best robe, save one, consisting of cloth of tissue of gold and fur of sables, which was likewise applied to the use of the chappel: at others he gave a chalice of gold, two phials of gold, and a tabernacle of gold, adorned with precious stones, and with the images of the Holy Trinity, and the Blessed Virgin, of Cristal."[55]

Lowth thought of Wykeham's timeless, and "sublime" foundations as works of art. In framing statutes and policies, Lowth observes, "the more simple the composition of his system, the

more surely will it attain its end, without disorder or impediment."
"Too much refinement will only give the greater scope and advantage to evasion." It is the bold, even irrational, stroke which Lowth
finds effective in charitable institutions such as Wykeham's
schools. The observation allows Lowth to expatiate in a manner
characteristic of mid-century esthetics about the nature of art. In a
work of art, he says as he approaches his summation of Wykeham's achievement, "the artist endeavours to express the most simple appearances of nature, her freest and most undisguised features, attitudes, and operations; and the first impressions of these,
upon a warm imagination, are commonly the liveliest and the
truest." In case we miss the point, Lowth elaborated his idea.
"The original drawings of a great Master, compared with the finished paintings which he has made from them, let us more intimately into the true spirit of his design; they lay open his whole
train of thinking, and discover the reasons of all the most minute
alterations which are made in the progress of the work...." Therefore we frequently "have reason to regret the effects of too much
study and application, of accuracy and correctness pursued too far;
when the cool endeavours of art have not been able to reach the
warm strokes of genius, and perhaps some particular parts of the
finished piece have even wanted the propriety and justness which
they had in the first composition."[56]

The opposition which Lowth is here making in 1758 is the one
which Joseph Warton makes in his *Essay on the Genius and Writings of Pope* (1756) and which Edmund Burke makes in his *Enquiry
into the Sublime and Beautiful* (1757), and Lowth's view accords
with thinking about primitivism of the mid-eighteenth century. On
the one hand, we have the proportion and rational structure of an
Alexander Pope, of the mode of Reason. On the other we have a
kind of Nature, (reminiscent of that we observed in eighteenth-
century Oriental prophecy), which nurtures in a medium of subjectivity the mind of the artist, whose spontaneous, primitive, and
imaginative strokes are seen as more effective than the rational
forms of the Classical mind. The parallel might be drawn with the
theories concerning early man which were prevalent in the mid-
century and which were so much part of the rise of Romanticism.
In their first expressions, races were imaginative, bold, warm,
spontaneous, close to, indeed, within Nature, it was thought. On
the other hand, when society had aged and structures had been
formed, wit, memory, morality, and judgment became the order of
the day.

For Lowth, William of Wykeham is a great original, even a "primitive," who achieved his immense goal through boldness and daring, which was one with emotional expression. He formed his Winchester school on the spot where he himself had gone to school; he was a father to his society; his greatness came from spontaneous expression, and the kind of work which Lowth raises to him, which he from time to time expressed in terms of architecture, was "primitive" in the same way as his benefactor's life.

Writing of Wykeham's great rebuilding of Winchester cathedral, Lowth notes: "he even chose to apply to his purpose some part of the lower order of pillars of the old Church, though his design was in a different Style of Architecture; that which we commonly call Gothic, with pointed arches and windows, and without key-stones, and pillars consisting of an assemblage of many small ones closely connected together; but which is more properly Saracen, for such was its origin: the Crusades gave us an idea of this form of architecture, which afterwards prevailed throughout Europe."[57] Like Edmund Burke's *Sublime and Beautiful*, Joseph Warton's *Essay on Pope,* and Robert Lowth's own *Lectures on the Sacred Poetry of the Hebrews,* Lowth's *Wykeham* appears to be constructed on a principle distinct from that of sequential form. Just as each portion of a Gothic design stands out as an individual statement, causing the reader to forget "the Whole" and producing an esthetic reaction in the viewer which makes him forget, and even revise, his sense of finite form, so, in Lowth's *Wykeham,* one "section" does not seem significantly to follow another. Each portion, full of detail, seems a new departure into unknown terrain where we are in the control of the writer's imagination. It is not the analytical skill or the reasoning behind Lowth's approach that we recall, but the moments: the morning opening of New College; the glittering clothes worn by courtiers around the doomed King Richard; the "*Wastelbred*" eaten by the poor old men at St. Cross; Roger de Cloune's escape with the building materials; the farthing's worth of pilchards provided for the poor; the cloak of cloth of tissue of gold and of sable given by King Henry VI to Winchester College.

These moments strike our imaginations; the reader does something with them himself: he begins to ponder, wonder, and imaginatively elaborate his own notion of the Middle Ages; and his concept becomes part of his individual creative vision. This artistic principle, which is essentially subjective, is intimately related to the

Romantic or pre-Romantic revolution of mid-century esthetics. It is fascinating to observe that the principle illuminates Robert Lowth's *Life of William of Wykeham* just as it characterizes Lowth's description of primitive Hebrew poetry, whose secret he perceived equally to exist not in the formal sequences of reason but in parallel formations of imagery. Apparently destroying the patterns of Time, the imagination thus afforded the reader the experience of "the Sublime," as Lowth's schoolboy experience of Wykeham's Medieval achievement now found the immortality of printed words.

CHAPTER 6

A Short Introduction to English Grammar

I   *The Background to Lowth's* Short Introduction

T HE writer of Lowth's obituary in *The Gentleman's Magazine,*
who referred equally to the *New Translationof Isaiah* and to
the *Short Introduction to English Grammar,* judged that "perhaps
the most enviable, as the most useful achievements, are what refer
to his own language; which owes to him what nothing said in it can
ever pay."[1] This observation is corroborated by such authorities as
Thomas Gray, who told William Mason in 1762, "I much like Dr.
Lowth's Grammar; it is concise, clear, and elegant";[2] Daniel Fenning, who noted that Lowth had "treated the subject in so clear
and comprehensive a manner, as to leave little to be done by succeeding grammarians";[3] Hugh Blair who found the *Short
Introduction* "the grammatical performance of highest authority
that has appeared in our time."[4] Hans Aarsleff, whose Princeton
study of language education in England between 1780 and 1860, is
a definitive, modern evaluation of the period in which Lowth's
small book was popular, observes the "profound influence"[5]
which Lowth had, not only in and but in Germany.

In Lowth's *Short Introduction,* we have perhaps the single most
popular and influential English grammar throughout the pre-
Romantic and Romantic periods in England, America, and even
Europe. Appearing anonymously in 1762, *A Short Introduction to
English Grammar* was issued again roughly once every two years
for the next seventy years, or until 1838. An "easy" version prepared by J. Ash[6] appeared in 1763 and was reissued at the same
rate until 1810. In America, during and after the struggle for independence, Lowth's *Grammar* appeared in Philadelphia, Hartford,

New York, and Wilmington. In 1841, the *Common School Journal*
reported "this Grammar is still used as a text-book, in Harvard
University, and a beautiful edition of it has lately been issued by the
Cambridge press."[7] Ash's *Lowth* also appeared in some sixteen
printings at regular intervals in New York, Massachusetts, Pennsyl-
vania, and Vermont. European versions of both grammars
appeared, especially in the late years of the eighteenth century.

Lowth's Preface is an interesting guide to the state of language
education in 1762. The English language was "of all the present
European languages by much the most simple,"[8] yet "a grammatical study of our own language makes no part of the ordinary
method of instruction which we pass thro' in our childhood."[9]
Lowth also stated in his Preface, "of all the ancient languages
extant that is the most simple, which is undoubtedly the most
ancient: but even that language itself does not equal the English in
its simplicity."[10] This view is a clue to Lowth's linguistic theory that
suggests that his *Grammar* sprang from a matrix of mid-century
concerns similar to those at the heart of the *Praelectiones* and the
Life of Wykeham. He saw in modern English the simplicity which
he found in the most ancient language, the Hebrew. The construction of Latin — or even Greek — syntax was a foreign and alien
element that had been relatively recently introduced into this
Northern European language. The true simplicity of English might
be sought in the "genius" of the "primitive" ages of England —
the Anglo-Saxon period and the Middle Ages.

However much the results of the English theorists of the last half
of the eighteenth century were to contribute to the broad stream of
European Romanticism, they found their evidence for sophisticated notions of primitivism among the antiquarians of the seventeenth and early eighteenth century. The earlier enquirers whose
approach to language and to theories of race illuminate our understanding of the nature of Lowth's *Short Introduction* include
Charles Butler (1560–1647), author of *The English Grammar or the
Institution of Letters, Syllables, and Words in the English Tongue,
whereunto is annexed an Index of Words Like and Unlike* (1633),
and James Greenwood (died 1737), who composed the monumental, *An Essay towards a Practical English Grammar describing
the Genius and Nature of the English Tongue: giving likewise a
Rational and Plain Account of Grammar in General, with a Familiar Explanation of its Terms* (1711). In the Evans Catalogue of the
sale of the Lowth library "on Wednesday, January 15 and five

following days" in 1823, Butler's *English Grammar* appears as item number 186 on page six; Greenwood's *Practical English Grammar,* in the edition of 1740, is item number 324 on page eleven.[11] We do not know that Lowth actually used Butler and Greenwood, but his own *Grammar* reproduces their basic features and attitudes.

Finding that the three characteristics of the English tongue are its antiquity, its copious elegance, and its generality — by which is meant "universality" — Butler writes that "The Hebrew being the language of our Grandfather Adam, which until the Confusion, all people of the earth did speak, must needs for antiquity, have the precedence; but the Teutonick (whereof the English is a dialect) being the language of unconquered Conquerors, hath continued in its primary seat of Germany, with little alteration, from the Confusion until this day."[12] By the "Confusion," Butler means Adam's expulsion from the Garden of Eden and the cacophony of the Tower of Babel which followed closely upon it.[13] The "genius" of the English language was close to that of Hebrew and, clearer in its more antique forms, could best be observed in Anglo-Saxon and Middle English. Few manifestations of this primitive movement did not also show antagonism to the Classical tradition. "For copiousness, no marvel if it exceed the Greek," writes Butler with huffy xenophobia, "so happy in composition; seeing it hath words enough of its own, to express any conceit; beside the store of borrowed words, which by some change it maketh her own."[14] As to universality, or "generality," the reader was to remember that "The Saxons, Jutes, Angles spread the Teutonic tongue through High and Low Germany and Denmark, Sweden, Lapland, Finland, Gothland, Norway, and the East part of Scotland, even from Berwick to the Orcades." "Ger" or "Gar" means "all" fittingly, we might note, for a language — German — which had been spread even into "Africk over-run by their Vandals."[15] For all its quaintness, Butler's history was grounded in fact, and not in the mythical history of, for example, Edmund Spenser's *Faerie Queene* (1590).

The scholarly details within these odd perspectives are appealing and correct. A student of Anglo-Saxon today might be surprised to read Butler's complaint at the disappearance of the "thorn," the tunic letter shaped something like a "p", "having a sound, that no other letter, or letters can express: wherefore it is a marvel how this so necessary a letter, and so much used in our English tongue was let slip; and Th having a different sound of its own came to be ad-

mitted in his stead: as in these words: the, this, these, that, those,
thou, thee. . . ."[16]

Butler shows the considerable inclination that was to grow in
"English" grammars which was to ignore the syntax of Latin and
to emphasize the material realities behind individual words. An
entertaining example, taken from Butler's twenty-seven page
"Index of Words like and unlike" that was appended to his *English
Grammar,* is his etymology of "nice," a word he finds derived
from hawking: "Nice or coy *curiousness* / a nias hauk, (not an
eyas), F. niais, It. *nidaso,* taken out of the Nest: as a hauk flown is
called a brancher."[17] In his copy of Butler, now in the Bodleian,
Edmond Malone, the eighteenth-century Shakespearean scholar,
has written in the margin next to this entry "wrong, for eyas is
right; from ey Teut. ovum."

The three elements which we discover in Butler's *English Grammar* — the phenomenological nature of the whole enquiry, the
assertively English character of the grammar, and the underscoring
of the "primitive" Anglo-Saxon source of the tongue — are, perhaps, even more noticeable in the only other grammar in the Evans
Catalogue of the Lowth library, James Greenwood's *Essay towards
a Practical English Grammar describing the Genius and Nature of
the English Tongue.* The most interesting feature of Greenwood's
Grammar is his debt to the major figures of the Royal Society; for
Greenwood's *English Grammar* opens with a dedication to Dr.
Richard Mead (1673–1754), Pope's physician and the leading medi-
cal authority of the time.

Among Mead's works was *A Mechanical Account of Poisons* in
which he gives an exact account of the mechanism of a snake's
fang. Mead swallowed venom in order to corroborate Galen's finding that skin puncture was a prerequisite of death. Typical of the
basic belief in physics and the "mechanical operation" of Nature in
his time is Mead's observation that the hard particles in the poison
mechanically produced in the blood the fatal effect. To his *Medica
Sacra,* which diagnosed the several ailments of Hezekiah, Jehoram,
Saul, Nebuchadnezzar, and Job as an abscess, dysentery, melan-
cholia, hypochondria, and elephantiasis, respectively, Lowth was
indebted in the *Praelectiones.* This wide-ranging *virtuoso,* whose
eclectic interest in all the material phenomena of Nature is both
typical of his time and indicative of the character of the *Grammar*
dedicated to him, was a member of the Council of the Royal
Society in 1705 and 1707 and became Vice-President in 1717. His

collection of coins, statuary, and curiosities was the largest in his day. The dedication to Mead points to the movement in which words and things began to approximate each other as single, limited, phenomena, objects similarly observable in the lens of the new science.

But Mead is only one of a handful to whom Greenwood confesses a considerable debt. "I must here confess," Greenwood notes toward the end of his Preface, "that I have been very much obliged in the following papers to Bp. WILKINS' *Real Character,* Dr. WALLIS, Dr. HICKS's *Saxon Grammar,* and some others. I must also take notice, that in two or three places I have made use of Mr. LOCK's expressions, because I liked them better than my own."[18] Wilkins, Wallis, and Hickes, along with Richard Mead, were the most prominent *virtuosi* of the scientific movement of the late seventeenth and early eighteenth centuries who demonstrated a Baconian, inductive interest in the phenomena of Nature in whatever shape they manifested themselves. John Wilkins (1614–1672) — a bishop, Cromwell's brother-in-law, one of the five chancellors of Oxford University during the Interregnum, and Warden of Wadham College — gathered around him the small group which was to change scientific thought towards the end of the seventeenth century; and he was, as much as Boyle, the founder of the Royal Society. His many scientific works include *The Discovery of a World in the Moon* to which he added a postscript of some present interest, a *Discourse concerning the Possibility of a Passage thither* (1640). His linguistic work, which Greenwood acknowledges, was entitled *An Essay towards a Real Character and a Philosophical Language* (1668). Characteristically, the *Essay* tended to view words as objects whose single material reality could be precisely defined, a development to whose dangers Swift pointed in *A Tale of A Tub.*

The work of George Hickes (1642–1715), titular bishop of Thetford and a prominent controversialist, suggests that the "scientific" study of language led to the popularization of Northern European culture and, finally, myth. Hickes was an authority on the Icelandic language, and he corresponded with Sir Hans Sloane about problems in Etruscan culture. Hickes, the polymath, published in 1689 his *Anglo-Saxon and Moeso-Gothic Grammar,* which was followed in 1703–1705 by his best known work, *Linguarum veterum septentrionalium thesaurus grammaticocriticus et archaeologicus,* or the *Grammatical, Critical, and*

Archaeological Thesaurus of the Ancient Northern Languages. It was Hickes' niece, Elizabeth Elstob (1683–1756), who edited in 1709 the *English-Saxon Homily on the Nativity of St. Gregory* and who published the *Rudiments of Grammar for the English-Saxon Tongue, first given in English* in 1715.

The third member of this triumvirate, John Wallis (1616–1703), who composed a history of the language in its Anglo-Saxon and Medieval phases as a Preface for Greenwood's *Practical English Grammar,* is in some ways the most interesting.[19] Also a guiding beacon and sustaining pillar of the youthful Royal Society, Wallis was, in short, the greatest English mathematician before Newton. As well as being the chief cryptologist to the Parliamentary forces — having broken the Royalist code before Carisbrooke Castle — and having composed *Arithmetica infinitorum* (1655), which prompted Newton to his binomial theorem, Wallis produced a grammar of the English language, the *Grammatica linguae Anglicanae* (1653). In a curious appendage to this work, *De loquela*, he perfected a description of the physical causes of the sounds of the English language, with which, it was reported, he successfully treated deaf mutes.

As Jonathan Swift's Gulliver was passing through the Grand Academy of Lagado, he encountered a professor of linguistics whose demonstration is of particular interest in our enquiry into the kind of English which Greenwood advocated: "Observing me to look earnestly upon a frame . . . he said, perhaps I might wonder to see him employed in a project for improving speculative knowledge by practical and mechanical operations."[20] Gulliver describes how "He then led me to the frame, about the sides whereof all his pupils stood in ranks, . . . the superficies was composed of several bits of wood, about the bigness of a dye, but some larger than others." "These bits of wood were covered on every square with paper pasted on them; and on these papers were written all the words of their language in their several moods, tenses, and declensions, but without any order."[21] Pupils turned the forty iron handles and wrote down the words which coincided. The "words of their language in their several moods, tenses, and declensions . . . without any order," which the pupils in the Academy "dictated to the four remaining boys who were scribes,"[22] "were all linked together by slender wires."[23]

These "slender wires" Greenwood proposed as the distinguishing feature of his *Practical English Grammar.* We may well see in

Greenwood the result of current, scientific investigation into the autonomy of the English language as a Northern, non-Classical phenomenon when he asserts that no other writers on English

have, in my opinion, taken the right method; for all of them forcing our English tongue too much to the Latin method ... have delivered many useless precepts concerning the Cases, Genders, and Declensions of Nouns; the Tenses, Moods, and Conjugations of Verbs, and other such like things, which our language hath nothing at all to do with; which things tend only to confound and perplex matters, rather than clear and explain them.[24]

"I have been obliged to pursue a quite different method," Greenwood observes,

neglecting the Latin way, and keeping close to what the particular nature of our tongue required; for the Syntax, or Construction of the Noun, is chiefly performed by the help of certain words called Prepositions, and the Conjugation being easily managed by the aid of certain words called Auxiliary or helping Verbs, that matter is performed with the greatest ease imaginable, that uses to create so much trouble in other languages.[25]

In Chapter VIII of his grammar "Of the PREPOSITIONS," which is twenty-five pages long, Greenwood returns to this theme even more explicitly. "The *English* tongue," he reminds his readers, "has no diversity of Cases (which the *Greeks* and *Latins* especially have) but does all by the help of *Prepositions,* which the *Greeks* and *Latins* did partly by Prepositions, and partly by the diversity or difference of Cases."[26]

We have noted in Lowth's works the close intimacy between "primitivism" and the scientific work of the Royal Society. The linguistic tradition to which Lowth's grammar belongs shows the same identification between the accounts of the native roots of English and modern, philosophical descriptions of the workings of English. Had not Locke, who had died in 1704, recognized in his *Essay Concerning Human Understanding* that prepositions, which were the native bonds by which the mind associated its separate ideas, had made our language no foreign-dominated artificial structure but a part of Nature herself? Greenwood writes "Besides words, says that great man, which are names of Ideas in the Mind, there are a great many others that are made use of to signify the Connection that the Mind gives to *Ideas* or *Propositions one with*

another.''[27] The words used to show the connection between ideas
"are generally called Particles; and it is in the right use of these that
the clearness and beauty of a good style particularly consists."[28]
"This part of *Grammar* has been, perhaps, as much neglected, as
some others over diligently cultivated," Locke had continued to
Greenwood's evident satisfaction; for he wrote "it is easy for men
to write one after another, of *Cases* and *Genders, Moods* and
Tenses, Gerunds and *Supines;* in these and the like, there has been
great diligence used ... yet he who would show the right use of
Particles, and what significance and force they have, must take a
little more pains, enter into his own Thoughts, and observe nicely
the several postures of the mind in discoursing."

After Greenwood's long introduction — one which is largely
drawn from direct quotation of Locke and one which reminds the
reader that particles are "carefully ranked into their distinct sub-
divisions," "Prepositions and Conjunctions"[29]—he offers a com-
prehensive list of the key prepositions of the English language:
"ABOVE. *Sax.* BUFAN, BUFON," "ABOUT. *Sax.* ABUTAN,"
"AFTER. *Sax.* AEFTER," "AGAINST. *Sax.* AGEN, ONGEAN,
TOGEANES," "AT. *Sax.* AET," "BEFORE. *Sax.* BEFORAN,"
"BEHIND. *Sax.* HINDAN, BEHINDAN." To this last entry
Greenwood adds, reflecting the common belief that Oriental
and primitive European languages were related, "*Heb.*
BEHAND."[30] From Saxon, "BENEOTH, BETWYNAN,
BETWEONAN, BEGEOND, BEGEONDAN, BE, BI, BIG," we
derived "beneath, between, beyond, and by." The "primitive" era
of Britain is shown to have been both topographical and linguistic.
Five pages anticipate the activities of the modern place-name
society. The word "LOWE, or Loe," for example, Greenwood
writes, "came from the Saxon Hlewe, or Hleaw, a Hill or Hillock;
as Houndslow, i.e., a Hill of Dogs, or a Hill fit for Hunting."[31]

II *The Substance of Lowth's* Short Introduction

Lowth notes in his Preface that English shares the virtue of simplicity with the most ancient language. Latin provides a multitude
of endings and subordinations; English, very few. It is, indeed, this
simplicity which explains the total neglect of the study of our language, "no part of the ordinary method of instruction which we
pass thro' in our chldhood." To Lowth, exclusive specialization
in Latin and Greek, as at Winchester we conclude, is wasteful for,

"A competent Grammatical knowledge of our own Language is the true foundation" for all literature and for the study of other languages. Therefore students in our schools should proceed from English to Latin. Since he has followed "easiness and perspicuity" throughout, he declares, and has tried to be of use to "the Learner even of the lowest class," he has decided that "universal Grammar" embodies principles common to all languages; from a grasp of his native tongue the student may proceed to others.

To Lowth, "Grammar treats of Sentences and the several parts of which they are compounded," and sentences are made up of "Letters, Syllables, Words." We discover in the section on "Letters" that "An articulate sound is the sound of the human voice, formed by the organs of speech"; "a consonant cannot be perfectly sounded by itself," "*J, j,* and *V, v* are consonants; the former having the sound of the soft *g,* and the latter that of a coarser *f.*" "The former may be called *ja,* and the latter *vee.*" The vowels, the peculiarities of *Y* and *W* — the former, a kind of *I;* the latter, both a vowel and a diphthong — the "Mutes" *b, c, d, g, k, p, q* and "Semi-vowels" *l, m, n, r, f, s* are covered in this review of the English Alphabet which, "like most others, is both deficient and redundant; in some cases, the same letters expressing different sounds, and different letters the same sounds."

Having dealt with "Grammar," "Letters," and "Syllables" in the first section ("in spelling, a syllable in the beginning or middle of a word ends in a vowel, unless the consonant *x* follow it, or two consonants, whereof the former is a liquid, or the same as the latter"), Lowth moves to the "nine Sorts of Words, or ... Parts of Speech" in his section "Words." These "parts of speech" are: *1* "the ARTICLE," *2* "the SUBSTANTIVE, or NOUN," *3* "the PRONOUN," *4* "the ADJECTIVE," *5* "the VERB," *6* "the ADVERB," *7* "the PREPOSITION," *8* "the CONJUNCTION," *9* "the INTERJECTION." To every section, he appends an "EXAMPLE" or "EXAMPLES." To this section "WORDS," he adds the following sentence with numbers that indicate the parts of speech:

> 1   2   7   2   5 1   2   4   7   2
> The power of speech is a faculty peculiar to man,
>
> 8   5   5   7 3 7 3   4   2
> and was bestowed on him by his beneficent Creator

7 1   4   8   6   4   2   8   9
for the greatest and most excellent uses; but alas!

6   6   5 3   5   3 7 1   4 7   2
how often do we pervert it to the worst of purposes?

In dealing with *1,* "the ARTICLE," he notes that "a substantive without any articld to limit it is taken in its widest sense." In Acts xxii, 4, "And I persecuted this way unto *the* death," the apostle intends "death in general." "The Definite Article therefore is improperly used," for the sentence should read "unto death" as in the original. Where the Roman Centurion says "Truly this was *the* Son of God," Matthew xxvii, 54 and Mark xv, 39, it is likely that "he only meant to acknowledge him to be an extraordinary person, and more than a mere man; according to his notion of Sons of God in the Pagan Theology." St. Luke's account supports the impression that Luke had no "proper and adequate notion of the character of Jesus, as the Son of God in a peculiar and communicable sense." "*A* Son of God" is the correct translation. Lowth sees in these instances the "excellence of the English language" and its superiority over Greek which "has only one Article."

Among the useful information that the section on the "SUB-STANTIVE" offers which have heavier emphases than any other matters, are the fundamental distinctions among English, Greek, and Latin. English, "to express different connections and relations of one thing to another, uses for the most part Prepositions." Now two cases only remain, the possessive and the nominative, which have distinctively different terminations. An affinity exists between the English language and Nature in the gender of animals, but all other substantives are neuter. This categorizing gives a great advantage in poetry and rhetoric, for personifications may be allotted either masculine or feminine gender.

The third kind of "WORD" Lowth investigates is the "PRO-NOUN." He deals with person, number, gender and case; he chastizes Richard Bentley for not explaining why he had properly complained of Milton's use of "ye" as the "Objective Case Plural"; and he selects examples from Sir Francis Bacon of the proper use of "his" as the possessive of "it" and from Dryden for the improper use of "whose" as the possessive of "which" when applied to things. In speaking of the possessives "mine" and "thine" used "when the Noun they belong to is understood," Lowth notes that

"...the Saxon *Ic* hath the Possessive Case *Min.; thu,* Possessive *Thin; He,* Possessive *His:* ... To the Saxon Possessive Cases *Hire, ure, eower, hira* (that is, *her's, our's, your's, their's*) we have added the *s,* the Characteristic of the Possessive Case of Nouns. Or *our's, your's,* are directly from the Saxon *ures, eoweres;* the Possessive Case of the Pronominal Adjectives *ure, eower;* that is *our, your.*" Noting that *"whose"* is properly *"who's,"* Lowth writes, "So the Saxon *hwa* hath the Possessive Case *hwaes*"; and he then adds, "note, that the Saxons rightly placed the Aspirate before the *w:* as we now pronounce it ... *what, when;* that is *hoo-át, hoo-én.*"

The "ADJECTIVE" deals largely with the three comparative forms. The double superlative "most highest" is admitted because of the "singular propriety" of the Supreme Being's position as *"higher than the highest."* Johnson, in his *Dictionary* (1755), had noted that *lesser* was "a barbarous corruption of *Less,* formed by the vulgar from the habit of terminating comparisons in *er."* *"Worser,"* Lowth adds, only sounds more barbarous "because it has not been so frequently used."

The section devoted to the "VERB," the second largest in the work, occupies some forty-five pages. The footnotes, which have increased from the beginning of the work, now frequently consume half of the page; and they offer examples from Addison, Sir Francis Bacon, Richard Bentley, the Bible, Clarendon, Dryden, John Gay, Milton, Pope, Matthew Prior, Sir Walter Raleigh, the Earl of Shaftesbury, Shakespeare, Bishop Sherlock, and Jonathan Swift. The derivations and etymologies that trace the Saxon and Anglo-Saxon roots of words are mainly from the work of Hickes, Ward, and Wilkins. Lowth deals much like a twentieth-century "grammar for beginners" might with person, number, tense, and mode. In his tables, the past subjunctive, "subjoined as the end or design, or mentioned under a condition, a supposition, or the like, for the most part depending on some other Verb" is given as,

1. I were	we	)	
2. Thou wert*	ye	)	were.
3. He were;	they	)	

The second person singular past subjunctive, "thou wert," necessarily differs from the second person singular of the ordinary, indicative past tense, "thou wast." A footnote asks, "shall we in deference to these great authorities allow *wert* to be the same with *wast,* and common to the Indicative and Subjunctive Mode?" "These authorities" are Addison, "I knew thou *wert* not slow to hear"; Dryden, "Remember that thou *wert*"; Milton, "Before the sun, / Before the heav'ns thou *wert*"; Pope, "All this thou *wert...*"; and Prior, "Thou who of old *wert* sent to Israel's court." Or, Lowth asks, should we "abide by the practice of our best ancient writers?"

Useful information that occurs not only in the text but in foot-notes along the way is expressed with calming clarity. "The peculiar force of the several auxiliaries is to be observed," he advises; "*do* and *did* mark the action itself, or the time of it, with greater force and distinction." "...Perdition catch my soul / But I *do* love thee!" and "This to me / In dreadful secrecy impart they *did*" from Shakespeare illustrate the point. It is interesting that the following distinction, still debated, was made two hundred years ago as it is now: "*will* in the first person singular and plural promises or threatens; in the second and third person only foretells: *shall* on the contrary, in the first person simply foretells; in the second and third persons commands or threatens." The footnote comments that such a distinction was not thus "formerly" and that *shall* simply expressed "the event" in the second and third persons. "So likewise *should* was used, where we now make use of *would.*" Turning to "IRREGULAR VERBS," Lowth offers twenty-five pages that are mostly tables that show their formation, that demonstrate derivations from Anglo-Saxon, and that present examples. He notes that "the formation of Verbs in English, both Regular and Irregular, is derived from Saxon," and "the Irregular Verbs in English are ... for the most part the same words which are Irregular Verbs in the Saxon."

The second half of Lowth's *Short Introduction* leaves the "Parts of Speech" plan which had begun with his numbered sentence, for he devotes sixty pages to different kinds of "SENTENCES" and parts of sentences, to a useful section on "PUNCTUATION," and to a "PRAXIS," or practice piece, for the parsing of six verses about John the Baptist that is largely taken from Luke iii, 1–7.

We half expect when we turn to the "SENTENCE" to find a description of a number of methods of subordinating parts of sentences into the many clauses of various kinds: adverbial clauses of time that begin with "when," of concession that begin with "although," and clauses of condition that commence with "if" or, if negative, with "unless." An estimate of Lowth's anti-Classical bent may be made in the contrast of his description of native English with Johnson's practice of building pyramids of architectural subordination of clause within clause, relative within relative, adverbial subordinate clause within adverbial clause. For Lowth, who was, as Pattison observed, perhaps the greatest Latinist of the century after Addison, his native English has only "Phrases"; and a phrase is "two or more words rightly put together in order to make a part of a Sentence; and sometimes making a whole Sentence." The "First Phrase" comprises a substantive in the nominative and a verb, "I am" or "Thomas is loved." In the second phrase, "the Substantive after the Verb agrees with the substantive before the verb, both being in the Nominative": "a calf becomes an ox," or "I am he." In the third kind of phrase, an adjective follows the verb, "life is short." In the fourth type, an adjective or object follows the verb. In the fifth kind, a verb follows another verb, "boys love to play." The sixth kind of phrase has no verb; it merely shows possession, as in the phrase "Milton's poems." The seventh kind of phrase shows apposition; the eighth is simply an adjective with a substantive; the ninth combines an adjective with an infinitive, "worthy to die"; the tenth combines an adverb with a verb; the eleventh a preposition; the "Twelfth Phrase" occurs "when the same quality in different subjects is compared by means of a conjunction, as in 'white as snow,' 'wiser than I.'" Although the discussion which follows this exposition follows no set system, it occasionally offers allusions to the former "Parts of Speech" and to paragraphs; but Lowth never goes beyond the simplicity of the opening observation that "the principal parts of a simple sentence are the Agent, the Attribute, and the Object."

Instead of attempting distinctions between confusing categories of clauses and between relative pronouns and adjectives, Lowth focusses simply on *the words* "who" "which" and "that" in his discussion of "Relatives."

The accuracy and clearness of the Sentence depend very much upon the proper and determinate use of the Relative, so that it may readily present its Antecedent to the mind of the hearer or reader without any obscurity or ambiguity. The same may be observed of the Pronoun and the Noun, which by some are called also the Relative and the Antecedent.

Sometimes the "Antecedent" is understood, as in "*Who* steals my

purse, steals trash...." This statement is the extent of his
admonishing and theorizing; for the rest of the discussion about
relatives is simple, helpful information with brief, even charming,
examples. He begins his exposition with "The RELATIVES *who,
which, that,* having no variation of gender or number, cannot but
agree with their Antecedent" and continues with the remarks that
"*who* is appropriated to persons," "*which* is used of things only,"
and "*that* is used indifferently both of persons and things: but perhaps would be more properly confined to the latter." The wonder is
that so simple a description of the language could have attracted
the majority of learners for a century in England and the United
States. Lowth's empathic awareness of the capacities of his readers,
a distinguishing mark of all his work, is very much in evidence
throughout.

III   *The Primitive Nature of Lowth's* Short Introduction

Robert Lowth's *A Short Introduction to English Grammar* is an
elegant, even charming, short essay compared with Greenwood's
comprehensive and pedantic account of the genius of the language.
With the advantages of large type and paper — over the small print
and format of Greenwood's — Lowth's study carries the unmistak-
able stamp of learning easily and gracefully worn. As in all of
Lowth's works, we find an air of gentleness, even simplicity, as
well as the broadest kind of scholarship; and this combination suggests a man unassertively at the top of his form.

Part of the simple attraction of Lowth's *Grammar* for children
and for the semi-literate is that each of his twenty-three sections is
unnumbered. Each is headed merely by a title, "Grammar," "Letters," "Syllables," "Example," "Article," "Substantive," "Pronouns," "Adjective," "Verb," "Irregular Verbs," "Adverb,"
"Preposition," "Conjunction," "Interjection," "Sentences,"
"Punctuation"; and these sections are followed by five sets of
"Example" and by a "Praxis," or by an extended analysis of a
simple piece of prose. In the elementary character of Lowth's head-
ings is to be found a major reason for the popularity of his exposition over so long a period of time.

The core of Lowth is the awareness of the special nature of the
undeclined Northern languages, that are as devoid of cases as of
declensions. His grammar, too, is held together by the "slender
wires" which Locke and Greenwood had observed to be the special

characteristic of the English language. In Lowth's description of prepositions, he remarks that "one great use of Prepositions in English, is to express those relations which in some languages are chiefly marked by Cases, or the different endings of the Noun."[32] Lowth speaks highly of James Harris' *Hermes* (1751) in his Preface. "Those, who would enter more deeply into this subject," he observes, "will find it fully and accurately handled, with the greatest acuteness of investigation, perspicuity of explication, and elegance of method, in a treatise entitled *Hermes*, by James Harris Esq.; the most beautiful and perfect example of analysis that has been exhibited since the days of Aristotle."[33] In speaking of the function of prepositions to show the relations between substantives, Harris had written, "those parts of speech unite of themselves in grammar, whose original archetypes unite of themselves in nature."[34]

The Nature which Lowth appears to have in mind, while universal, has been particularly kind to the English in the matter of prepositions which *A Short Introduction* like Greenwood's *Practical English Grammar* finds to be especially Saxon. In dealing with the "Substantive," in his sixth section, Lowth notes that "the English language, to express different connections and relations of one thing to another, uses, for the most part, Prepositions."[35] Even those few embryonic case endings that the English language has, Lowth notes with a loyalty to Northern Europe that is strongly reminiscent of Butler, are derived from the Teutonic: "the English being derived from the same origin as the German, that is, from the Teutonic, is not wholly without them."[36] The footnote to the word "Teutonic" offers the reader a Latin quotation from Hickes' *Linguarum veterum septentrionalium thesaurus,* the thesaurus of the ancient Northern languages of 1703–1705 to which Greenwood was so indebted, and points to the continuation in modern English of the divisions of Anglo-Saxon rhetoric.[37] Of Hickes' observation Lowth remarks, "to which may be added the degrees of comparison, the form of which is the very same in the English as in the Saxon."[38]

Discussing the "Verb," Lowth observes, "*Do* and *have* make the Present Time; *did, had,* the Past; *shall, will,* the Future: *let,* the Imperative Mode; *may, might, could, would, should,* the Subjunctive. The Preposition *to* placed before the Verb makes the Infinitive Mode. *Have* and *be* through their several Modes and Times are placed only before the Perfect and Passive Participles respectively;

the rest only before the Verb itself in its Primary Form."[39] This advice is illuminated by a footnote which occupies the greater part of three pages and begins, "Bishop Wilkins gives the following elegant investigation of the Modes in his *Real Character,* Part iii, Chap. 5. 'To show in what manner the Subject is to be joined with his Predicate, the Copula between them is affected with a Particle, which from the use of it is called *Modus,* the manner or *Mode.*'"[40]

To Hickes' works, Lowth makes several references. In a footnote such as "if it be true, as I have somewhere read, that the Modes of the Verbs are more numerous in the Lapland tongue than in any other, possibly the Laplanders may be provided with an Interrogative Mode,"[41] he confesses also that expert as a source. Characteristic is the note to "contractions from *beated, bursted, casted,* &c.,"[42] which reads "they follow the Saxon rule: Verbs which in the Infinitive end in *dan* and *tan*... (that is, in English, *d* and *t;* for *an* is only the Characteristic termination of the Saxon Infinitive); ...in the Preterite and Participle Preterite commonly for the sake of better sound throw away the final *ed;* as *beot, afed* (both in the Preterite and Participle Preterite), for *leoted, afeded;* from *beotan, afedan.* Hickes, Grammat, Saxon, cap. 9."[43] Again, observing that the prepositions "to" and "for" in English retain, or contain, the force of the Latin dative case, Lowth refers his readers to an "Anglo-Saxon Poem in Hickes' Thesaur., Vol. I, p. 231."[44]

Lowth's library most likely included the Tyrwhitt *Chaucer* and the Middle Scots *Aeneis* of Gavin Douglas, for these works are on the Evans list of the 1823 sale. Moreover, the reference just cited concludes that "the word *worth* is not the Adjective, but the Saxon verb *weorthan,* or *worthan, fieri, to be, to become*; which is often used by Chaucer...."[45] Typical of Lowth's discussion is the exposition of irregular verbs with its emphasis on the Teutonic nature of English and with its repeated allusion to Chaucer. Lowth quotes a number of verbs which change "i" to "ou" when forming the past, "bind," "find," "grind," and "wind."[46] "That all these had originally the termination *en* in the Participle, is plain from the following considerations," he continues, "*drink* and *bind* still retain it; *drunken, bounden;* from the Saxon, *druncen, bunden:* and the rest are manifestly of the same analogy with these. *Begonnen, sonken,* and *founden,* are used by Chaucer; and some others of them appear in their proper shape in the Saxon; *scruncen, spunnen, sprungen, stungen, wunden.* As likewise in the German, which is only another offspring of the Saxon: *begunnen, geklun-*

gen, getruncken, gesungen, gesuncken, gespunnen, gesprungen, gestuncken, geschwummen, geschwungen."[47]

On the next page, Lowth continues the discussion and refers once more to Chaucer and to the moving spirit behind the scientific movement whose influence is so apparent in the *Short Introduction to English Grammar:* "*hangen,* and *scoten,* are the Saxon originals of the two first Participles; the latter of which is likewise still in use in its first form in one phrase; a *shotten* herring. *Stuck* seems to be a contraction from *stucken,* as *struck* now in use for *strucken.* Chaucer hath *comen* and *wonnen: becommen* is even used by Lord Bacon."[48]

The movement in which words and things began to approximate each other earlier in the century shows its influence in the frequently rural images which pages of Lowth's *Grammar* evoke; they are fresh, traditional, and, in a sense, strongly redolent of a world of Medieval practicality. The world that some people picture as the eighteenth century is one of artificiality, wigs, velvet coats, and metropolitan smugness; but this portrayal seems unreal as we read Lowth's list of "substantives." "In English, the Substantive Singular is made Plural, for the most part, by adding to it *s;* or *es,* where it is necessary for the pronunciation: as, *king, kings; fox, foxes; leaf, leaves;* in which last, and many others, *f* is also changed into *v,* for the sake of an easier pronunciation, and more agreeable sound. Some few plurals end in *en:* as *oxen, chicken, children, brethren;* and *men, women,* by changing the *a* of the Singular into *e.*[49] The footnote here reminds us "and anciently, *eyen, shoen, housen, hosen;* so likewise anciently *sowen, cowne,* now always pronounced and written *swine, kine.*"[50] These, we learn, are forms "retained from the Teutonic";[51] and we are then reminded of the euphonious "*mouse, mice; louse, lice; tooth, teeth; foot, feet; goose, geese*" which are all "directly from the Saxon: *mus, mys; lus, lys; toth, teth; fot, fet; gos, ges.*"[52]

It is possible to depict Lowth as a grammarian too concerned with "correctness." One commentator complains that Lowth "came out definitely on the side of logical 'correctness' as against practice" and that, "to him, even such writers as Addison and Pope were guilty of incorrectness."[53] A reasonable amount of instruction in the formation of tenses for the guidance of ostlers, dairymaids, country school mistresses, foreigners, and apprentices, not to mention school children, might clearly involve a suggestion of the correct and incorrect. It is preferable, on the whole, to keep tenses distinct, and it is not reasonable to tell inexperienced students that they may use the nominative case of the pronoun when the rest of the English speaking world uses the objective case. Such a charge ignores Lowth's purpose and readership.

The space which Lowth devotes to incorrectness in writers such as Pope, Dryden, or Swift is small compared with his larger concern — a depiction of the simplicity and ancient character of the English language. Lowth's *Short Introduction* was widely used, a major factor in a huge liberalizing movement in which he inculcated the adoption of English in all its traditional, Northern integrity and in which he rejected Classical models. The mid-eighteenth century was precisely the time during which the Classicism of the Augustan prose of Pope, Dryden, and Swift was challenged. Johnson's rotund, architectural paragraphs of complex, Latinate subordination were the last important instances of Classical style in the history of English prose. Lowth's *Grammar,* one of the earliest and most influential of handbooks to the language, is remarkable for having encouraged a distinct kind of native English based on such older sources as Anglo-Saxon and Middle English. In effect, Lowth's *Short Introduction* is an application of his lifelong awareness of the relevance of "the first ages" to the good of his fellow men. It is diverting to realize that Lowth's *Short Introduction* was the most widely read grammar during the period which saw the rise of Romanticism — the period during which poetry began to be written in what Wordsworth called the "language really used by men."[54]

CHAPTER 7

Isaiah, A New Translation

WHEN Lowth became Bishop of London in 1777, he moved to the ancient palace of the bishops of London at Fulham. The short memoir of Lowth in *The Gentleman's Magazine* and later substantially reprinted as a small pamphlet[1] gives few details of this, or any other, period of his life. Even though the bishops of London had special jurisdiction over colonial churches, and Lowth's tenure of the London bishopric covered the tumultuous years of 1777–87, hardly a piece of paper with Lowth's name on it exists in Lambeth Palace among the papers of the bishops of London.[2] It is from this period of his life, however, that we have a most charming and revealing anecdote which suggests Lowth's elegance and simplicity. John Wesley (1703–91), Lowth's close contemporary, had devoted his entire life to the criticism of the established church; and it had resulted in the movement which produced the Methodist Church. No one, it might seem, would be less sympathetic to Wesley than Robert Lowth, who was with the exception of the Archbishops of York and Canterbury, at the pinnacle of the Anglican church structure. Lowth was dining in the same company as John Wesley, and a nice point in an age of ceremony was whether the Anglican luminary or the reformer should take precedence at table. Each demurred, until Lowth thought to say that, since he was deaf in one ear he should sit below the aged Wesley in order not to miss any of his words; indeed, he added the hope that he might sit at Wesley's feet in the world to come. His "whole behaviour," Wesley wrote in his *Journal*, was "worthy of a Christian bishop."[3]

The sweetness and the elegance of Isaiah combined with its form and sublimity may have persuaded Lowth to rank this prophet, in the 1740's, as "the most perfect model of the prophetic poetry,"[4] and may have led him in 1778 to issue a new translation of the prophet. Isaiah held a special place in Lowth's affections. Differing from Ezekiel, the most sublime and roughest of the three major

141

prophets, Isaiah had received the greatest amount of attention in
the Oxford lectures. It was Lowth's translation into Latin of the
ode from chapter fourteen of Isaiah which Smart had praised in the
highest terms,[5] and Lowth's own estimation of it had increased
over the years; he now found that the celebrated ode "stands
among all the monuments of antiquity unrivalled."[6]

The central place of *Isaiah, A New Translation, with a Preliminary Dissertation* (1778) in Lowth's work suggests that his longer
consideration of the prophet was not an afterthought but a return
to central issues regarding the nature of Oriental poetry. Although
this translation is not as widely read as the *Praelectiones,* it is
unwise to study the latter, especially in the translation of the pedestrian Gregory, without reference to the discussions in Lowth's
Isaiah that were written in English by his own hand after more than
a quarter of a century had elapsed since 1753 when the earlier work
was published.

I   *The Dissertation*

"An attempt to set in a just light the writings of the most sublime
and elegant of the Prophets" could now be made for the first time,
the newly-appointed Bishop of London told George III in the
Dedication. "An inadequate or even false idea" had governed all
other translations, for it had been universally accepted that "the
Prophecies of Isaiah are written in Prose." Lowth stated that he
would examine the books of the Old Testament acknowledged to be
poetic, analyze "every known part of the poetical character," and
demonstrate the similarity between them and Isaiah. Although
Lowth admits that his former work "seems to have met with the
approbation of the learned," he indicates new objectives: "here I
shall endeavour to treat it more at large; to pursue it further, and to
a greater degree of minuteness" than he had in the *Praelectiones*.
Moreover, he wished his theories about Isaiah to be considered "by
way of supplement . . . as well as of themselves to place the subject
in the fullest and clearest light."

Giving twice as many examples, Lowth goes into greater detail
about the varieties of "Synonymous Parallelism." The pattern of
"Bow thy heavens, O Jehovah, and descend; / Touch the mountains, and they shall smoke" in Psalm cxliv, in which the repetition
is reinforced by each line's consisting of "double members, or two
propositions," is found also in Isaiah lxv, "And they shall build

houses, and shall inhabit them; / And they shall plant vineyards, and shall eat the fruit thereof," etc. Within the second division, of "Antithetical Parallelism," "when two lines correspond with one another by an Opposition of terms and sentiments," he finds a range of forms that run from "an exact contraposition of word to word ... down to a general disparity, with something of a contrariety," as in "Yet a little while, and the wicked shall be no more; / Thou shalt look at his place, and he shall not be found: / But the meek shall inherit the land; / And delight themselves in abundant prosperity," an acrostic or alphabetical poem from Psalm xxxvii. In Isaiah ix, "The bricks are fallen, but we will build them with stone, / The sycamores are cut down, but we will replace them with cedars," etc., Lowth says that "the Opposition lies between the two members of each," but the lines offer an example of "Synthetic Parallelism" and are a not uncommon example of the fusing of two kinds.

Ecclesiastes, Job, Micah, Proverbs, the Psalms and the Song of Solomon offer examples of the last kind of parallelism, "Synthetic or Constructive"; in this division of the topic, Lowth elaborates a complex explanation about the "correspondence and equality between different propositions ... noun answering noun, verb to verb, member to member, negative to negative, interrogative to interrogative" that is somewhat beyond the scope of his Oxford exposition. He cites Isaiah, lviii, 5–8, that begins,

> Is such then the fast that I choose?
> That a man should afflict his soul for a day?
> Is it, that he should bow down his head like a bulrush?
> And spread sackcloth and ashes for his couch?
> Shall this be called a fast;
> And a day acceptable to Jehovah?

To the characteristics of Oriental poetry not investigated previously he also adds "the distinction of Hebrew Verses into Longer and Shorter"; and, of special interest to an understanding of the Oriental ode is the comment that "the closing pause of each line is generally very full and strong: and in each line commonly, towards the end ... there is a small rest, or interval, depending on the sense and Grammatical construction, which I would call a Half-pause."

Lowth finds additional applications of the theory of parallelism that are of great use not only to the translator but also to "an Interpreter; and [that] will often lead him into the meaning of obscure words and phrases." Indeed, "inveterate mistakes, which have disgraced the Text above two thousand years ... are happily corrected, and that, I think, beyond a doubt, by the Parallelism supported by the example of similar passages." Pointing to the interdependence of form and meaning, Lowth demonstrates the application of his key *leitmotif* of *mashal,* meaning equally "authority," "force," and "power," and "to speak parabolically" or "in parables." For Isaiah xxviii, 14, the King James' version gave "Wherefore hear the word of the Lord ye scornful men THAT RULE this people which is in Jerusalem." The correct reading, Lowth says, is "Wherefore hear ye the word of Jehovah, ye scoffers; / Ye who to this people in Jerusalem UTTER SENTENTIOUS SPEECHES?" This apt example he follows with "an instance still more remarkable of the influence which the Parallelism has in determining the sense of words" in Isaiah xxviii, 15, which reads, "'We have entered into a covenant with death; / And with the grave we have made... / what?'" he asks. None of the available manuscripts suggests "an agreement, a bargain, a treaty, or something to the same sense." It is the principle of parallelism "that determines it to this meaning; and that so clearly, that no doubt at all remains concerning the sense of the passage."

To Lowth, the Old Testament has something of the same glamor that Shaftesbury found in Mt. Atlas. In North Africa, his travelers saw "the revolutions of past ages, the fleeting form of things, and the decay even of this our globe." No one could investigate farther than he had, notes Lowth, into the form of Hebrew poetry. The ends of the lines are "infallibly marked"; but Hebrew, like other Oriental languages, is destitute of vowels; therefore its true quantities are lost having "lain now for two thousand years in a manner mute and incapable of utterance." "Scanty relics of a language formerly copious" still exist. But his pride in contemporary scholarship joins the esthetic of "the Sublime" as he airs the ability of contemporary paleography to exhume from the first ages a complex artifact like a ruined monastery in a noble park.

A consideration of the distinction between Lowth's *Praelectiones* and his *Isaiah* must include the greater degree of scholarship on a national scale which had come to fruition in the quarter-century that separates his works. Among the scholars whom he names, two especially, Charles Godfrey Woide (1725–1790) and Benjamin Kennicott (1718–1783), did epoch-making work on the manuscripts of the Old Testament; and they did so with his direct support and influence. In fact, without Lowth, the scholarship which finally made possible his *Isaiah* and which amounted to a unique intellectual venture might not have been undertaken. A fascinating sidelight on the nature of "Orientalism" in the third quarter of the eighteenth century is that the upsurge of Biblical scholarship that Lowth fostered increased the dependence of translators on a variety of Oriental languages such as the Coptic and the Arabic. Woide, a Pole who became expert in the language of Lower Egypt, emigrated to England on account of his extreme Protestant views, published a Latin-Egyptian Dictionary, and was in charge of Hebrew and Arabic manuscripts in the new British Museum. On Lowth's recommendation and with royal financial support, Woide had worked extensively in the libraries of Paris; and especially useful to Lowth was Woide's collation of a second-century Coptic version of Isaiah at St.-Germain-des-Prés. Lowth notes that the superiority of the Coptic version had been attested to by the great John Ernest Grabe, the editor and the champion of the authoritative manuscript discovered in Alexandria.

Of greater stature, perhaps, than Woide was Lowth's colleague, Benjamin Kennicott, who, the son of a barber, had made his way through and beyond the university by diligence and talent. Inspired by Lowth, he had pursued all his life the goal of an accurate text. Subscriptions amounting to almost ten thousand pounds had maintained him during a lifelong career spent collating manuscripts in ducal and royal libraries in Denmark, France, Holland, and Sardinia. He had married late and his elderly wife, a "blue-stocking" friend of Mrs. Garrick and Fanny Burney, was renowned for having learned Hebrew after marriage in order to help her husband. Since Lowth had had the benefit of Kennicott's labors before their publication, he had paid him the most respectful compliments. When the first part of Kennicott's massive Variorum Edition of the Old Testament appeared in 1776 shortly before Lowth's *Translation,* Lowth wrote that six hundred manuscripts of the Old Testament had been "collated or consulted, in most parts of Europe; and have been in part published, and the whole will, I hope, soon be completed." He termed the Variorum Old Testament "a work the greatest and most important that has been undertaken and accomplished since the Revival of Letters."

To Lowth, the Renaissance had sanctified a system of syllable emphasis of a much later date than the composition of the text.

What had "in effect" existed before Kennicott and Woide was "an Interpretation of the Hebrew Text made by the Jews of late ages, probably not earlier than the Eighth Century"; and it had informed the version of 1611. This sandy foundation was eroded by all kinds of contingent difficulties. Not only had erroneous emphases or "pointing" been given "divine authority" but the belief had existed that the Old Testament had been transmitted "down to the present times pure, and entirely free from all mistakes, as it came from the hands of the authors." God's "constant miraculous superintendence" is hardly born out, Lowth noted sardonically, by any parallel case, for "Almighty God has not thought such a miraculous interposition necessary in regard to ... the New Testament." In fact, the greater the number of transcribers, as also Malone was discovering in his Shakespearean investigations, the greater the number of errors: "the stream generally becoming more impure, the more distant it is from the source."

The Old Testament contained the oldest poetry extant, and the practices of copyists, Lowth claimed, were incredible: they simply left mistakes unerased and re-wrote; at the edge of the page, they cut or shifted letters only with the regularity of the margin in mind. In the first authority, the Greek Version of the "Seventy Interpreters" or the Septuagint, the version of Isaiah is more "ill rendered" than almost any book. "The words omitted in different places amount to the number of fifty," not including "particles, prepositions, and pronouns affixed." Other frequent mistakes are in proportion. Both the Arabic and Coptic versions, as well as many whole or fragmentary ones which Lowth lists, are therefore entirely indispensable to a reasonable reading. Yet Lowth advises that we must remember that Aristotle's *Poetics* "continues to be the great Code of Criticism; the fundamental principles of which are still plainly deducible." "If the Iliad or the Aeneid had come down to us with more errors in all the copies than are to be found in the worst Manuscript ... the Fable, the Mythology, the Characters, the great constituent parts, would still have been visible and apparent."

II *The Translation*

Lowth's *New Translation* capitalizes the first stanza of Isaiah, for he uses it as a title. Similar practices are repeated during the prophecy; and these, with other literary divisions — such as

Lowth's favorite Chapter Fourteen into "preamble," "ode," and "oracle" — give the appearance of an anthology. More importantly, Lowth uses parallelism throughout a Biblical work for the first time. The lines *look* like verse; and, indeed, since they were in English similar to prose, they gave impetus to a practice followed by Smart and Blake; and by Macpherson in Northern primitive poetry such as *Ossian*. The first chapter begins,

1.　　　THE VISION OF ISAIAH THE SON OF AMOTS,
　　　WHICH HE SAW CONCERNING JUDAH AND JERUSALEM;
　　　IN THE DAYS OF UZZIAH, JOTHAM, AHAZ, HEZEKIAH,
　　　KINGS OF JUDAH.
2.　　　HEAR, O ye heavens; and give ear, O earth!
　　　For it is JEHOVAH that speaketh.
　　　I have nourished children and brought them up;
　　　And even they have revolted from me.
3.　　The ox knoweth his possessor;
　　　And the ass the crib of his lord:
　　　But Israel knoweth not Me;
　　　Neither doth my people consider.
4.　　Ah, sinful nation! a people laden with iniquity!
　　　A race of evil doers! children degenerate!
　　　They have forsaken JEHOVAH;
　　　They have rejected with disdain the Holy One of
　　　　　Israel;
　　　They are estranged from him; they have turned
　　　　　their back upon him.
5.　　On what part will ye smite again, will ye add
　　　　　correction?
　　　The whole head is sick, and the whole heart faint:
6.　　From the sole of the foot even to the head, there
　　　　　is no soundness therein;
　　　It is wound, and bruise, and putrifying sore:
　　　It hath not been pressed, neither hath it been bound;
　　　Neither hath it been softened with ointment.
7.　　Your country is desolate, your cities are burnt
　　　　　with fire;
　　　Your land, before your eyes, strangers devour it:
　　　And it is become desolate, *as if destroyed by an*
　　　　　inundation.
8.　　And the daughter of Sion is left, as *a shed* in
　　　　　a vineyard;
　　　As a lodge in a garden of cucumers, as a city
　　　　　taken by siege.

The difference between the Lowth and the King James version is not, at first sight, extensive. His verbal changes, however, can be radical on occasion. He insists that "as overthrown by strangers," the last phrase of Stanza 7 in the King James version, is a misreading and that "as if destroyed by an inundation" is the correct translation. The other italicized words in the quotation indicate that it is in the area of material reality that his translation differs most. For example the "cottage in a vineyard" of Isaiah i, 8, is now a common or garden "shed."

In Isaiah iii there is an inventory of female ornament. Chapter 1 of this present book discussed the difference between William Lowth's approach to "the nose jewels" of Isaiah iii, 21 and Robert's emphasis. Where William, who used the King James version, is theological, Robert is anthropological; where William is spiritual, Robert is materialistic. Robert's entire translation bears out this sense of exclusive exotic appeal to the senses. Some of Robert's changes reflect the difference between Jacobean and Georgian dress; for example the "chains," "wimples," and "hoods" of stanzas 19, 22, and 23 become "pendents," "cloaks," and "turbans." The total effect is of a difference in the incisiveness of the images; everything appears more clearly etched than in the King James Authorized Version. Robert Lowth's translation reads:

iii, 16. Moreover JEHOVAH hath said:
    Because the daughters of Sion are haughty;
    And walk displaying the neck,
    And falsely setting off their eyes with paint;
    Mincing their steps as they go. . . .
17. *Therefore will the Lord humble the head of the*
        daughters of Sion;
    And JEHOVAH will expose their nakedness.
18. In that day will the Lord take from them *the*
        ornaments,
    Of the feet-rings, and the net-works, and the
        crescents;
19. *The pendents,* and the bracelets, and *the thin*
        vails;
20. *The tires,* and *the fetters,* and *the zones,*
    And *the perfume boxes,* and *the amulets;*
21. The rings, and the jewels of the nostril;
22. *The embroidered cloaks, and the little purses;*
23. *The transparent garments,* and the fine linen *vests;*
    And the turbans, and the mantles:

24. *And there shall be, instead of perfume, a
      putrid ulcer;*
   And, *instead of well-girt raiment,* rags;
   And, instead of *high-dressed hair,* baldness;
   And, instead of *a zone,* a girdle of sackcloth:
   A sun-burnt skin, instead of beauty.

Lowth's changes in phrasing include *"the ornaments, / Of the feet-
rings"* which had been "their tinkling ornaments about their feet"
(18); *"the embroidered cloaks"* which were "the changeable suits
of apparel" (22); *"there shall be, instead of perfume, a putrid
ulcer"* which was formerly "and it shall come to pass that instead
of sweet smell, there shall be stink" (24); and *"a sun-burnt skin,
instead of beauty"* for "and burning instead of beauty" (24).
Important changes in real meaning occur in 16 where "walk with
stretched forth necks and *wanton eyes"* has become Lowth's "And
walk displaying the neck / *and falsely setting off their eyes with
paint"*; in 20, where *"the tablets"* have been changed into *"the
perfume boxes";* and in 23, in which *"the glasses,* and the fine
linen..." have given way to *"the transparent garments,* and the
fine linen *vests."*

Lowth had written thirty years earlier at the conclusion to Lecture VII, "Poetic Imagery from Common Life" when he was intro-
ducing Isaiah xiv to his audience: "Figure to yourselves a vast,
dreary, dark sepulchral cavern, where the kings of the nations lie,
each upon his bed of dust, the arms of each beside him, his sword
under his head, and the graves of their numerous hosts round about
them." After twenty-five years this triumphal ode appears even
more splendid: "Behold! the king of Babylon is introduced, they
all rise and go forth to meet him; and receive him as he approaches!
'Art thou also come down unto us? Art thou become like unto us?
Art thou cut down and withered in thy strength, O thou destroyer
of the nations!'" As he says in the notes, "for beauty of disposition, strength of colouring, greatness of sentiment, brevity, perspicuity and force of expression," it "stands among all the monuments of antiquity unrivalled." Smart wrote of Lowth's Latin version that it was "one of the best performances that has been published for a century."[7] The tone is reminiscent of *Ossian,* and the
situation is similar to Gray's *The Bard* in which the prophet foretells the downfall of a successful tyrant. This high-point of Lowth's
entire translation now reads:

9. Hades from beneath is moved because of thee,
     to meet thee at thy coming:
  He rouseth for thee the mighty dead, all the great
     chiefs of the earth;
  He maketh to rise up from their thrones,
     all the kings of the nations.

10. All of them shall accost thee, and shall say
     unto thee:
  Art thou, even thou too, become weak as we?
     art thou made like unto us?

11. Is then thy pride brought down to the grave; the sound
     of thy sprightly instruments?
  Is the vermin become thy couch, and the earthworm
     thy covering?

12. How art thou fallen from heaven, O Lucifer, son
     of the Morning!
  Art cut down to the earth, thou that didst subdue the
     nations!

13. Yet thou didst say in thy heart: I will ascend
     the heavens;
  Above the stars of God I will exalt my throne;
  And I will sit upon the mount of the divine presence,
     on the sides of the north:

14. I will ascend above the heights of the clouds; I will
     be like the most High.

15. But thou shalt be brought down to the grave, to the sides
     of the pit.

16. Those that see thee shall look attentively at thee; they
     shall well consider thee:
  Is this the man, that made the earth to tremble; that
     shook the kingdoms?

The incantatory effect of the repetitive form adds a hypnotic elevation to the poem — one that is impressive even now when these esthetic matters are not perhaps as timely. The contrasts of a few stanzas of the 1611 translation suggest the heightening which the parallelism and some of the other changes made by Lowth have afforded:

11. Thy pomp is brought down to the grave, and the
    noise of thy viols: the worm is spread under thee,
    and the worms cover thee.

12. How art thou fallen from heaven, O Lucifer, son
    of the morning! how art thou cut down to the ground,

which didst weaken the nations!
13. For thou hast said in thine heart, I will ascend
    into heaven, I will exalt my throne above the stars
    of God: I will sit also upon the mount of the
    congregation, in the sides of the north:
14. I will ascend above the heights of the clouds; I
    will be like the most high.

III   *The Notes to* Isaiah

The Notes to the *New Translation,* which occupy an entire volume, cover twice as many pages as the introductory Dissertation
and the prophecy together; and they are an indispensable guide to
the nature of the English sense of "the Oriental" in the last part of
the eighteenth century. Like the similarly extensive notes to William
Beckford's Arabian fantasy *Vathek* (1786), with which they share
the authority of Sir John Chardin, Thomas Harmer, Henry Maundrell, Pococke, Thomas Shaw, Lady Mary Wortley Montagu, and
other travelers, Lowth's notes enable us to resurrect the early
Romantic image of the East. The note to Isaiah i, 6, "It hath not
been pressed...," begins "the art of medicine in the East consists
chiefly in external applications." Sir John Chardin, frequently
cited in the *Praelectiones,* had observed that "plasters, ointments,
oils, frictions ... are made use of in the East upon the belly and
stomach in most maladies," for the Orientals were ignorant "of the
art of making decoctions and potions." Jean-Baptiste Tavernier
(1605–1689) in his *Travels in India* had noted that "they have a certain preparation of oil and melted grease, which they commonly
use for the healing of wounds." Lowth reminds his readers that
"Wine, cleansing and somewhat astringent," along with "oil,
mollifying and healing," were used by the good Samaritan.
   To Isaiah i, 8, which Lowth translates as "And the daughter of
Sion is left, as a shed in a vineyard; / As a lodge in a garden of
cucumbers," he appends the authority of Harmer, who is also frequently mentioned in Lowth's lectures, for "a little temporary hut
covered with boughs, straw, turf" for the use of the watchman during the ripening season. Frederick Hasselquist, the Swedish traveler
and naturalist (1722–1752), had written in his *Travels* that Eastern
foxes and jackals were common in Palestine "especially during the
vintage"; for they often destroyed the "fruits of the gourd kind,
melons, watermelons, cucumbers, &c.," that are "in great request
in the Levant on account of their cooling quality." Tavernier had

attested to the attractions and reliability of what Lowth called "cucumers": "Les concombres dans le Levant ont une bonté particulière, & quoiqu'on les mange crus, ils ne font jamais de mal" ("the cucumbers of the Levant are especially good, and however much one eats them raw, one is never sick").

How eclectic the term "Oriental" was, and with what liberating enjoyment men related Hebrew scripture to the exotic and colorful literature of travel, is suggested by Lowth's typical allusion to Antonio Ulloa's (1716–1795) *Voyage to South America.* Illuminating Isaiah i, 18, "though your sins be as scarlet.... though they be red as crimson...," Lowth observes that "this colour was produced from a worm, or insect, which grew in a coccus, or excrescence, of a shrub" as in "the Opuntia of America"; he then reminds his readers of the insect which lives in the *kermes* oak in Provence and of the derivation of the word "crimson" from Arabic, *kermez.*

One of Lowth's most intriguing expansions was of the "wanton eyes" of "the daughters of Sion" of Isaiah iii, 16, which refers, he says, to "falsely setting off their eyes with paint." Lowth's interest in cosmetics had been heightened by the recent excavations at Herculaneum, which were contemporaneous with his own inquiries. "I have a metalline mirror found in Herculaneum, which is not above three inches square," he relates in the note to Isaiah viii, 1; and he here offers a three page essay about cosmetic practices in the East, a curious interest and expertise for a Bishop of London. The Italian traveler, Pietro della Valle (1586–1652), to whom we have alluded before as an authority on jewelry, drawing a picture of his Assyrian wife who was born in Mesopotamia and educated at Baghdad, described "her eye-lashes, which are long, and according to the custom of the East, dressed with stibium." Sandys had noted in Turkey that the black powder that women used on their eyes was "brought from the kingdom of Fez, and called *Alcohole;* which by the not disagreable staining of the lids doth better set forth the whiteness of the eye." Shaw, to whom also Lowth had referred previously, described the application "performed by dipping first into the powder a small wooden bodkin of the thickness of a quill, and then drawing it afterwards through the eye-lids over the ball of the eye." Alexander Russell (1715?–1768) had confirmed this method in his *Natural History of Aleppo.*

The attention which Lowth has given to the ode of Isaiah xiv concentrates upon a parabolic style that is of central interest in our definition of Lowth's notion of Oriental poetry. In the *Praelectiones,* Lowth had dealt with *mashal,* or *mashalim,* in Lecture XIV, "The Sublime in General." His description of this parabolic style "which denotes figurative language" that expresses an intense "spirit of sublimity," "energy and enthusiasm," had comprised one strain of poetry, one not necessarily prophetic. The special character of this style was to offer sharp images of sense, often from common life, in a powerful, authoritative manner which produced an overpoweringly sublime effect on the reader. In the note to Isaiah xiv, Lowth draws together his earlier remarks about prophetic poetry and *mashal* or the parabolic style. "I take this to be the general name for the poetic style among the Hebrews," he comments. This style includes every kind of verse, the sententious, the figurative and, above all, "the sublime." The verb *mashal,* he repeats, means "to rule, to exercise authority; to make equal, to compare one thing with another" in "acute, weighty, and powerful speeches." In Balaam's first prophecy in Numbers xxiii, in Job's final speeches, and in Isaiah xiv, this style affords "the first and most eminent examples extant of the truly great and beautiful in poetic style."

These examples from Lowth's notes in *Isaiah, A New Translation* suggest the variety and extent of the knowledge he offers. "Daily Life in the East" is the scarcely submerged theme of these four hundred or so pages of notes; and the topics include not only medicine, horticulture, dyes, cosmetics, and poetic theory but also agriculture, architecture, anthropology, military strategy, townplanning, and viniculture. The extent to which the growth of recent knowledge of the East permeates his version of the prophet is indicated by the number of times he cites and quotes not only modern Biblical scholars but contemporary observers. In Lowth's "Index of Persons," Chardin has twenty-two entries; Harmer, twenty-three;[8] and other figures, such as Maundrell, Pococke, Sandys, Shaw, Tavernier, Lady Mary Wortley Montagu, and Ulloa add up to a total of travelers' observations approaching eighty notations or references, the largest block of citations to any one source in Isaiah, a prophecy which is a mere sixty or so short chapters.

IV *The Significance of Lowth's* Isaiah

The question is, of course, to what extent and in what respects we may discover a repetition of Lowth's *Praelectiones* in his *New*

Translation of Isaiah, his first application of the central doctrine of parallelism to an extended Biblical work. The allusions to the *Lectures*, which were not translated into English until 1787, the year of Lowth's death, serve as a control; they reveal the emphases which stayed with him for more than twenty-five years when he returned to the subject of his triumph. In discussing Isaiah xi, 6-8, which begins,

> Then shall the wolf take up his abode with the lamb;
> And the leopard shall lie down with the kid:
> And the calf, and the young lion, and the fatling
>   shall come together;
> And a child shall lead them . . . ,

Lowth notes that "the idea of the renewal of the Golden Age, as it is called, is much the same in the Oriental writers, with that of the Greeks and Romans: the wild beasts grow tame; the serpents and poisonous herbs become harmless; all is peace and harmony, plenty and happiness." After Lowth has presented quotations from Virgil, Horace, and Theocritus among the Classical writers and then from the Arabian and Persian poets, "Ferdusi" and "Ibn Onein" (these last from Sir William Jones' researches into Oriental poetry),[9] Lowth states that "I have laid before the reader these common passages from the most elegant of the ancient poets, that he may see how greatly the Prophet on the same subject has the advantage upon the comparison; how much the former fall short of that beauty and elegance, and variety of imagery, with which Isaiah has set forth the same ideas."

It is, perhaps, unfortunate that Lowth was a bishop; for it is difficult to assume that his interest in the Prophet Isaiah and in the whole of Hebrew literature was secular. But such was the case, and his approach is that of a non-theological student of comparative ancient literature and of its common images and techniques. He appears now, in *Isaiah,* even more culturally relative than he had been. With Shakespeare, Milton, Virgil, Homer, the Arabs, and the Persians, the prophet is presented in dramatic isolation as the greatest of the early poets, a secular eminence which was less exposed in the earlier lectures.

Isaiah xiv contains, Lowth notes, "one of the boldest Prosopopoeias, that ever was attempted in poetry; and is executed with astonishing brevity and perspicuity." The personifying of the dead

kings who arise to speak to the defeated Babylonian monarch,
however, is only one aspect of his admiration of this highpoint. In
Lecture I of the *Praelectiones,* he had memorably distinguished
between the epic and the ode. The epic achieved its effect by "con-
ducting the reader through a varied and delightful scene" like a
spreading fire "making its impression ... more especially by its
continuance." The greatest and most poetic of forms, above the
rest of poetry as poetry was above prose, the ode "strikes with an
instantaneous effect, amazes, and as it were storms the affections"
like "a flash of lightning." Because the ode has the special property
of revealing a mind in the grip of strong emotion, it had become
central to the Oriental movement. This emphasis is now strengthened in Isaiah xiv and its "Ode of supreme and singular
excellence."

Biblical paraphrases from the earliest years of the century, as we
observe in *Young Paraphrase on Part of Job* (1719), had combined modern images with the most ancient and original poetry.
This blurring of the temporal perspective was furthered by the
nature of prophecy, which told of events far distant in incisive,
familiar terms, and by the nature of "the Sublime," the experience
of the timeless Infinite through sense responses to the objects of
Nature. Lowth had strengthened this impetus towards timelessness
as a centrally desirable characteristic of great poetry by his investigation of the Hebrews' "Mystical Allegory." He had shown in
Lecture XI that the foretelling of a temporally local event could
allude, at the same moment and by the same images, to the distant
restoration of the church. A "sublime" effect of this kind is central
to Isaiah xl, the notes to which explain that "I have not the least
doubt that the return of the Jews from the captivity of Babylon is
the first, though not the principal, thing in the Prophet's view. The
Redemption from Babylon is clearly foretold; and at the same time
is employed as an image to shadow out a Redemption of an infinitely higher and more important nature."

The use of the past tense to refer to the present, in Isaiah xlii —
another aspect of the disorientation of time — is central to the fervid, irrational effect he describes, and so is the powerful emphasis
on metaphor throughout. Simile, the comparison most used in the
epic, referred to things known by judgment and reason, calmly sur-
veyed objects in the memory, and compared like with like. The role
of imagination, as he had pointed out in Lecture XII on "Comparison," was to force together in the heat of creation things

thought by reason to be dissimilar. The image of the defeated
Sennacherib and host in Isaiah xxix, "And like as a dream, a vision
of the night, / So shall it be with the multitude of all the nations,
... As when a hungry man dreameth; and lo! he seemeth to
eat; / ... But he awaketh, and he is still faint..." draws from him
this comment: "Sennacherib and his mighty army are not compared to a dream, because of their sudden disappearance; but ...
to what happens to a hungry and thirsty man, when he awakes
from a dream, in which fancy had presented to him meat and drink
in abundance; and finds it nothing but a vain illusion.... The
image is extremely natural, but not obvious; it appeals to our
inward feelings, not to our outward senses; and is applied to an
event in its concomitant circumstances exactly similar, but in its
nature totally different." Parallel but inferior moments in Homer,
Virgil, and Lucretius follow, as well as the instruction to "See De S.
Poes. Hebr. Praelect. XII."

Lowth's long allusions suggest that the notes are an extension to
the *Lectures* of thirty years earlier, but they have a characteristic
that is even more central to the nature of Oriental poetry as it was
seen in the eighteenth century. This subject concerns "their manner
of exhibiting things divine, spiritual, moral and political, by a set of
images taken from things natural, artificial, religious, historical; in
the way of metaphor or allegory." Of course, he observes, "all
poetry has chiefly recourse to natural images, as the richest and
most powerful source of illustration." "But it may be observed of
the Hebrew poetry in particular," he goes on with studied emphasis, "that in the use of such images, ... in the way of illustration or
ornament, it is more regular and constant than any other poetry
whatsoever."

This note to Isaiah ii, 13-16 is particularly concerned with the use
of images of the "cedars of Libanus and oaks of Basan" for
"kings, princes, potentates of the highest rank" or "ships of Tar-
shish and works of art and invention employed in adorning them,
for merchants, men enriched by commerce and abounding in all the
luxuries and elegancies of life..."; and Lowth strikes in this note a
theme to be taken up over and over again: Hebrew poetry did not
employ abstractions nor refer to vague and unseen things. It was
constructed throughout, like our Imagist poetry of the modern era,
from concrete images appealing to the senses; and it was imbued, as
Richard Aldington said of Hilda Doolittle's verse, with "a kind of
accurate mystery."[10] Isaiah xiii, 10, begins, "Yea the stars of

heaven, and the constellations thereof, / Shall not send forth their light: / The sun is darkened..." The "Note" to this passage observes "to express happiness, prosperity, the instauration and advancement of states," etc., the poets made use of images "taken from the most striking parts of nature, from the heavenly bodies, from the sun, moon, and stars; which they describe as shining with increased splendour and never setting, the moon becomes like the meridian sun, and the sun's light is augmented sevenfold." To indicate defeat, disaster, the downfall of nations they use the opposite images, "the stars are obscured, the moon withdraws her light, and the sun shines no more ... all things seem tending to their original chaos."

The most striking and memorable descriptions of the effect of "the Sublime" in eighteenth-century prose occur in Lowth. In Lecture XVI, "Of Sublimity of Sentiment," he had pictured the journey of the mind and imagination, appropriately in an age of astronomy, "through all the dimensions of space, length, breadth and height" as the intellect flew to "the boundaries of creation" and then "into the void of infinity: whose vast and formless extent ... impresses it with the sublimest and most awful sensations, and fills it with a mixture of admiration and terror." The images producing this effect, he observes in the same lecture, might be "quite inconsistent with the Divine Being, and derived from an ignoble source"; for, "from ideas which in themselves appear coarse, unsuitable, and totally unworthy of so great an object, the mind naturally recedes, and passes suddenly to the contemplation of the object itself, and of its inherent magnitude and importance."

This combination of the most lowly and "unworthy" images and of the most magnificent, cosmos-searching sense of sublime elevation which is isolated and described in Lecture XVI of the *Praelectiones* now appears, in retrospect, to be most vivid and significant. Not only did the Hebrews consistently employ imagery of ordinary life and of natural objects to achieve their most characteristic great effects, but also at the heart of their poetry was this technique, as it were, of opposites or of inappropriate response. "Of metaphors, allegories, and comparisons of the Hebrew poets, in which the Divine Nature and attributes are represented under images taken from brutes and other low objects; of their effect, their sublimity, and the causes of it; see De. S. Poes. Hebr. Praelect. XVI," Lowth writes of Isaiah xxxi, 4, "For thus hath JEHOVAH said unto me: / Like as the lion growleth, / Even the young lion over his prey; ...

So shall JEHOVAH God of Hosts descend to fight."

This allusion only appears to be perfunctory because Lowth had earlier returned to the theme in one of the most poetic of his frequently inspired literary observations, about Isaiah i, stanza 24,

> Wherefore saith the Lord JEHOVAH God of Hosts,
>   the Mighty One of Israel:
> Aha! I will be eased of mine adversaries;
> I will be avenged of mine enemies.

The comment on this stanza is the longest literary-analytical passage in the Notes, and it begins with a psychological *aperçu* which reminds us of Lowth's victory over Warburton: "Anger, arising from a sense of injury and affront, especially from those who, from every consideration of duty and gratitude, ought to have behaved far otherwise, is an uneasy and painful sensation: and revenge, executed to the full on the offenders, removes that uneasiness, and consequently is pleasing and quieting at least for the present."

But, as to whether or not we may apply such peculiarly human psychology to the Almighty, Lowth explains that "This is a strong instance of the metaphor called Anthropopathia; by which, throughout the Scriptures, as well the historical as the poetical parts, the sentiments, sensations, and affections; the bodily faculties, qualities and members of men, and even of brute animals, are attributed to God." The reason is: "We have no idea of the natural attributes of God, of his pure essence, of his manner of existence, of his manner of acting: when therefore we would treat on these subjects, we find ourselves forced to express them by sensible images." "Necessity leads to beauty," he notes. Metaphor consists in bringing together the unlike, and this most beautiful of metaphors, "used with great elegance and sublimity in the sacred Poetry," brings together the most concrete of unelevated objects and the highest abstract idea.

He returns to the theme of the closing paragraphs of Lecture XVI and writes, perhaps even more eloquently,

what is very remarkable, in the grossest instances of the application of it, it is generally the most striking and the most sublime. The reason [was:] when the images are taken from the superior faculties of the human nature, from the purer and more generous affections, and applied to God, we are apt to acquiesce in the notion; we overlook the metaphor, and take it as a proper attribute: but when the idea is gross and offensive, as in this passage of Isaiah, where the impatience of anger, and the pleasure of revenge, is attributed to God, we are immediately shocked at the application, the impropriety strikes us at once; and *the mind casting about for something in the Divine Nature analogous to the image, lays hold on some great, obscure, vague idea, which she endeavours in vain to comprehend, and is lost in immensity and astonishment.* See De S. Hebr. Prael. XVI. sub. fin. (my italics).

The publication of the *Praelectiones* in 1753 and its frequent reissuing had resulted in "numerous attempts to follow the translation theory implicit in parallelism,"[11] the most important of which was Smart's *Jubilate Agno.* Lowth's *Isaiah, A New Translation,* provided "a practical example to follow" and "results were soon forthcoming,"[12] as one scholar has noted recently. Even more importantly, however, we have invaluable proof that in the extended work of Lowth, the major authority on Oriental primitivism in the late as in the mid-eighteenth century, the most sublime poetry ever written was shown to be a response to material objects even more sharply realized than in neo-Classical verse. Imagination did not deal with large, vague abstractions; on the contrary, it was primarily concerned with ordinary things in an eternal, timeless and dimensionless, world formally represented in the stasis of parallelism.

It is significant that Smart followed Lowth's principle of parallelism in his verse, and it is more instructive in understanding the effect of primitivism on the workings of Romantic verse that Smart made central and most effective in his poem such local and domestic phenomena as "my cat Jeoffry" who "camels his back to bear the first notion of business" and that, Wordsworth in the mountains of the primitive Lake District, records in one of his most important demonstrations of creative imagination a sublime moment in which,

> . . . fixed resemblances were seen
> To implements of ordinary use,
> But vast in size, in substance glorified;
> Such as by Hebrew Prophets were beheld
> In vision — forms uncouth of mightiest power
> For admiration and mysterious awe.
>
> (*The Excursion,* II, 864–69)

It is intriguing to observe also that in Lowth, whose *Isaiah*, like his *Praelectiones*, maintained its popularity well into the nineteenth century, we discover the roots not only of Romantic Orientalism but those of nineteenth-century writers such as Edward Fitzgerald (1809–1881) whose *Rubáiyát of Omar Khayyám* (1859), like the prose of the demonic traveller, Sir Richard Francis Burton (1821–1890), struck the authentic prophetic note, at once sublimely mysterious and packed with sharply observed phenomena.

CHAPTER 8

The Stature of Robert Lowth

I Eighteenth-Century Critics of Lowth

WILLIAM Cowper, Edward Gibbon, Samuel Johnson, Hannah More, Christopher Smart, Joseph Warton, Thomas Warton the Younger, John Wesley, and John Wilkes gave Lowth the recognition for a variety of achievements which few men in any century earn. Even when we take into account William Cowper's extreme susceptibility, his recognition of the "early genius" of Lowth's schoolboy verse is remarkable. "I thank you for Mr. Lowth's verses," his letter to "dear friend," Unwin, began, "they are so good, that had I been present when he spoke them, I should have trembled for the boy, lest the man should disappoint the hopes such early genius had given birth to. It is not common to see so lively a fancy so correctly managed, and so free from irregular exuberances, at so unexperienced an age: fruitful, yet not wanton, and gay without being tawdry."

Cowper noted that "the Sublime" was Lowth's strength even as a fledgling poet. "When schoolboys write verse," he wrote, enlarging on his theme, "if they have any fire at all, it generally spends itself in flashes, and transient sparks, which may indeed suggest an expectation of something better hereafter, but deserve not to be commended much for any real merit of their own. Their wit is generally forced and false, and their sublimity, if they affect any, bombast." But such was not the case with Lowth: for "Lowth seems to have stepped into excellence at once, and to have gained by intuition, what we little folks are happy, if we can learn at last, after much labour of our own, and instruction of others...."[1]

Gibbon's *Autobiography* or *Memoirs,* which is "only incidentally a personal autobiography," is, as Trevor-Roper has recently written, "a history of the making of *The Decline and Fall of the*

161

Roman Empire.''[2] Recognition of an equal, perhaps, accounts for the exception enjoyed by Lowth in an Oxford which Gibbon paints in colors of Medieval squalor fifty years after his unfruitful stay there. The celebrated retort which Lowth had made to Warburton in the *Letter to the Author of the Divine Legation* is used by Gibbon to contrast his own less happy experience. "A venerable prelate, whose taste and erudition must reflect honour on the society in which they were formed, has drawn a very interesting picture of his academical life,"[3] he observes; "'I was educated (says Bishop Lowth) in the University of Oxford. I enjoyed all the advantages, both public and private, which that famous seat of learning so largely affords. I spent many years in that illustrious society, in a well-regulated course of useful discipline and studies, and in the agreeable and improving commerce of gentlemen and of scholars;...'"[4] Gibbon did not enjoy these advantages public and private which Oxford afforded more easily a member of the Wykehamist "Society" than a solitary young man emerging from a childhood of delicate health: he wrote "To the University of Oxford *I* acknowledge no obligation; and she will as cheerfully renounce me for a son, as I am willing to disclaim her for a mother."[5]

The trouble was blamed by Gibbon on the Oxford system in which, "instead of being paid by voluntary contributions, which would urge them to increase the number, and to deserve the gratitude of their pupils, the Oxford professors are secure in the enjoyment of a fixed stipend, without the necessity of labour, or the apprehension of control."[6] Gibbon makes clear that an exception was Lowth, a great teacher as well as great scholar. "There still remains a material difference between a book and a professor," he observed:

The hour of the lecture enforces attendance; attention is fixed by the presence, the voice, and occasional questions of the teacher; the most idle will carry something away; and the more diligent will compare the instructions which they have heard in the school, with the volumes which they peruse in their chamber. The advice of a skilful professor will adapt a course of reading to every mind and every situation; his authority will discover, admonish, and at last chastise the negligence of his disciples; and his vigilant enquiries will ascertain the steps of their literary progress. Whatever science he professes he may illustrate in a series of discourses, composed in the leisure of his closet, pronounced on public occasions, and finally delivered to the press. I observe with pleasure, that in the University of Oxford

Dr. Lowth, with equal eloquence and erudition, has executed this task in his incomparable *Praelectiones* on the Poetry of the Hebrews.[7]

It would be surprising if Lowth, the most celebrated of the professors of poetry at Oxford, and also an author of a Medieval biography and a widely acclaimed *Grammar,* had not attracted the attention of Boswell. Armed with a letter from a fellow Scot, Boswell found the then Bishop of Oxford at home on the morning of Saturday, April 12, 1772, in his house in Duke Street, Westminster. Boswell observed that Lowth was a "neat," "judicious," and "little" man — the last observation probably exaggerated since other accounts tell us that Lowth was a well-built man — and that "his abilities as a writer" were "well known."[8] In a letter to William Temple in 1779, Boswell added a few remarks to this assessment. He noted that Johnson had not read *Isaiah, A New Translation* but had been told it was "a great work," and then Boswell underlined for later readers the distinction in temperament he saw between himself and Lowth. "I do not think Lowth an engaging man; I sat a good while with him this last spring. He said Dr. Johnson had *great genius.* I give you this as a specimen of his talk, which seemed to me to be neither discriminating, pointed, nor animated. Yet he certainly has much curious learning and a good deal of critical sagacity."[9]

Johnson held a distinctly high opinion of Lowth. The sweep of his teasing observation to Boswell the Scot that "all Scotland could not muster learning enough for Lowth's prelections"[10] does not detract from its impressiveness when we remember the intellectual status of Edinburgh, "the Athens of the North," in the eighteenth century. Himself a lexicographer and a grammarian, Johnson thought well of Lowth's *Short Introduction to English Grammar.* "The Reverend Mr. Astle of Ashbourne," one of the wraiths who people Boswell's *Life,* had evidently known Johnson from his earliest years and had once asked him for advice on furthering his education. "Dr. Johnson ... recommended to him the following books,"[11] Boswell writes; the list includes one grammar of the English tongue: *"Clarendon's History — Watt's Improvement of the Mind — Watt's Logic — Nature Displayed,"* it reads, and then *"Lowth's English Grammar."*[12] Such attention, along with Johnson's remark about Lowth's learning to George III in 1767,[13] confirms our sense that the greatest men of the time recognized in Lowth an outstanding mind. Johnson's verdicts, read in conjunction with his praise of "Spence on Pope's Odyssey, and Trapp's Praelectiones Poeticae" in his "General Plan of Education,"[14] also points to an awareness of the strengthening of the appointments to the professorship of poetry at Oxford, consolidated by Lowth's *Praelectiones*.

The breadth of Lowth's appeal and the recognition of his Oriental work in the movement of feeling appear in Hannah More's lines about his *Isaiah* in her poem, "Sensibility." Hannah More, "the most powerful versificatrix in the English language,"[15] spoke for her readers when she noted that, in addition to Lowth's great eminence as a Classicist — "though Latian bards had gloried in his name" — he had added to his laurels by bringing to England the authentic note of Oriental prophecy:

> Illustrious Lowth! for him the muses wove
> The fairest garland from their greenest grove.
> Though Latian bards had gloried in his name,
> When in full brightness burnt the Latian flame;
> Yet fired with nobler hopes than transient lays,
> He scorned the meed of perishable praise,
> Spurned the cheap wreath by human science won,
> Borne on the wing sublime of Amos' son,
> He seized his mantle as the Prophet flew,
> And caught some portion of his spirit too.

The work of William F. Stead,[16] W. H. Bond,[17] Arthur Sherbo[18] and Sophia Blaydes[19] has brought to the attention of scholars the influence of Lowth's description of parallelism as discussed in the *Praelectiones* on Smart's *Jubilate Agno*. It is now widely accepted that a major distinguishing mark of that poem — its echoing, antiphonal structure — was the direct result of Lowth. These findings have given Lowth a firmly established mansion in the house of prosody. The parallelism which Lowth found central to Hebrew, primitive poetry was a more fitting verse pattern than the "conjunction disjunctive"[20] of the poetry of Pope for the pre-Romantic and Romantic poetry of the late eighteenth century which attempted to suggest the stasis of "the Sublime" in the phenomena of Nature. Writing of the *parabolic* style of Hebrew verse, Lowth had noted a "strict . . . analogy between the structure of the sentences and the versification."[21] Inseparable from English verse since the disappearance of Medieval Romance, had been a complex counterpoint of syntax and meter in which the management of the caesura played an important part. In the parallelism of Hebrew poetry, not only did object, as it were, answer object, noun noun, and adjective adjective across the sequence of succeeding lines, to suggest the motionless quality of eternity, but the machinery of complex syntactical subordination that included the caesura — a major resource in, for example, the verse of Pope or John Donne — was absent.

"Genius, judgement, and learning," had conspired to make Lowth's *Praelectiones* "truly admirable,"[22] Smart wrote in the "Literary Observations" of *The Universal Visiter* for January, 1756; and he then praised "its elegance, novelty, variety, spirit, and (I had almost said) divinity"[23] and called it "one of the best performances that has been published for a century."[24] Although Smart here praised the translation of Lowth's favorite ode from the fourteenth chapter of Isaiah on the fall of the Babylonian king, he returned to the poem, all of whose ninety-two lines he had printed in the previous *Universal Visiter,* in his article in February, "Further Remarks on Dr. Lowth's celebrated PRELECTIONS."[25] His statements are worth dwelling upon since not only his *Jubilate Agno* but his *A Song to David* was to be composed in the next few years. Noting Lowth's ode's "elevated and striking" nature, Smart chose one peculiar, technical feature among "some beauties, which, as they have a singularity in their excellence," would not, he felt, "in general be taken notice of, without such pointing out."[26] Lowth had "most judiciously fixed upon the ALCAIE, as a measure the best adapted to the sublimity of his subject," and he had made a "noble" use of it.

By omitting the caesura common to Latin as to English verse, especially to verse syntactically complex, Lowth had produced the equivalent in Latin of Oriental parallelism, giving an incantatory effect suitable for an ode prophesying triumph over a monstrous tyrant. "The pause, or breaking-place, usual in the *Alcaie,* being here omitted," Smart observed, "gives a grandeur and rapidity which are due to the magnificence of the expression."[27] Smart's closing image suggests a deep sympathy between the sensibilities of the poet and Lowth. "The stile is accurate to the most classical exactness," he wrote, "and yet so perspicuous in its purity, that it has all the easiness of a limpid stream, though as elaborate as the waterworks at *Versailles*."[28]

Lowth's Latin was judged by Pattison the best since Addison, but we have something here beyond modern Classical verses.

Smart's water images convey not only a combination of the brilliance of a million individual droplets but also the presence of a
profound as it were, infinite, organizing power behind the scenes.
No analogy could more sharply convey the sense of utter clarity of
detail and yet simultaneity of Smart's unique effect in *A Song to
David,* nor, incidentally, the combination of concreteness and the
sublime that Lowth himself saw as central to Oriental verse. It
seems likely that in composing *A Song to David,* which appeared in
1763, Smart recalled the grandeur and rapidity of Lowth's ode —
whose form has an overall similarity to that of *A Song* — and the
benefits of the caesura-less verse that Lowth had invented. It is
pleasant to read that, when Smart was released from his madhouse
confinement in 1763, Hawkesworth wrote that "he had lately
received a very genteel letter from Dr. Lowth, and is by no means
considered in any light that makes his company as a gentleman, a
scholar, and a genius less desirable."[29]

The work of Thomas Warton the Younger reminds us that the
major achievement of the Wykehamist Romantics, both antiquarians and poets, was the consolidation of the idea of the primitive past as the subject of verse. The role of historical criticism in
our own day should not blind us to the novelty of Thomas Warton's *History of English Poetry* whose first volume appeared in
1774. It is significant that, along with Chatterton's "Rowley"
poems, Warton praised Lowth's contribution to the recovery of
English primitivism in his *Life of Wykeham.* Lowth had "admir-
ably characterized" the "genius" of the reign of Richard II, its
"splendour and gallantry," Warton, the Camden Professor of History in the University of Oxford observed; Lowth's was "the hand
of a master."[30] A more subtle form of flattery is suggested in
Thomas Warton's own poem, *Verses on Sir Joshua Reynold's
Painted Window at New College, Oxford.* Many years earlier, in
1729, Robert Lowth, as a schoolboy at Winchester, had praised the
window of Wykeham's other "Seinte Marie College" chapel in his
poem *The Genealogy of Christ as it is represented on the East Window in Winchester Chapel.* It is interesting to consider that Thomas
Warton's "brawny Prophets, that in robes so rich, / At distance
due, possess the crisped niche," like the "Patriarch's that sublimely
reared / Diffuse a proud primeval length of beard,"[31] point to the
influence of a young Winchester schoolboy.

Joseph Warton in discussing Pope's "Messiah" in his *Essay on
the Genius and Writings of Pope,* had noted that "misery and

destruction" were depicted by Isaiah in the "distress and desola-
tion" of Babylon.[32] Like Smart, Warton turned to Lowth's translation of the fourteenth chapter of Isaiah: "Accordingly, a noble ode
on the destruction of Babylon, taken from the fourteenth chapter
of Isaiah, has been written by Dr. Lowth; whose Latin prelections
on the inimitable poesy of the Hebrews, abounding in remarks
entirely new, delivered in the purest and most expressive language,
are the richest augmentation literature has lately received; and from
which the following passage, gradually unfolding the singular
beauties of this prophecy, is here closely, though faintly translated,
and inserted as a pattern of just criticism."[33] And Warton inserts
his own translation of Lowth's *Ode prophetica* and also several
pages from Lecture XIII of Lowth's analysis of the ode, because
they contained a "pattern of just criticism."

The year 1797 with Joseph Warton's nine-volume edition of Pope
found this judgment of Lowth strengthened. Discussing Lowth's
"Prelections on the Poetry of the Hebrews," the aging Warton
notes, forty years after his *Essay on Pope*, "these Prelections,
abounding in remarks entirely new ... have been received and read
with almost universal approbation, both at home and abroad"[34] —
strong evidence of Lowth's European reputation and its growth in
the last half of the eighteenth century. Again, Warton's comments
about his fellow Wykehamist are a preamble to the superiority of
Lowth's "sublime" verse over Pope's. In the first place, Pope had
made use of "the old translation of Isaiah" when writing his
"Messiah," for he did "not have recourse to the more accurate and
more animated version of Bishop Lowth."[35] "I find and feel it
impossible to conclude these remarks on Pope's Messiah," Warton
continued, now as previously, "without mentioning another poem
taken also from Isaiah, the noble and magnificent ode on the
Destruction of Babylon, which Dr. Lowth has given us in the thirteenth of his Prelections on the Poetry of the Hebrews; and which,
the scene, the actors, the sentiments, and diction, all contribute to
place in the first rank of the sublime."[36]

In 1794, incapable of letting old wars lie forgotten, Richard
Hurd, in "a preliminary dissertation" to yet another edition of
Warburton's *Divine Legation*, returning to the Lowth-Warburton
battle of 1765, remarked of the late Robert Lowth: "his friends did
his character no service by affecting to bring his merits, whatever
they were, into competition with those of the bishop of Gloucester,"[37] Warburton. As for Lowth's "Latin Lectures on Hebrew

Poetry" and his "English Version of the Prophet Isaiah," Hurd
commented "the former is well and elegantly composed, but in a
vein of criticism not above the common"; the latter he found
"chiefly valuable, as it shows how little is to be expected from Dr.
Kennicott's work."[38] It was not inappropriate that Lowth's friend,
Joseph Warton should speak the last word in the battle. "It has
been constantly a matter of surprise," he observed tartly, to hear
an eminent prelate pronouncing lately, with a dogmatical air, that
these Prelections, 'are in a vein of criticism not above the common.' Notwithstanding which decision, it may safely be affirmed,
that they will long survive, after the commentaries [by Warburton]
on Horace's Art of Poetry, and on the Essay on Man, are lost and
forgotten."[39]

The interest of the irreligious John Wilkes in Bishop Lowth's
work seems, perhaps, unlikely; but R. C. Alston tells us that the
notes in the 1769 copy of Lowth's *Short Introduction* in Winchester
College Library are in Wilkes' hand.[40] Also Wilkes wrote, as we
have seen, the review of the 1763 edition of Lowth's *Praelectiones,*
by then a work of European reputation, which appeared in the
Gazette Littéraire de L'Europe on September 30, 1764.[41] Wilkes
complained that Lowth had not treated the pastoral poetry of the
Hebrews fully enough, but he admitted that "the most striking
picture of . . . the first ages [is] to be drawn from the Jews."[42] It is especially interesting that Wilkes should show in these phrases that he
recognized that Lowth's topic was "primitive" verse written by the
very first men. Lowth had shown that the first men had sung before
employing logic and abstract meaning, and he had "proved that
some of their oldest prophecies and parts of their history were poetry."[43] Metaphor drawn from the objects of Nature, Wilkes commented, was the strength of Hebrew poetry: "Sometimes they are
drawn from the great objects of nature, the sun, moon, and stars,"
and "The mountains of Lebanon and Carmel are frequently introduced by the sacred writers."[44] Wilkes, the composer of the sala-
cious *Essay on Woman,* was shocked at "the strength and boldness
of their [Oriental] metaphors," for "it must be confessed that they
had no true notions of delicacy, or even of decorum."[45] "The
variety of their allusions to child bearing, and other things of the
fair sex, very justly shock our manners, and give us strange ideas of
that age."[46]

The essential combination of lowly "objects of nature" and "the
Sublime" which is at the heart of Lowth's appreciation of Hebrew

poetry and of poetry in general is central for Wilkes. "It is an eternal fault of the modern poets to draw their comparisons from objects not known,"[47] he remarks, giving the example which Warton had cited a few years earlier in his *Essay on the Genius and Writings of Pope* (Pt. I, 1756). "Pope's swains enjoy as serene a sky, and complain of the scorching heat, as much as those of *Theocritus* and *Virgil*."[48] "The Jewish poetry is ... very happy in marking the variety and distinct character of all ... objects familiar to the Jewish nation,"[49] and yet "the variety of sublime sentiments in the Prophets is altogether astonishing."[50] Lowth had observed of Ezekiel, the prophet most frequently alluded to in the verse of English poets of the pre-Romantic and Romantic eras, that in sublimity he was not even excelled by Isaiah.[51] Wilkes faithfully conveyed to his Parisian editor the gist of Lowth's description of this, the most imaginative of the three major prophets. "He is wild, vehement, and strong, but ungraceful and turbid. He is so rapid that it is difficult to mark his progress ... there is neither beauty nor grace in him, but there is much fire and force; he seems a mind strongly agitated, and therefore cannot fail to agitate his readers."[52] The secular drift of Wilkes' review is a useful reminder of Lowth's non-religious bias. Drawing to a close, Wilkes offers Lowth's comparison of the prophet Ezekiel with a Greek dramatist. "All his perfection, and all his faults are in Aeschylus,"[53] the poet of the *Essay on Woman* observed. It is remarkable that this most turbulent English demagogue of the eighteenth century perceived brilliantly the sometimes obscure significance of Lowth, one which has only become apparent after two centuries.

II *The Significance of Lowth's Work*

Lowth is the major mid-eighteenth-century expert on perhaps the most important image in the Romantic movement, "primitivism." The Oriental and Medieval, or Gothic, aspects of "primitivism" are essentially two sides of the same coin — a new form of literary expression which succeeded the poetry of Reason of the early eighteenth century and which significantly paved the way for the early nineteenth-century flowering of the Romantic movement.

It is important to observe that Lowth's lectures on Hebrew poetry were lectures on the nature of poetry in general. Lowth is concerned to tell his readers about the nature of what he takes to be the earliest poetry in the world because he supposes that this poetry is the best poetry ever written and because he supposes that all poetry is composed in a context which is similar to that experienced by "original" man. From 1708 the professors of poetry at Oxford University had lectured on and even written poetry of this Oriental kind, but Lowth brought the activity to a new and unprecedented state of refinement. He systematized mid-century poetry, and concentrated men's attention onto characteristics of literature which without him might have been neglected.

The central fact in the poetry which he analyzed was that it was poetry of the *emotions*. He denigrated reason, which he saw, like Bishop Berkeley, as a source of untruth and of uncreative obscurity. Lowth undermined the role of sequential thought in poetry. The overall effect of poetry of reason built on a sequential model is a formal one; in it the sense of a middle and an end significantly follows that of a beginning. Lowth's claim that the verse pattern of the Hebrews, which he called "parallelism," was the truest and most poetic of forms reversed the assumptions of Pope's heroic couplet. Lowth focused attention on a new kind of poetic truth in which the effect was not of judgments that smoothly succeeded each other but of a psyche agitated by emotion that obsessively returned again and again to obscure vortices of understanding with which it could not deal. Instead, the reader's mind lurched forward, unwillingly and hesitatingly, from image to image, leaving obscurities unresolved and associating concepts irrationally up and down the progress of the poem like the water insect in Coleridge's image of the understanding: sometimes moving against the current, sometimes with it.[54]

In Lowth, elevated ideas are suggested by low ideas. In him we see clearly enunciated in poetry the revolution in thought which was engaging philosophy throughout the eighteenth century. In John Locke's *Essay Concerning Human Understanding*, two ideas become associated with each other through the agency of cause and effect — or by memory operating on a temporal model. We recall one idea because the idea related to it in our minds happened *at the same time* in the past (*Essay*, II, xxxiii). Lowth stated unequivocally at the end of his sixteenth lecture that a mind experiencing extreme emotion does not associate ideas by means of cause and effect. Rather, the images of the lowliest, most vulgar objects in nature give the most sublime effect. The mind, we conclude, is creative; it makes new associations continually and changes "reality" in the act of creating poetry. This forceful statement of the mind's asso-

ciative activity under creative duress provides a link between concepts of primitive creativity and a major concern of eighteenth-
century philosophy, "the association of ideas," which anticipates
the connection which the philosopher David Hartley (1705–57)
made in his *Observations on Man* (1749) between association and
prophecy (and dreams) that was significant in the development of
the verse of Wordsworth and Coleridge.

In the mid-eighteenth century, a prophet was deemed to be a
poet; and a poet a prophet. This understanding of the poet's
powers is enunciated most clearly in Lowth. The very nature of true
poetry he pronounced to be prophecy. Poetry was, in Lowth, a
triumph over the forms of Time (and Space). The mind, highly
charged with emotion, made patterns of futurity out of its experience. This phenomenon, we might suggest, is of significance for
an understanding of writers and of the human mind at large; and it
is possibly the single most important concept in the Romantic
movement.

Peripherally, we might observe another interesting characteristic
of the kind of poetry which Lowth isolated in description and
analysis. The poetry of Lowth's fellow Wykehamist, William Collins, struck an important new note. In, for example, the *Ode on the
Poetical Character* (1746), patterns of time disappear, because of
the ambiguous "originality" of the poet's activities, which include
identification with the creative activity of God and with the "most
sublime" of the prophets, Ezekiel. We feel that personal memory
dissolves and that the very being of the poet is at risk; that his iden-
tity disappears and that it is perhaps remade during the reading of
the poem. The reader, we might add, experiences something of the
same kind of threat. The poetry is one of process during which significant things happen to the reality of the reader as well as to that
of the poet. This rich insecurity, the central characteristic of mid-
eighteenth-century poetry, we might well trace to Lowth's
achievement.

The concept of poetry in Lowth is that of the first man ever to
exist in the act of creating his emotional response to a totally new
world. Each of us, we conclude, is essentially, an "original"; for
we are continually and most importantly re-experiencing the celebration of Nature which the first inhabitants of earth might be said
to have experienced. This image of the poet as the original man,
explicitly emphasized in Lowth, is, of course, at the very heart of
the cosmos of William Blake whose poetry, which is largely "Orien-

tal'' prophecy, appears to owe many of its characteristics to the kinds of perceptions we have seen in Lowth. Perhaps most importantly, the link between Lowth's theories and Blake's practice may be observed in the concept of the nature of *the word* in "primitive" "original" poetry.

Memory, as we have observed, is of little importance in Lowth's notion of poetry. The mind is continually creative, rejecting the old, as it subjectively makes new forms out of the cosmos whose celebration is its major activity. In a mind prophetically engaged, words cease to become signs which activate pictures in a computer memory bank — in our cognitive machinery. Rather, words, which are always significantly new, are products of the original mind (like the earliest man creating his language as he sought to express himself), and they appear to the reader as isolated moments of "becoming" and of total newness. Hence, the poetry which derived from Lowth's field of enquiry was an experience of "ongoingness" in which categories of generality were avoided and a continual particularization beckoned the reader to create himself anew. The optimism of power over the cosmos suggested by this kind of poetry, we must note, is at the very core of the Romantic mind.

The description and the popularization of an emotional mode which offers an experience of continual simultaneity in which a sense of a beginning, a middle and an end are powerfully absent; in which the mind makes unpredictable associations, heuristically forming its own cosmos, triumphing over Time and Space; in which the self of the poet (prophet) as well as that of his audience is renewed and recreated in an ongoing experience of pervasive originality; in which even the nature of words is changed from the prosaic to the creative — these are the achievement of Lowth's mid-eighteenth-century career. This sense of poetry he made available to Christopher Smart, to William Blake, to Edward Young, and to Thomas Gray. Young's *Night Thoughts,* perhaps, was the major immediate example of the genre which Lowth hâd analyzed, Blake's verse following several decades after. A poem like Thomas Gray's *The Bard* (begun in 1755) appears, in a Welsh context, to follow Lowth's lectures with impressive faithfulness — even down to the discovery among the Welsh of a parallel construction similar to the Hebrew.

It is important to observe that Lowth's lesser contribution to Medievalism or Gothicism in his *Life of Wykeham* offers a kind of Medieval artifact which approximates his description of Oriental verse. *Wykeham* is also emotional; it produces an ambiguous sense of where the Middle Ages "are"; it makes associations apparently without a rational, formal plan; the role of the author, Lowth himself, in regard to his great benefactor, is curiously obscure; while the sense of the objects of that Medieval world is surrealistically intriguing, and suggests the area of perception investigated in Coleridge's Medieval poem *Christabel* (1798), especially the relationship of objects suspended between the creative mind and the — dissolving — forms of memory. Thomas Warton the Younger recognized in his *History of English Poetry* Lowth's Gothic achievement. But we must add a word concerning the equally "primitive" nature of Lowth's grammar, his *Short Introduction,* which combined novelty with availability, and which made crystal clear for generations of simple people who became, in part, the reading public of the Romantic poets, the native, Anglo-Saxon roots of the English language.

The major application of Lowth's description of Oriental poetry was made by Christopher Smart in his *Jubilate Agno* (written 1759–63, first published 1939) and *A Song to David* (1763). We have noted above Smart's high opinion of Lowth and the probable effect of the prophetic ode from Isaiah, but it is necessary to dwell at length on Lowth's overall influence on Smart. A major emphasis in Lowth's analysis was that the most sublime poetry had been composed by the use of the most down-to-earth imagery of everyday objects, and Smart's characteristic charm is related to the imagery of everyday objects in his own mid-eighteenth-century world. "For I will consider my cat Jeoffry," Smart sang in *Jubilate Agno.* "For having consider'd God and himself he will consider his neighbour. / For if he meets another cat he will kiss her in kindness. / For when he takes his prey he plays with it to give it a chance. / For one mouse in seven escapes by his dallying." (*Jubilate Agno* [*Rejoice in the Lamb*], Fragment B1, 697, 715–18).

In Smart's *A Song to David* the imagery of everyday eighteenth-century life includes this list of products of England's colonies, especially those in the East:

> The wealthy crops of whit'ning rice,
> 'Mongst thyine woods and groves of
> spice,
>   For ADORATION grow;
> And, marshall'd in the fenced land,
> The peaches and pomegranates stand,

> Where wild carnations blow.
> (Stanza LX)

These crops were, of course, more familiar to eighteenth-century colonial travelers than to Ezekiel or Isaiah. This use of everyday imagery repeats in modern England the practices of the Hebrew bards and gives a strong sense of images poised between two eras. The effect belongs neither to one time nor one spatial location. This sublime ambiguity is equally pronounced in Lowth's lectures and in his Isaiah.

Most importantly, Smart appears to have followed Lowth's description of the several kinds of parallelism of Hebrew verse. Lowth's analysis of the "timeless" effects of parallel structures occurs in Lowth's Lecture XIX on "Prophetic Poetry." It is fascinating to observe that Smart specifically claimed for himself in *Jubilate Agno* the role of a prophet: "For it will be better for England and all the world in a season, as I prophecy this day. / For I prophecy that they will obey the motions of the spirit descended upon them as at this day" (*Jubilate Agno,* Fragment C, lines 58–9).

In prophetic poetry, Lowth had found that "in two lines (or members of the same period) things for the most part shall answer to things, and words to words, as if fitted to each other by a kind of rule or measure" (II, 34). The principle of "things answering to things" and with remarkable frequency, "words answering to words" is at the very heart of Smart's technique. In *A Song to David,* the pattern of one stanza repeats with few variations the displacement of things in the previous one:

LXV

> For ADORATION, beyond match,
> The scholar bulfinch aims to catch
>   The soft flute's iv'ry touch;
> And, careless on the hazle spray,
> The daring redbreast keeps at bay
>   The damsel's greedy clutch.

LXVI

> For ADORATION, in the skies,
> The Lord's philosopher espies
>   The Dog, the Ram, and Rose;
> The planet's ring, Orion's sword;

> Nor is his greatness less ador'd
> In the vile worm that glows.

We observe especially the ironic effect of the two final lines of these stanzas and the submerged similarity of the "damsel's greedy clutch" and "the vile worm," an association which recalls William Blake's *Sick Rose* (1793).

Lowth's analysis of Hebrew form began with an account of "sacred hymns ... alternately sung by opposite choirs" (II, 25). "From the Jewish, the custom of singing in alternate chorus was transmitted to the Christian Church," Lowth observed (II, 31). To this antiphonal, echoing pattern Lowth traces the development of the parallel construction of prophetic poetry. So faithful is Smart's imitation of the ancient Hebrew forms as observed by Lowth that he forms portions of *Jubilate Agno* on a patterning of "Let" verses which were the mirror image of a series of "For" stanzas which answered them, as it were, from the page facing. On the one side, the "Let" lines read,

45. Let Areli rejoice with the Criel,
        who is a dwarf that towereth above others.

Let Phuvah rejoice with Platycerotes, whose
        weapons of defence keep them innocent.

Let Shimron rejoice with the Kite, who is of
        more value than many sparrows.

Let Sered rejoice with the Wittal — a silly bird
        is wise unto his own preservation.

Let Elon rejoice with Attelabus, who is
        the Locust without wings.

50. Let Jahleel rejoice with the Woodcock
        who liveth upon suction and is pure from his diet.

On the other side of the page the "For" lines respond, one by one,

45. For I am a little fellow, which
        is intitled to the great mess by the benevolence of God my father.

For I this day made over my inheritance
        to my mother in consideration of her infirmities.

For I this day made over my inheritance
        to my mother in consideration of her age.

> For I this day made over my inheritance
>   to my mother in consideration of her poverty.

50. For I bless the thirteenth of August, in which
    I had the grace to obey the voice of Christ in my conscience.

(Fragment B1, "Let" and "For" lines 45–50)

As a recent editor has pointed out in his edition of Smart,[55] the combination of the "Let" and "For" lines, which appear harmless considered separately, associates Smart's mother and family with the scavenging kite, locust, and wittal, and Smart himself with the foolish, chattering woodcock and gullible heron (criel).

Smart's line is powerful because, like the Hebrew line suggested by Lowth, and like the line later of Walt Whitman (1819–92), it is a single incantatory thrust, without caesura, which combines poetic form *and* syntactical shape in one linguistic gesture. This line contrasts with the English classical line traditional since the late Middle Ages, for example, in Pope, which set in a sophisticated counterpoint the syntactical pattern against the metrical rhythm.

Among the three kinds of parallel structure that Lowth found in Hebrew verse, the first kind he noted was "synonymous parallelism, when the same sentiment is repeated in different, but equivalent terms" (II, 35). Many of the above examples illustrate this basic echoing device, which produced the startling, brilliant recurrence of imagery Lowth found so effective and characteristic of the Hebrew spirit. Another example from Smart (*Jubilate Agno,* Fragment A, 42–3) suggests how persistent Smart's use of synonymous parallelism was:

> Let Solomon praise with the Ant, and
>   give the glory to the Fountain of all Wisdom.
> Let Romamti-Ezer bless with the
>   Ferret — the Lord is a rewarder of them,
>   that diligently seek him.

In *A Song to David* the pattern of Stanza XII, with its parallel single lines,

> Serene — to sow the seeds of peace,
> Rememb'ring, when he watch'd the fleece,
>   How sweetly Kidron purl'd —
> To further knowledge, silence vice,
> And plant perpetual paradise

> When God had calm'd the world,

is closely followed in Stanza XIII, in order to dramatize powerful stanzaic opposites:

> Strong — in the Lord, who could defy
> Satan, and all his powers that lie
> In sempiternal night;
> And hell, and horror, and despair
> Were as the lion and the bear
> To his undaunted might.

Many of Smart's lines conform to the strict exact reiteration of verb for verb and phrase for phrase found in Lowth's first category, and Smart even has rare sub-categories like the "triplet parallelisms" (Lowth II, 42) of his description of "Jeoffry's" toilet,

> For fourthly he sharpens his paws by wood.
> For fifthly he washes himself.
> For sixthly he rolls upon wash.

> (Fragment B1, lines 708-10)

Other lines in Smart's verse correspond to Lowth's third category, the looser "synthetic" or "constructive parallelism" "in which the sentences answer to each other, not by the iteration of the same image or sentiment ... but merely by the form of the construction" (II, 48-9). Occasionally, as in stanzas XII and XIII above, we recall Lowth's remaining category, the antithetic parallelism "when a thing is illustrated by its contrary being opposed to it" (II, 45). The "Let" and "For" lines both numbered "15" in Fragment B1 also embody something of this antithetical principle. The "Let" line 15 reads "Let Ephah rejoice with Buprestis, the Lord endue us with temperance and humanity, till every cow have her mate!" Smart's "For" line reads, "For I am come home again, but there is nobody to kill the calf or to pay the musick."

Smart's use of Lowth's concept of "parallelism" exploited the poetic possibilities of the echoing pattern. The sequential habits of traditional syntax are disrupted, and the reader seems to enjoy an experience of constant simultaneity as if all the objects of nature danced in his mind in an infinite creation. The interesting added observation which we must make of Smart's Lowthian achievement in *Jubilate Agno* and in *A Song to David* is that nowhere as in these two poems may we find so pleasing and persuasive a demonstration of the authenticity of George Berkeley's philosophical suggestion that all phenomena exist subjectively without Time and Space in man's perceiving mind, and in the mind of the Creator in infinite simultaneity.[56] Smart's poetry seems like the naive but infinite celebration of Creation in all its forms by a primitive, newly created mind that wonders at the novel words which come pouring from the imagination, as if words too, as Lowth's work had suggested, were part of the poet-prophet's ever-original creative act.

In placing Lowth's significance in the more *general* history of ideas in the eighteenth century we must note the following. Thomas Burnet observed in his *Archaeologicae philosophicae*, the work from which Coleridge took the epigraph for *The Ancient Mariner,* that readers "may perhaps imagine that when Plato talks of his aethereal earth's being adorned with jewels, and filled and beautified with splendid bodies, he is only indulging in a sportive imagination."[57] "I have often observed (with Admiration)," Burnet continued, "that the prophets and sacred authors always make use of these figures, in their descriptions of paradise, as well as of the New Jerusalem, and adorned this subject with jewels ... as if all things in that state were irradiated with a new and special light."[58] Burnet is the origin of the distinctive eighteenth-century "Sublime," the infinite response to the objects of Nature solely through the senses; and the union of this theory with the writing of the Old Testament prophets is a notable feature of his work.

For Burnet, the jeweled vision of the prophets was proof of the eternal dimensions of the other world, the "Mundane Egg" from which our world had emerged some six thousand years before. Among his examples, Burnet includes Ezekiel. The vision of Ezekiel concerns the granting of the gift of poetry. At the heart of the first chapter, in which the prophet sees whirlwinds, turning wheels, amber, beryl, and "the likeness of four living creatures," was a throne of sapphire: "And above the firmament that was over their heads was the likeness of a throne, as the appearance of a sapphire stone" (Ezekiel i, 26). Lowth's father, William, had gone into detail about the "terrible" power of Ezekiel in his *Commentary* on the prophets. For Lowth, whose favorite prophet was Isaiah, Ezekiel was the most sublime. "In sublimity," he declared in his lecture on the characteristics of the prophets, "he is not even excelled by Isaiah." In effect, Ezekiel was the most sublime of all the original poets.

Ezekiel's vision was, first, of the gift of poetry; and, understandably, this gift was related to his ability to perceive nature in its eternal aspect, in effect, like God. It is clear that "the sapphire throne" may well be thought to represent the sky itself as seen by God. As *Guardian No. 86* had noted of the war horse in Job and in the metaphor of the grasshopper, Nature was seen in Oriental poetry apart from the dimensions of Time and Place. For Young, Collins, Gray, Smart, and Wordsworth, poets whose work is intimately related to the gradual development of Romanticism from the mid-eighteenth century to the height of the Romantic movement, Ezekiel and the sapphire throne have a special significance. It is impossible to establish that all these poets were familiar with Lowth; and it is equally difficult, as well as useless, to claim that these passages would not have occurred without Lowth's studies of Oriental poetry. It is, perhaps, sufficient to point to the likelihood that all these writers following the prophetic manner knew Lowth's work and, more importantly, to indicate the centrality of the passages cited in the growth of Romanticism.

Young, who composed *Night Thoughts* during the time that Lowth was giving his lectures on the sacred poetry of the Hebrews, explicitly compared his own vision in *Night Thoughts* with that of Ezekiel. At the climax of the poem in "Night IX," Young images the cosmos "like a precious gem, / Though little, on the footstool of His throne!" (IX, 1514–1515) around which "in heavenly liveries ... Azure, green, purple, pearl, or downy gold..." the angels stand. At the center of the night sky, the "Bard of Welwyn," the most celebrated poet-prophet of the century, sees,

> Orb above orb ascending without end!
> Circle in circle, without end, enclosed!
> Wheel within wheel; EZEKIEL! like to thine!
>
> (IX, 1097–99)

Two important poems written at this time take the nature of poetry as their special topic. Both are to a significant extent "Oriental," and both are concerned with the problems and opportunities for poetry in the mid-eighteenth century. One is Collins' *Ode on the Poetical Character* (1746); the other is Gray's *The Progress of Poesy,* written in 1754; and both take as their central, climactic image the sapphire throne of Ezekiel. Collins images the poetic gift as created simultaneously with the earth on the first day of Creation by the union of God and Fancy on a throne borrowed from the Ancient Hebrews: "Long by the loved Enthusiast wooed, / Himself in some diviner mood, / Retiring sat with her alone, / And placed her on his sapphire throne" (29-32). In Gray, the Pindaric Ode is, as it were, subsumed as his poem "progresses" by an older, more timeless tradition than that of Pindar. The blindness of the greatest English poet, Milton, is explained in the poem by his approaching that "new and special light" of the Old Testament prophets. Milton, says Gray, "rode sublime,"

> Upon the seraph wings of ecstasy,
> The secrets of the Abyss to spy.
> He passed the flaming bounds of Place and Time,
> The living throne, the sapphire blaze.
>
> (*Progress of Poesy*, 96–99)

The poem closes, prophetically, with a vision of glory imaged in the most ancient, timeless terms. The great English poet of the future might not show "the pride nor ample pinion" of Pindar, but "oft before his infant eyes would run / Such forms as glitter in the Muse's ray / With orient hues, unborrowed of the sun" (118-20).

It is not surprising to note these images in Smart, whose relationship with Lowth is, perhaps, more clearly understood at this time. Gems play an important part in this poet, "The jasper of the master's stamp, / The topaz blazing like a lamp..." (*Song to David,* 154-56); but we should note that Smart too identifies his poetry with that of Ezekiel. "Gamma supports the glorious arch / On which angelic legions march," he declares, "and is with sapphires paved" (*Song to David,* 187–89).

In Wordsworth's *The Excursion,* there is a significant moment at which "the Solitary," cynical since his experiences in the French Revolution, tells of his part in the search for a poor old man lost in the storm. As this simple primitive was discovered and carried back to his home by the mountain people, the Solitary saw a renewing vision:

> Fabric it seemed of diamond and of gold,
> With alabaster domes, and silver spires,
> And blazing terrace upon terrace, high
> Uplifted ...
>
> (II, 839–42)

"Oh, 'twas an unimaginable sight!" he declares, "Clouds, mists, streams, watery rocks and emerald turf,''

> Clouds of all tincture, rocks and sapphire sky,
> Confused, commingled, mutually inflamed,
> Molten together, . . .
>
> Right in the midst, where interspace appeared
> Of open court, an object like a throne
> Under a shining canopy of state
> Stood fixed . . .

(II, 854–56; 861–64)

At this moment Wordsworth points to the similarity of this vision to that of ''Hebrew Prophets'' and to their images of ''implements of ordinary use, but vast in size,'' and he does so with a strong suggestion of Lowth's central theme of the parabolic nature of Hebrew poetry, and a distinct suggestion also of what we have noted as ''inappropriate response.''

Lowth was the product of a profound cultural shift from the certainty that the perspectives of Greece and Rome stretch back to a moment in historical time, to an awareness of the mythologizing processes of original man that are ever-present in all men. His work is, incidentally, one outcome of the battle between the Ancients and Moderns of the earlier years of the eighteenth century; for he demonstrated that Modern man, in constantly repeating ''original'' experience of ''the first ages,'' achieved greater things than the Ancients of a comparatively recent, limited, Classical era.

Of immediate significance in the history of ideas is the evidence that a study of Lowth suggests that the Oriental movement was a major branch, or tributary, of the mid-eighteenth-century poetry of feeling or sentiment. ''The language of poetry I have more than once described as the effect of mental emotion,'' he declared in Lecture XVII. Extensive physiological disturbance occurred when poetry was created by man, of which it was so much a natural part. ''For its origin,'' he says in the same lecture, the art of poetry was indebted to the effects wrought ''upon the imagination, the senses, the voice, and the respiration by the agitation of passion.''

The absence of memory from the poetic process is the most radical claim that Lowth makes about the nature of the first poetry and, incidentally, about all lyric and prophetic verse. Imitation is still, for him, the function of literature; but it is an imitation which negates that neo-Classical principle; for it is the imitation of the mind itself in the process of knowing. As he wrote in Lecture XVII, "When a passion is expressed ... the mind is immediately conscious of itself and its own emotions; it feels and suffers in itself a sensation either the same or similar to that which is described." In Lowth's view, true poetry was an extension of Nature in which the reader experienced a disturbing dissolving of the self as objective reality and also a fusion with the process of the poet's mind — a characteristic of the poetry of Lowth's fellow Wykehamists, Collins and Young, as well as of Smart and Blake, also "Oriental" poets. Since this verse, the pattern to some degree of all Romantic poetry, involved a response to a real and sometimes surreal awareness of Nature, its author created, as God had, something totally new and unprecedented. The poet, along with Adam and Eve, dwelt in the eternal dimensions of paradise; and he observed, like a *Deus Creator* himself, the phenomena of Time and Place from the realm of the Eternal; he saw, like the poet of Job, all things as if "in the eye of the Creator."[59]

The wider significance of this memory-less art is illuminated by the contrast of Lowth's view with Pope's. Pope's *Pastorals,* for example, present the concept of man as a divided being, as both an experiencer of an external Nature and at the same moment a comparer or contraster of the present with previous experience, of his own time and of the men of the ages of Theocritus, Virgil, and Spenser — the poets that Pope echoes. The division of the *Pastorals* into seasons also holds each one in a double vision of itself and of the context of time. Indeed, the major intent of all Classical and neo-Classical art is to observe things within a context; and the divided or fallen man is inseparable from this vision.

Lowth's perception of the poetry of earliest man agrees with Johann von Schiller's, whose essay *On Naive and Sentimental Poetry* (1795)[60] suggests two cultural realities. In "naive" art, original man was not distanced from Nature, nor did he project feeling, as it were, *onto* natural objects — a process which involves separation and distancing. Lesser poets of the time, whom Schiller terms "sentimental," objectified Nature as decisively as had Pope; but their mirror was clouded with feeling. Lowth's view of early Hebrew verse is similar to Schiller's concept of "naive" poetry; and he is, in effect, the major English voice in a European movement which influenced German Romantic philosophy more strongly than that of any other country, in the area where anthropology mingles with esthetic theory. Herder is, of course, the best known example of Lowth's influence in Germany; Douglas Bush has noted the contribution of Lowth's "discourses on the sacred poetry of the Hebrews ... to Herder's immensely fruitful conception of myth, poetry, and religious symbolism."[61] It is important to note that Herder's famed dictum, "Man is an animal that sings," may be found in all its significance throughout Lowth's observations about Oriental verse.

For Lowth, as for Herder, the centrally human activity which distinguished man from other animals was linguistic and mental. This difference in mankind had manifested itself as poetry from the earliest moment of existence as a visceral necessity and as one inseparable from the functions of breathing and feeling. Man's ability to cope with reality and to form a creative link with what appears to be external Nature is at the heart of this view of poetry as a form of knowledge that relates man's finite experience to a timeless cosmos through man's interpretative myths. In broad terms, a grasp of Lowth is a clue to the extensive understanding of Blake who posed an identical contrast between the sterile finite world and the creative infinite. In our own day, Wallace Stevens, especially in *Sunday Morning,* once more posits the powerful claim that man is eternal; man is one with and is not separated from the sky, "this dividing and indifferent blue."

There is a deeply held prejudice that literature is an art which "refers" to topics that move readers in "real" life; and that one derivative of such art is poetry. This idea, true of some poetry, carries with it a concept of words as signs for objects in Nature that are external to the work. The belief assumes that each word refers *back* in time to the poet's and to the reader's former experience. Although Pope's verse clearly depended on this mechanism, the mid-eighteenth-century thinkers felt their way toward a quite distinct, not to say revolutionary, notion of words, both in their philosophy and in their poetry. In the concept of "the first ages," there was some awareness, never far from Blake, for example, or Wordsworth, that words had existed before their meanings had been defined — that there was, in effect, central to language, a preintellectual non-referential element that was to be observed in the speech of contemporary "originals" such as children, idiots, and the uneducated poor. Herder's axiom of the gestation of man's language simultaneously with himself points to such a belief.

Lowth's concept of the parabolic character of Oriental poetry — his view of the mind's soaring reaction away from the actual meaning of a "lowly" word when applied to God, his sense that poetry always referred to the future since the greatest poetry was prophecy, and his elevation of the passionate ecstatic inspiration of the agitated present moment — suggests a very close affiliation with this new linguistic sense. If poetry was heuristic, a new creation, then words, the building-blocks of verse, were objects in Nature just like trees, horses, and fish; and they had their own properties. Their referential activity was no longer the important function. This sense of words is an important part of Berkeley's theory of words, which, like Lowth's parallelism, has links with eighteenth-century poetry. In the *Principles of Human Knowledge,* which itself offers a modern parallel to the mental and emotional activity of the first men which Lowth describes, Berkeley had written, "the communicating of ideas marked by words is not the chief and only end of language" (*Introduction,* 20).

Again, Berkeley observes: "the passions of fear, love, hatred, admiration... and the like arise, immediately ... upon the perception of certain words, without ideas coming between." Berkeley's "absolute denial" of "*general abstract ideas*" (*Introduction,* 19), which parallels Lowth's description of their rejection by primitive poets, suggests another aspect of the concreteness of words and also the closeness between Lowth's view of primitivism and the greatest age of philosophy England has seen. Although we cannot absolutely apportion the influence between Lowth and Berkeley, it is clear that Smart's *Jubilate Agno* and *A Song to David,* which reveal the influence of Lowth's Oriental concepts, which use words as objects with an instantaneous, sublime effect, and which contain a parallel denial of abstractions (as, for example, in Smart's celebrated "quick peculiar quince" where objects and derivative values are of equal verbal value) might have come from either Lowth or Berkeley or from both sources.

Lowth's various works provide examples of the era's widespread exploitation of the images of the past — Oriental, Medieval, linguistic, and poetic — which had been made possible largely by the growth of the influence of science in the previous hundred years. There is a distinction to be made between the imaging of the past by means of an elaborate myth — such as the derivation of poetry by way of Apollo, Linus, Musaeus, and Orpheus found in Julius Caesar Scaliger's *Poetics* and somewhat modified, in Pope — and of a past built on the everyday "real" materials of people long dead, on monkish deeds, ancient manuscripts, archaeological finds, and musty chronicles. The materialist view of the past is as misleading as the mythic one, for the people at the time of historical incidents did not give the same central significance to their material world which their later discoverers and interpreters do. Indeed, all histories are equally selective.

The point, however, needs to be made that Lowth's work depended on an enormous unearthing in his century of the materials of history. Hearne is the very type of antiquarian fostered by the Royal Society without whose activities it is to be doubted that the age of Lowth would have arrived. The past is an idea present in the minds of contemporary men which might be used in various ways. It is significant that Lowth, like Giambattista Vico,[62] was able to employ his era's new-found awarenesses to enhance the contemporary view of man. Lowth's picture of history is not a sequence of inherited progress from stage to stage, but an account of perfectible, godlike man's rising, in his own terms only, to timeless achievements.

Without Chardin, Harmer, Hickes, Kennicott, Rymer, Wilkins, Woide, and other recent *virtuosi,* Lowth could not have constructed the "first ages," that ubiquitous image that appears in all his works. Probably his greatest significance to us in our understanding of his age is related to this dependence on modern scholarship, a dependence that Swift satirized so extensively and effectively. The presence of these authorities in Lowth's work reminds us that the myth of the first ages was as transient as any vision of golden gods and goddesses on Mt. Olympus. The world, after all, was *not* a mere six thousand years old; Job was not the oldest poem ever written — and, if it were, that fact would signify little in a world which was to become in the nineteenth and twentieth centuries two hundred billion years old.

What is significant is that Lowth combined the feeling and emotion pre-eminent in his own day with the concrete images of the primitive worlds he investigated and that he made out of them something of great value in the genesis of Romanticism. He showed in his fashionable talk of "the Sublime" that man reaches through his emotions and imagination to eternal forms; and to do so he uses the lowliest of materials, the immediate and particular things of the everyday world. Indeed, Lowth demonstrated that man could inhabit the whole cosmos by the unaided use of his senses on the material objects of Nature around him — as had the earliest Hebrews. Lowth's was an extraordinary activity even for an eighteenth-century bishop, for only in a broad sense could his effort be called "religious." Poetry promised to free man from his fallen status in Creation, and it hinted at the dissolving of heaven and hell which Blake was to proclaim. Ironically, it was on a basis of antiquarian history that Lowth anticipated the central tenet of the Romantic movement that is defined in Coleridge's definition of the primary imagination as "the living power and prime agent of all human perception ... a repetition in the finite mind of the eternal act of creation in the infinite I AM."[63]

Notes and References

Preface

1. S. T. Coleridge, *Biographia Literaria,* ed. J. Shawcross (Oxford, Clarendon Press, 1907), I, 202. References to this work below will be to *Biographia Literaria.*

2. Robert Lowth, *De sacra pöesi Hebraeorum praelectiones academicae* (Oxford, 1753). *Lectures on the Sacred Poetry of the Hebrews,* trans. G. Gregory (London, 1787). References hereafter to this work will be to *Lectures.*

3. Arnaldo Momigliano, "On the Pioneer Trail," *The New York Review,* XXIII, 18 (Nov. 11, 1976), 36.

4. Isaiah Berlin, *Vico and Herder: Two Studies in the History of Ideas* (London, Hogarth Press, 1976).

5. *The Life of William of Wykeham, Bishop of Winchester* (London, 1758). This work will be indicated below as *Wykeham.*

6. *A Short Introduction to English Grammar* (London, 1762). Given below as *A Short Introduction.*

7. *Isaiah, A New Translation* (London, 1778).

Chapter One

1. William Lowth, *A Commentary upon the Larger and Lesser Prophets* (London, 1714–25). This work first appeared in fragments as smaller commentaries.

2. William Lowth, *A Commentary upon the Larger and Lesser Prophets,* 3rd ed. (London, 1730), p. 7. Later references are to *Commentary.* William Lowth died in 1732; this is the last edition of his *Commentary* during his life.

3. John Harris, *Navigantium atque itinerantium bibliotheca: or a Compleat Collection of Voyages and Travels, consisting of above four hundred of the most authentick writers.* 2 vols. (London, T. Bennet, 1705). This work was revised and enlarged 1744–8, and re-issued 1764.

4. *Lectures,* II, 89.

5. *Commentary,* p. 254.

6. *Ibid.,* p. 254. See Marcus Fabius Quintilianus, *Institutio oratorio,* VI, ii, 24, *"quae 'deinosis' vocatur, rebus indignis, asperis, invidiosis addens vim oratio."* "This is known as *deinosis,* that is to say, language

giving additional force to things unjust, cruel or hateful . . . ''

7. The date of Longinus', *Peri hypsous, On the Sublime,* is uncertain. For a recent translation in which substantial doubt is cast on Longinus' authorship see D. A. Russell, *'Longinus' On the Sublime* (Oxford, Clarendon Press, 1964).

8. *Commentary,* p. 134.

9. Anthony, Earl of Shaftesbury, *Characteristics of Men, Manners, Opinions, Times,* 2nd ed. corr. (London, 1714), II, 389–90.

10. Edmund Burke, *Philosophical Enquiry into the Origin of our Ideas of the Sublime and Beautiful* (London, R. & J. Dodsley, 1757), Part I, Section xv.

11. Flavius Josephus, *Flavii Josephi opera,* ed. J. Hudson, 2 vols. (Oxford University Press, 1720). William Lowth contributed significantly to Hudson's definitive edition.

12. A. K. Cook, *About Winchester College* (London, Macmillan, 1917). Hereafter given as Cook.

13. *Ibid.,* pp. 16–17.

14. *Ibid.,* pp. 17–18.

15. See W. Thomas, *Le Poète Edward Young (1685–1765), Étude Sur Sa Vie et Ses Oeuvres* (Paris, 1901), p. 21.

16. Joseph Spence, *Observations, Anecdotes, and Characters of Books and Men* (London, W. H. Carpenter, 1820).

17. Samuel Johnson, Preface, *The Preceptor,* I, (Section vi), (1748). See Allen T. Hazen ed., *Samuel Johnson's Prefaces and Dedications* (Port Washington, N.Y., Kennikat Press, 1937) p. 184. See also G. B. Hill ed., *Boswell's Life of Johnson,* rev. Powell, 2nd ed., (Oxford, Clarendon Press, 1964) V, 317, n 1. Hereafter referred to as *Boswell.*

18. Joseph Spence, *Letters from the Grand Tour,* ed. Slava Klima (Montreal & London, McGill-Queen's University Press, 1975), p. 237.

19. Joseph Addison, *The Spectator, 357* (1712). See also *Lectures,* I, 284.

20. W. E. H. Lecky, *A History of England in the Eighteenth Century* "New Edition" (London, Longmans, 1897), I, 105.

21. *Wykeham,* p. vi.

22. Henry Nettleship ed., *Essays by the Late Mark Pattison* (Oxford, 1889), II, 136. This work hereafter referred to as Pattison.

23. Peter Hall, *Sermons and Other Remains of Robert Lowth* (London, J.G. & F. Rivington, 1834), p. 38. Hereafter cited as Peter Hall.

24. Edward Gibbon, *The Memoirs of the Life of Edward Gibbon,* ed. Birkbeck Hill (London, 1900), p. 55. Hereafter referred to as *Memoirs.*

25. Apparently Lowth preached on freedom of religion and on the abolition of slavery. See Peter Hall, p. 35.

26. Joseph Spence, *Observations, Anecdotes and Characters of Books and Men,* ed. James M. Osborn (Oxford, Clarendon Press, 1966), I, 472; II, 603.

27. *Isaiah, A New Translation,* 3rd ed. (London, 1795), II, 91. Hereafter referred to as *Isaiah.*

28. Pattison, II, 135.

29. *Ibid.,* "The 'classic elegance of Lowth' became a standard phrase and continued to be so till into the present century."

30. *Boswell,* II, 36–37.

31. Pattison, II, 137.

32. See below pp. 166.

33. The overwhelming importance of minute "particulars" in the esthetics of the mid-eighteenth century *and* the influence of Lowth's friend Joseph Spence in this regard on Joseph Warton, only somewhat less close to Lowth, is explored by William Darnall MacClintock, *Joseph Warton's Essay on Pope* (Chapel Hill, 1933, repr. New York, 1971), p. 10. Lowth's dependence on "particulars" both in his Orientalism and in his Gothic writing suggests a fundamental "Wykehamist" esthetic in which particulars played a central part.

34. Wykeham, p. iv.

35. *Ibid.,* pp. v–vi.

36. Johann David Michaelis, "Praefatio Editoris," *De sacra pöesi Hebraeorum, Thesaurus antiquitatum sacrarum* XXXI (Venice, 1766), cxxxviii*ff.*

37. Paul Henry Lang, *George Frideric Handel* (New York, W. W. Norton, 1966), p. 360.

38. *Isaiah,* II, 47.

39. *Ibid.,* 48.

40. *Ibid.*

41. Doreen Ingrams, *A Time in Arabia* (London, J. Murray, 1970), p. 32.

42. *Gentleman's Magazine,* LVII, Pt. 2 (1787), 1028.

43. Lecky, III, 272.

44. *Gentleman's Magazine,* LVII, Pt. 2 (1787), 1028.

Chapter Two

1. Thomas Hearne, *Remarks and Collections of Thomas Hearne,* ed. C. E. Doble (Oxford, 1886), II, 120.

2. *Ibid.*

3. *Ibid.,* p. 141.

4. Frederick Morgan Padelford, *Select Translations from Scaliger's Poetics* (New York, Holt, 1905), p. 15.

5. "There is mention of *Orpheus, Linus,* and *Musaeus,* venerable names in antiquity...." See Alexander Pope, "An Essay on Homer," *The Iliad of Homer,* Books I–IX, ed. Maynard Mack (London and New Haven, Methuen, 1967), pp. 65–66.

6. Gerardi Joannis Vossii, *De artis poeticae, natura ac constitutione*

(Amsterdam, 1647). Cf. *"De origine pöematum magna quaestio est ...
neque alio nos juvat, quam quod idem dicat, ante bellum Trojanum
suisse,"* Vossius, p. 77.

7. Joseph Trapp, *Lectures on Poetry, Read in the Schools of Natural
Philosophy at Oxford* (London, C. Hitch & C. Davis, 1742), pp. 4–5.
Given below as Trapp.

8. *Ibid.,* p. 28.

9. *Ibid.* Cf. Vossius, p. 78. "Puto enim, triumviros istos Pöesios,
Orphea, Musaeum, Linum, non fuisse: sed esse nomina ab antiqua
Phoenicum lingua, qua usi Cadmus, aliquamdiu posteri."

10. Trapp, p. 28.

11. *Ibid.,* p. 5.

12. *Ibid.*

13. Cf. Bush on Herder; Douglas Bush, *Mythology and the Romantic
Tradition in English Poetry* (Cambridge, Mass., Harvard University
Press, 1937), p. 47.

14. Vossius, p. 81.

15. Trapp, p. 28.

16. *Ibid.,* cf. "Of Lyric Poetry," p. 203: "That this is the most ancient
kind of poem, is pretty evident. *Jubal,* in sacred Writ, is said to be the first
inventor of musical instruments; and little doubt is to be made, but vocal
music was added to them."

17. *Ibid.,* p. 203.

18. *Ibid.,* p. 174.

19. *Ibid.,* p. 204.

20. *Ibid.*

21. S. T. Coleridge, *Biographia Literaria,* I, 11, "...a point was looked
for at the end of each second line ... a *conjunction disjunctive* of epi-
grams ... not poetic thoughts ... thoughts *translated* into the language of
poetry."

22. Trapp, p. 203.

23. "At Oxford, as we all know, much will be forgiven to literary merit;
and of that he had exhibited sufficient evidence by his excellent ode on the
death of the great Orientalist, Dr. Pocock[e] ... this ode, which closed the
second volume of the *Musae Anglicanae* ... is by far the best lyric composition in that collection; nor do I know where to find it equalled among
the modern writers. It expresses with great felicity images not classical in
classical diction; its digressions and returns have been deservedly recommended by Trapp as models for imitation."

Samuel Johnson, "Edmund Smith," *Lives of the English Poets,* ed.
Birkbeck Hill (Oxford, Clarendon Press, 1905), II, 12. See also "... he
repeated some of them, and said they were Smith's best verses," *Boswell,*
III, 269.

24. Trapp, 208. Smith's Latin reads: *"Quin nunc requiris tecta viren-
tia / Nini ferocis, nunc Babel arduum, / Immane opus! crescentibusque /*

Vertice sideribus propinquum! / Nequicquam; amici disparibus sonis / Eludit aures nescius artifex, / Linguasque miratur recentes, / In patriis peregrinus oris. / Vestitur hinc tot sermo coloribus, Quot Tu, Pococki, dissimilis Tui / Orator effers..." "The Confusion of Tongues" of the Tower of Babel was a central concept in the movement towards the "primitive" and "original." See discussion of Butler's *Grammar* (1633) and Wallis' preface to Greenwood's *Grammar* (1711) in Chapter VI, below.

25. *Ibid.,* p. 208.

26. *Ibid.*, pp. 203–4.

27. *Ibid.,* p. 207.

28. "If at his title Trapp had dropped his quill, / Trapp might have passed for a great genius still; / But Trapp, alas! (excuse him if you can) / Is now a scribbler, who was once a man." Edward Young, *The Universal Passion,* Satire I, 81-84.

29. Jonathan Swift, *The Journal to Stella, Satires and Personal Writings by Jonathan Swift,* ed. William A. Eddy (London, Oxford University Press, 1932), p. 335.

30. *Ibid.,* p. 353. Swift became friendlier to Trapp later. Cf. "I hope they sent you my Scrutore. I gave the key of it at Oxford to Mr. Trapp..." and "You will recommend him [*i.e.,* Mr. Pilkington "my chaplain"] to Jo. (Dr. I mean) Trapp." *The Correspondence of Jonathan Swift,* ed. Harold Williams (Oxford, Clarendon Press, 1963), II, 32, and IV, 62.

31. Ambrose Philips' "Modern" *Pastorals* employed images of contemporary rural life. Pope's *Pastorals* followed Classical models of Virgil and Theocritus. Both appeared in Tonson's *Poetical Miscellany, the Sixth Part* (1709) with several translations, Biblical and Classical, by newly appointed Professor of Poetry Joseph Trapp.

32. Alexander Pope, *The Correspondence of Alexander Pope,* ed. George Sherburn (Oxford, Clarendon Press, 1956), I, 105. Cromwell to Pope, Nov. 20, 1710.

33. *Ibid.,* p. 106. Pope to Cromwell on Nov. 25, 1710.

34. Samuel Johnson, "The Preface to the Preceptor, containing a General Plan of Education," *The Works of Samuel Johnson* (Oxford, W. Baynes & Son, 1825), V, 240.

35. See Chapter VI for an account of Greenwood. "Dr. Wallis's Preface, with Additions," Greenwood's first page announces. Wallis died several years before the work appeared.

36. "Phrase that time has flung away, / Uncouth words in disarray, / Tricked in antique ruff and bonnet, / Ode, and elegy, and sonnet," from Samuel Johnson's "Lines written in Ridicule of certain Poems published in 1777."

37. Warton used the Medieval octosyllabic couplet. His role as a metrical innovator who passed on to later poets, Scott, Morris, Byron, the meters as well as myths of Northern Europe may have been significant.

38. *Isaiah,* II, 376.

39. The opening lines of Warton's *The Universal Love of Pleasure.* See also, Sir William Temple, "Of Poetry," *Critical Essays of the Seventeenth Century,* ed. J. E. Spingarn (London, Oxford University Press, 1908–1909), re-issued Bloomington, University of Indiana Press, 1957, III, 107.

40. Smart printed the almost one hundred lines of Lowth's *"Ode Prophetica; In Occasum Regis Regnique Babylonici"* in his *The Universal Visiter and Monthly Memorialist,* January, 1756.

41. *Catalogue of the Library of the Late Rev. Robert Lowth including the LIBRARY of his Father the Celebrated Bishop of London, Author of the Hebrew Praelections, Translation of Isaiah, etc., which will be sold by Auction by Mr. Evans, at his House No. 93, Pall-Mall on Wednesday, January 15 and five following days* (London, 1823).

42. Our investigation, including correspondence with the present head of the Lowth family, suggests that "I. H. Lowth" is an error. By his wife, Mary, whom he married in 1752, Lowth had eight children, Thomas Henry, Robert, William; Mary, Frances, Martha, Margaret, and Charlotte. Like his father, Thomas Henry was a Wykehamist who duly became a Fellow of New College. He won the undergraduate Latin poetry prize in 1773, the graduate English Essay prize in 1776. How likely that Spence should give the literary son of his famed friend a copy of Thomson's *Seasons* that he had had from the poet's own hand! "T. H. Lowth" died in 1778, as did all but two of Lowth's children, before the Bishop's own death.

43. William Wordsworth, *The Prelude,* ed. Ernest de Selincourt, 2nd ed. rev. Helen Darbishire (Oxford, Clarendon Press, 1959), p. 522.

44. Alan Dugald McKillop, *The Background of Thomson's Seasons* (Minneapolis and London, University of Minnesota Press, 1942), p. 151.

45. J. Warton *et al.,* eds., *The Works of Alexander Pope* (London, B. Law etc., 1797), I, xxxvi.

46. *Ibid.*

47. Joseph Spence, *An Essay on Mr. Pope's Odyssey, in Five Dialogues,* 2nd ed. (London, 1737), p. 2. Hereafter cited as Spence.

48. *Ibid.,* pp. 2–3.

49. *Ibid.,* p. 2.

50. *Ibid.,* p. 3.

51. *Ibid.,* pp. 212–13. For a study of the concept of prophetic poetry in the eighteenth century, see Murray Roston, *Prophet and Poet, the Bible and the Growth of Romanticism* (Evanston, Northwestern University Press, 1965). Given hereafter as Roston.

52. Spence, pp. 214–15.

53. Anne Lefèvre Dacier, *L'Iliade* (Paris, Rigaud, 1711); *L'Odyssée* (Paris, Rigaud, 1716). *L'Iliade* was translated into English in 1712 by Ozell, Oldisworth, and Broome. See *Madame Dacier's Remarks upon Mr.*

Pope's ... Homer ... made English by Mr. Parnell (London, E. Curll, 1724).

54. Sir John L. Myres, *Homer and his Critics,* ed. Dorothea Gray (London, Routledge & Kegan Paul, 1958), p. 57. Giambattista Vico (1668–1744), whose views on the nature of the idea of the past are pertinent to Lowth, has recently undergone a revival of interest. See *Giambattista Vico,* ed. Tagliacozzo and White (Baltimore, Johns Hopkins Press, 1969).

55. See John, Lord Sheffield ed., "Notes on ... Editions of the Greek and Roman Classics," *The Miscellaneous Works of Edward Gibbon* (London, J. Murray, 1814), V, 582.

56. Spence, p. 215 f. Anthony Blackwall (1674–1730) was author of *An Introduction to the Classics* (London, John Martlock, 1718) as well as of his celebrated literary appreciation of the Scriptures, *The Sacred Classics Defended and Illustrated* (London, C. Rivington & W. Cantrell, 1725, 1731).

57. Spence, p. 285.

58. *Ibid.,* pp. 285–86.

59. *Ibid.,* p. 286.

60. *Ibid.*

61. *Ibid.* See Section I, "The Moralists," *Characteristics.*

62. William Darnall MacClintock, *Joseph Warton's Essay on Pope, a History of the Five Editions* (Chapel Hill, 1933), p. 10.

63. MacClintock's quotation is from Spence, pp. 279–80.

64. *Lectures,* I, 114.

65. Spence, p. 48.

66. *Ibid.,* p. 50.

67. "John Lizard," *Guardian No. 86, The Guardian,* ed. Alexander Chalmers (London, F.C. & J. Rivington, etc., 1822), II, 24. Given below as *The Guardian.*

68. John Wallis, "Dr. Wallis's Preface, with Additions," James Greenwood, *An Essay towards a Practical English Grammar,* 4th ed. (London, J. Nourse, 1740), p. 2. I have used the fourth edition of Greenwood since it appears to have been the one in Lowth's Library.

69. Joseph Addison, *The Spectator,* ed. Donald F. Bond (Oxford, Clarendon Press, 1965), III, 514. Later references will be to *Spectator.*

70. *Ibid.*

71. *Lectures,* I, 112.

72. Hugh Blair, *Lectures on Rhetoric and Belles Lettres* (London and Edinburgh, W. Strahan, T. Cadell, etc., 1783), I, 114–15.

Chapter Three

1. Robert Arnold Aubin, *Topographical Poetry in XVIII-Century England* (New York, The Modern Language Association of America,

1936), p. 86. *Katherine Hill* appeared in *The London Magazine,* II (1733), 35–36. See Aubin, p. 298. (Modern spelling: *C*atherine.)

2. William Cowper, *Letters of William Cowper,* ed. J. G. Frazer (London, Macmillan, 1912), I, 182.

3. *Commentary,* p. 134.

4. Spence, pp. 214–15.

5. *Lectures,* I, 282.

6. Joseph Addison, *Spectator,* II, 219.

7. *Ibid.,* 220.

8. *Ibid.,* 220–21.

9. *Ibid.,* 221.

10. *Ibid.*

11. *Ibid.,* 223.

12. Joseph Addison, *Spectator,* III, 338.

13. *Ibid.*

14. *Ibid.,* 338–39.

15. *Ibid.,* 338.

16. *Lectures,* I, 284.

Chapter Four

1. The *Praelectiones* embodied a Latin text, Hebrew, Greek and Latin quotations in the text and in the numerous footnotes. The challenge in book design was great, and the work is a highwater mark in eighteenth-century printing. The Clarendon Press had been founded recently from the profits of Edward Hyde, Earl of Clarendon's *The History of the Rebellion and Civil Wars in England* (Oxford University Press, 1702–1704). The press started a tradition of masterly printing of which Lowth's *Praelectiones* were, perhaps, the first great example.

2. *Pattison,* II, 135.

3. Typical of the "Oriental" items in the *Catalogue of the Library of the Late Rev. Robert Lowth, including the LIBRARY of his Father, The Celebrated Bishop of London,* Bodleian Catalogue, "Mus. Bibl. III. 8° 96," are number 1001, p. 34, "Shaw's Travels in Barbary and the Levant, with the Supplement ... Oxford, 1738," and number 1002, "Sandys' Travels in Turkey, etc., 1632." Lowth's use of Oriental travelers may be observed in I, 88, of the *Lectures,* where Chardin's '*Travels*' is cited on the Arab use of verse for recording history; in I, 136, where Maundrell's '*Travels*' tells of the *fauna* of the Middle East; in I, 132, where Sandys recounts the melting of snow in the summer in the Lebanon. Several of Lowth's travelers stand out here. George Sandys (1578–1644), Elizabethan translator of Ovid, visited Turkey, the pyramids, and Palestine. His '*Travels*' were repeatedly re-issued. Izaak Walton alludes to his account of the carrier pigeon service between Aleppo and Babylon in the *Compleat Angler.* Edward Pococke (1604–1691), on whom Smith com-

posed the masterly ode praised by Trapp, was chaplain to the "Turkey Merchants" at Aleppo, as well as first Professor of Arabic. His *Specimen historiae Arabum,* which is cited by Lowth in I, 88 along with Chardin, was one of the first two books in Arabic to come off the University press.

4. Thomas Burnet, *The Theory of the Earth* (London, 1684, 90), I, 139-40. A distinction is made in the present argument between the "sublime" of Longinus (author of *Peri hypsous,* or *On the Sublime*) to whom Lowth alludes occasionally, and the new "Sublime" of the eighteenth century which begins with this passage in Burnet and runs through Addison, Burke and Young. In large part, Lowth's lectures belong to the latter tradition.

Chapter Five

1. Francis Jeffrey, *Contributions to the Edinburgh Review,* 2nd ed. (London, Longman, 1846), III, 483.

2. William Warburton, *The Divine Legation of Moses,* 10th ed., with a discourse by Richard Hurd (London, T. Tegg, 1846), I, 110.

3. *Ibid.,* p. 111-12.

4. Edward Gibbon, *The Memoirs of the Life of Edward Gibbon,* ed. Birkbeck Hill (London, 1900), p. 177.

5. *Ibid.,* pp. 177-78.

6. *Ibid.,* p. 179.

7. *Ibid.*

8. Pattison, II, 134.

9. *Ibid.,* p. 135.

10. *Ibid.*

11. *Ibid.,* p. 137.

12. *Ibid.*

13. *Ibid.,* p. 137.

14. *Ibid.,* p. 138.

15. William Warburton, *The Divine Legation of Moses Demonstrated,* 4th ed. (London, 1765), III, "An Appendix concerning the Book of Job." See Pattison, II, 140.

16. Pattison, II, 140.

17. Rev. John Wesley, *Sermons on Several Occasions* (New York, Lane & Scott, 1848), II, 346.

18. Pattison, II, 139.

19. [Robert Lowth] *A Letter to the Right Reverend Author of The Divine Legation of Moses Demonstrated, in Answer to THE APPENDIX to the Fifth Volume of that Work,* by A Late Professor in the University of Oxford (Oxford, 1765), pp. 62-63. Pattison, II, 141. Referred to hereafter as *A Letter.*

20. Pattison, II, 143.

21. *Ibid.,* p. 139.

22. *A Letter,* p. 63. Pattison quotes this celebrated central part of Lowth's reply, pp. 141–42.

23. *A Letter,* p. 63.

24. *Ibid.,* p. 64.

25. *Ibid.,* pp. 64–65.

26. *Ibid.,* p. 65.

27. Isaac Disraeli, "WARBURTON and his Quarrels," *The Calamities and Quarrels of Authors,* "A New Edition," ed. "his son The Right Hon. B. Disraeli" (London, 1859), see *n.,* p. 237.

28. Pattison, II, 143.

29. Peter Hall, p. 4.

30. *Lectures,* I, 114.

31. Blair, *Lectures on Rhetoric and Belles Lettres,* I, 114–15.

32. *Ibid.*

33. *Boswell,* II, 36.

34. *Ibid.,* pp. 36–37.

35. *Wykeham,* p. iii.

36. *Ibid.,* p. iv.

37. Lowth's dedication in *Wykeham* provoked a *Letter to the Rev. Dr. Lowth . . . in Vindication of the Fellows of New College* (1758). Lowth replied in the *Answer to an Anonymous Letter &c.* (1759).

38. *Wykeham,* pp. 326–27.

39. Spence, pp. 279–80.

40. *Ibid.,* pp. 280–81. The "orrery" was named after its inventor [1713], Charles Boyle, Earl of Orrery.

41. Joseph Warton, *The Genius and Writings of Pope,* 4th ed. (London, 1782), I, 43–46.

42. *Wykeham,* p. 300.

43. *Ibid.,* p. xxiii.

44. *Ibid.*

45. *Ibid.,* pp. 7–8.

46. *Lectures,* I, 113–14.

47. *Wykeham,* pp. 216–19.

48. *Ibid.,* p. xi.

49. *Ibid.,* pp. 75–6.

50. Cook, pp. 26–7.

51. *Wykeham,* p. 89.

52. *Ibid.,* p. 179.

53. *Ibid.,* p. 180.

54. *Ibid.,* pp. 181–82.

55. *Ibid.,* pp. 196–7.

56. *Ibid.,* pp. 185–7.

57. *Ibid.,* p. 211.

Chapter Six

1. Anon. "Biographical Memoirs of the late Bishop of London," *The Gentleman's Magazine,* LVII, Pt. 2 (1787), 1029.

2. Edmund Gosse, ed., *The Works of Thomas Gray,* rev. ed. (London, Macmillan, 1902–06) III, 129.

3. Daniel Fenning, *A New Grammar of the English Language* (London, S. Crowder, 1770), p. iv.

4. Hugh Blair, *Lectures on Rhetoric and Belles Lettres,* "A New Edition" (London, Tegg, 1853), p. 101.

5. Hans Aarsleff, *The Study of Language in England 1780–1860* (Princeton, Princeton University Press, 1967), p. 43.

6. John Ash, *Grammatical Institutes or an Easy Introduction to Dr. Lowth's English Grammar* (London, E. & C. Dilly, 1763).

7. Arthur G. Kennedy, *A Bibliography of Writings on the English Language* (Cambridge and New Haven, 1927), pp. 208–09. See also R. C. Alston, *English Grammars Written in English* (Leeds, 1965), pp. 32–38; 42–48.

8. Preface, *A Short Introduction,* p. iii.

9. *Ibid.,* p. vii.

10. *Ibid.,* p. iii.

11. Anon., *Catalogue of the Library of the late Rev. Robert Lowth, including the LIBRARY of his Father,* Bodleian Catalogue, "Mus. Bibl. III. 8° 96," pp. 6 and 11.

12. Charles Butler, *The English Grammar or the Institution of Letters, Syllables and Words in the English Tongue, Whereunto is annexed an Index of Words like and unlike* (Oxford, 1633), p. 1.

13. The theorists of primitivism, whether Oriental or Northern European, found the beginning of their languages: for Pococke, Syriac, Arabic, Ethiopian, Aramaic; for Butler, German, and hence, English, in the "Confusion," the Tower of Babel.

14. Butler's *Grammar,* p. 2.

15. *Ibid.*

16. *Ibid.,* p. 21.

17. The "Index of Words like and unlike" is unnumbered but, of course, is alphabetized.

18. James Greenwood, *An Essay towards a Practical English Grammar describing the Genius and Nature of the English Tongue; giving likewise a Rational and Plain Account of Grammar in General, with a Familiar Explanation of its Terms,* 4th ed. (London, 1740), p. "A4." Hereafter given as Greenwood. (See also 1st ed. [1711], p. "A 4").

19. Wallis died in 1703, and Greenwood's *Grammar* did not appear until 1711. This Preface, with additions by Greenwood, continued to be a marked feature in Greenwood's later editions, running to forty-one pages in the fourth edition.

20. Jonathan Swift, *Gulliver's Travels,* ed. Herbert Davis (Oxford, Blackwell, 1959), pp. 182-4.

21. *Ibid.,* p. 184.

22. *Ibid.*

23. *Ibid.*

24. Greenwood, p. 39. (Cf. 1st ed., pp. 34-5).

25. *Ibid.*

26. *Ibid.,* p. 86.

27. *Ibid.,* p. 84, (1st ed., p. 69). Cf. John Locke, *An Essay Concerning Human Understanding,* ed. John W. Yolton, Everyman's Library (London, 1961), II, 72f. Cited hereafter as *Essay.*

28. Greenwood, p. 84.

29. *Ibid.,* p. 85.

30. *Ibid.,* pp. 87-93. (Cf. 1st ed. pp. 73ff).

31. *Ibid.,* p. 223. (1st ed., p. 205).

32. *A Short Introduction,* pp. 91-92.

33. *Ibid.,* pp. xiv-xv.

34. James Harris, *Hermes, or a Philosophical Inquiry concerning Universal Grammar,* 3rd ed. (London, I. Nourse & P. Vaillant, 1771), pp. 263-64.

35. *A Short Introduction,* p. 24.

36. *Ibid.,* p. 25.

37. *Ibid., n.* 7.

38. *Ibid.*

39. *Ibid.,* p. 59.

40. *Ibid.,* pp. 59-60.

41. *Ibid.,* p. 115, *n.* 9.

42. *Ibid.,* p. 68.

43. *Ibid.,* pp. 68-69, *n.* 4.

44. *Ibid.,* p. 132, *n.* 6.

45. *Ibid.*

46. *Ibid.,* p. 79.

47. *Ibid.,* pp. 79-80.

48. *Ibid.,* p. 81.

49. *ibid.,* p. 23.

50. *Ibid.,* p. 23, *n.* 4.

51. *Ibid.,* p. 24.

52. *Ibid.*

53. A. S. Collins, "Language 1660-1784," *The Pelican Guide to English Literature* (Harmondsworth, Penguin, 1957), IV, 136-37.

54. "The principal object then, proposed in these poems, was to choose incidents and situations from common life, and to relate or describe them throughout, as far as was possible, in a selection of language really used by men...." Preface to the 2nd edition, Samuel Taylor Coleridge and William Wordsworth, *Lyrical Ballads.* See *Lyrical Ballads,* ed. W. J. Owen

(London, Oxford University Press, 1967), p. 156.

Chapter Seven

1. Anon., "Biographical Memoirs of the late Bishop of London," *The Gentleman's Magazine,* LVII, Pt. 2 (1787). Substantially similar in content and brevity is *Memoirs of the Late Robert Lowth* (London, 1787). Both are, perhaps, by his son, Robert.

2. See, e.g., *The Fulham Papers in the Lambeth Palace Library,* ed. William W. Manross (Oxford, Clarendon Press, 1965).

3. John H. Overton and Frederic Relton, *The English Church ... to the end of the Eighteenth Century (1714–1800),* (London, Macmillan, 1906), p. 172. See also A. S. Wood, *The Burning Heart* (Exeter, Paternoster Press, 1967), p. 204. Lowth's sympathy might be explained by the "primitive" aspects of the Methodist movement. The Wesleyan phenomenon in the eighteenth century may be viewed as a social application of theories of "primitivism" just as Charles Wesley's "hymns" related to the "primitive" songs thought to have been sung by the earliest men. One branch of the Methodist Church became known as "the Primitive Methodists."

4. *Lectures,* II, 84–85.

5. Christopher Smart, "Literary Observations," *The Universal Visiter* (January, 1756), p. 25; (February, 1756), pp. 73–74. Cited below as Smart.

6. *Isaiah,* 3rd ed. (London, 1795). See note to Isaiah xiii. For the sake of brevity, all references to Lowth's *Isaiah* indicate only the section of the work, e.g., "Dissertation" or in "Notes," the chapter and verse under discussion.

7. Smart, p. 25.

8. Chardin and Harmer appear some fifty times in the volume of *Notes* to Lowth's *Isaiah, A New Translation.* Sir John Chardin (1643–1712), born in Paris, traveled to Persia at the age of twenty-one and became the Shah's agent for gems. His *Journal du Voyage ... en Perse et aux Indes Orientales* was translated into English in 1686. His work was praised, especially by Sir William Jones (1746–1794), famed late-eighteenth-century Orientalist. In the Preface to his *Journal,* Chardin confessed "my favourite design," *Notes upon Passages of the Holy Scriptures, illustrated by Eastern Customs and Manners.* This MS. was lost until 1770, when its recovery by relatives led to its incorporation in the second edition of Thomas Harmer's *Observations* in 1776, a discovery which accounts for the extensive use of Chardin and Harmer in Lowth's *Isaiah* (1778). Thomas Harmer (1714–1788), a Norwich-born Independent minister, was less widely traveled, but Lowth's dependence on his works, *Observations on Divers Passages ... from ... Voyages and Travels,* first edition, 1764, and *Outlines of a New Commentary on Solomon's Song ... by ... help of Instructions from the East,* corroborates the impression

gleaned from a variety of travellers that Lowth's work was significantly influenced not only by the mid-century awareness of "the East" in general, but by the light that modern, "scientific" observers used to illuminate the Scriptures.

9. Jones, the best-known Orientalist of the younger generation, followed Lowth in demanding a reader's complete knowledge of Eastern countries. His *Essay on the Poetry of the Eastern Nations* (1772) shows his debt to Lowth, which he acknowledged gratefully. See *Works* (London, G.G. & J. Robinson, 1799, 1801), II, 417 and 483.

10. Peter Jones ed., *Imagist Poetry*, (Harmondsworth, Penguin, 1972), Introduction, p. 36. See also Jones' citation of the early Imagists' ambition to compose "poems in a sacred Hebrew form," p. 15.

11. Roston, p. 136.

12. *Ibid.,* p. 137.

Chapter Eight

1. J. G. Frazer, ed., *Letters of William Cowper,* I, 181–82.

2. Edward Gibbon, *The Decline and Fall of the Roman Empire,* ed. H. R. Trevor-Roper (Sadler & Brown, Chalfont St. Giles, England, 1966), p. 1. Gibbon shared with Lowth the time-span of the New Chronology of six thousand years or thereabouts. It was in this perspective that his Roman Empire descended from the position it had held in the neo-Classical mind. This great historian began also with the Jews whose characteristics, inherited by the early Christians (see especially Gibbon, Chapter XV), contributed significantly, in Gibbon's view, to the downfall of the European civilization of Rome.

3. *Memoirs,* p. 49.

4. *Ibid.* See Lowth, *Letter to the . . . Author of the Divine Legation,* pp. 64–5.

5. *Memoirs,* p. 50.

6. *Ibid.,* p. 54.

7. *Ibid.,* p. 55.

8. James Boswell, *Boswell for the Defence, 1769–1774,* ed. William K. Wimsatt, Jr., and Frederick A. Pottle (New York, McGraw-Hill, 1959), p. 108.

9. *Letters of James Boswell,* ed. C. B. Tinker (Oxford, Clarendon Press, 1924), II, 285–86.

10. *Boswell,* V, 57–58, *n.* 3.

11. *Ibid.,* IV, 311.

12. *Ibid.*

13. *Boswell,* II, 37.

14. Samuel Johnson, *The Works of Samuel Johnson* (Oxford, 1825), V, 240.

15. Sir W. Forbes, *Account of the Life and Writings of James Beattie*

(London, Roper, 1824), p. 30.

16. Christopher Smart, *Rejoice in the Lamb,* ed. William Force Stead (London, J Cope, 1939), Appendix IV, "On the Verse-form," pp. 296–300.

17. W. H. Bond, "Christopher Smart's *Jubilate Agno,*" *Harvard Library Bulletin,* IV (1950), 39–52.

18. Arthur Sherbo, *Christopher Smart, Scholar of the University* (East Lansing, Michigan State University Press, 1967), pp. 105–06, 158–59, 214.

19. Sophia B. Blaydes, *Christopher Smart as a Poet of his Time, a Reappraisal* (The Hague and Paris, Mouton, 1966), pp. 98ff.

20. *Biographia Literaria,* I, 11.

21. *Lectures,* I, 99.

22. Smart, p. 25.

23. *Ibid.*

24. *Ibid.*

25. *Ibid.,* pp. 73–74.

26. *Ibid.,* p. 73. The terms Smart uses are consciously those of a practicing poet concerned with technique. The next sentence at this point reads, "There is an uncommon degree of merit in what I venture to call the mechanical part of the ode, *viz.* the structure of the versification."

27. *Ibid.*

28. *Ibid.*

29. See Sherbo, p. 196.

30. Thomas Warton the Younger, *The History of English Poetry* (London, A. Murray, 1870), p. 170.

31. Thomas Warton the Younger, *Verses on Sir Joshua Reynolds' Painted Window at New College, Oxford,* ll. 13–16; 71–74.

32. Joseph Warton, *The Genius and Writings of Pope* (London, 1782), I, 14.

33. *Ibid.,* pp. 14–15.

34. J. Warton, *et al.,* eds., *The Works of Alexander Pope,* with Notes and Illustrations (London, 1797), I, 106.

35. *Ibid.,* p. 93, *n.* 1.

36. *Ibid.,* p. 106.

37. Richard Hurd, *The Life of the Author;* "first printed in MDCCXCIV," in *The Divine Legation of Moses Demonstrated,* by the Right Reverend William Warburton, 10th ed. (London, 1846), I, 49.

38. *Ibid.*

39. Joseph Warton, *The Works of Pope,* I, 106.

40. R. C. Alston, *English Grammars Written in English* (Leeds, 1965), p. 43.

41. Wilkes' review of Lowth's *Praelectiones* is preserved in the Wilkes Collection, Vol. III, fols. 2 and 3, the William L. Clements Library, University of Michigan. In the same collection are thirty-two letters between Wilkes and his editor, Suard. See Gabriel Bonno, "Lettres Inédites de

Suard à Wilkes," "Univ. of Calif. Publ. in Modern Philology," No. 15 (Berkeley and Los Angeles, 1932), 161-280. See also *The Contributions of John Wilkes to the Gazette Littéraire de L'Europe,* by Louis Bredvold, (Ann Arbor, 1950).

42. Bredvold, p. 15. Wilkes' fashionable interest in the primitive "first ages" is further suggested by his review of the Ossianic *Some Specimens of the Poetry of the Antient Welsh Bards,* trans. the Rev. Evan Evans (London, 1764), which appeared in the *Gazette* for November 4, 1764. Clearly *au fait* with Northern as well as Oriental myth, Wilkes wrote of Gray's *Bard,* "nothing was ever more happily imagined, and the execution equals the idea. . . . We will venture to say that this single ode of Mr. Gray's has not been excelled by the English in the variety and grandeur of images. . . ."

43. Bredvold, p. 12.

44. *Ibid.,* p. 13.

45. *Ibid.,* p. 12.

46. *Ibid.*

47. *Ibid.,* p. 13. Like Gregory, Lowth's translator, Wilkes emphasized that the *Praelectiones* dealt with the nature of poetry in general, as well as that of the Jews. Wilkes wrote, "it is extremely difficult to suggest any new ideas on a subject so frequently handled . . . notwithstanding the difficulty. . . . Mr. Lowth has presented poetry in general to us in a variety of new aspects. . . ." (Bredvold, p. 12).

48. Bredvold, pp. 13-14.

49. Bredvold, p. 13.

50. *Ibid.,* p. 14.

51. Lowth, II, 89.

52. Bredvold, p. 15.

53. *Ibid.*

54. "The little animal *wins* its way up against the stream, by alternate pulses of active and passive motion, now resisting the current, and now yielding to it in order to gather strength and a momentary *fulcrum* for a further propulsion." S. T. Coleridge, *Biographia Literaria* (chapter vii), I, 85-6.

55. Marcus Walsh ed., *Selected Poems of Christopher Smart* (South Hinksey, Oxford, Carcanet, 1972), pp. 12-13.

56. It is difficult to isolate any section of George Berkeley's works, for all argue the subjectivity of Time and Space. But *A New Theory of Vision* eds. A. A. Luce and T. E. Jessop (London & New York, Nelson, 1948), Section 46ff., offers a critique of our notion of external Space, and *Principles of Human Knowledge* eds., Luce and Jessop (London & New York, Nelson, 1948), Section 90ff., suggests broader implications of the subjectivity of all objects of thought, perhaps especially the abstraction "Time."

57. Thomas Burnet, *Theory of the Visible World,* trans. "Mr. Foxton" (London, 1729), p. 74. The *Archaeologicae philosophicae* (1692) was translated in two parts in 1729; the first bore its Latin title, the second,

this, in itself highly suggestive of the debt *The Ancient Mariner* owed to Burnet's cosmology.

58. Thomas Burnet, *Theory of the Visible World,* pp. 74–75.

59. "John Lizard," (Edward Young?), *The Guardian,* II, 22.

60. See especially Schiller's discussion of Young and of Young's counterpart, Klopstock in *Naive and Sentimental Poetry and On the Sublime,* trans. Julius A. Elias (New York, F. Unger, 1966), p. 135. The essay first appeared in German in 1795.

61. Douglas Bush, *Mythology and the Romantic Tradition,* p. 42.

62. Cf. A. William Salomone, "Pluralism and Universality in Vico's *Scienza Nuova,*" *Giambattista Vico, An International Symposium,* ed. Giorgio Tagliacozzo and Hayden V. White (Johns Hopkins, 1969), pp. 518ff.

63. *Biographia Literaria,* I, 202.

Selected Bibliography

PRIMARY SOURCES

De sacra poesi Hebraeorum praelectiones academicae Oxonii habitae. Clarendon Press, Oxford, 1753. *Lectures on the Sacred Poetry of the Hebrews.* Trans. G. Gregory. "To which are added the principal notes of Professor Michaelis and notes by the translator and others," 2 vols. London: J. Johnson, 1787. *Lectures on the Sacred Poetry of the Hebrews.* Trans. G. Gregory. 2 vols. London: 1787. Reprinted in facsimile with a useful Introduction by Vincent Freimarck, in the series *Anglistica & Americana,* Georg Olms Verlag, Hildesheim, W. Germany, No. 43, in 1969.

The Life of William of Wykeham, Bishop of Winchester. With a Supplement. London: A. Millar and R. and J. Dodsley, 1758.

A Short Introduction to English Grammar, with Critical Notes. Published anonymously. London: A. Millar and R. & J. Dodsley, 1762. *A Short Introduction to English Grammar,* 1762, was reprinted as a "Scolar Press Facsimile," by The Scolar Press Ltd., Menston, Yorkshire, England, 1967.

A Letter to the Right Reverend Author of the Divine Legation of Moses Demonstrated. Oxford: Clarendon Press, 1765.

Isaiah, A New Translation, with a Preliminary Dissertation and Notes, critical, philological and explanatory. 2 pts. London: J. Dodsley, T. Cadell, 1778.

SECONDARY SOURCES

ALSTON, R. C. *English Grammars Written in English.* Leeds: E. J. Arnold, 1953. Contains a useful record of eighteenth-century grammars, among which Lowth's was reprinted almost every two years until the mid-nineteenth century.

ANON. *Memoirs of the Life and Writings of the Late Right Reverend Robert Lowth D.D. F. R. SS. LOND. and GOETTING. Lord Bishop of London.* London: W. Bent, 1787. The Advertisement reads, "the following Memoirs were written originally for the Universal Magazine, and were printed in that Miscellany of November last." Authentic but dull, this brief anonymous life, perhaps by Lowth's son, Robert, is substantially the same as the "Biographical Memoirs," which appeared in *The Gentleman's Magazine.*

ANON. "Biographical Memoirs of the late Bishop of London." *The Gentleman's Magazine,* LVII, Pt. 2 (1787).

ATKINS, J. W. H. *English Literary Criticism: 17th and 18th Centuries.* London: Methuen, 1951. Unexceptional but useful outline of the major figures. Readers will find Chapter VI, "The Widening Outlook: Lowth, Young, Gray, the Wartons, Hurd," comprehensive.

BELL, H. E. "A New College Scandal of the Seventeen-Twenties." *Historical Essays 1600–1750.* Eds., Henry E. Bell and R. L. Pollard. New York: Barnes and Noble, 1963. This essay, part of a collection in honor of David Ogg, historian, of Wykeham's New College, Oxford, deals with some matters glanced at in Lowth's *Life of Wykeham,* and reminds us of the stature of Lowth, the historian.

BOND, W. H. "Christopher Smart's *Jubilate Agno.*" *Harvard Library Bulletin,* IV (1950), 39–52. Recalls the influence of Lowth's discovery of "parallelism" in Hebrew poetry on Smart's *Jubilate Agno.*

BREDVOLD, LOUIS. *The Contributions of John Wilkes to the Gazette Littéraire de L'Europe.* The University of Michigan Contributions in Modern Philology, No. 15. Ann Arbor: University of Michigan Press, 1950: Contains an account of Wilkes' perceptive review of Lowth's *Praelectiones.*

BURKE, EDMUND. *A Philosophical Enquiry into the Origin of our Ideas of the Sublime and Beautiful.* Ed., J. T. Boulton. London: Routledge and Paul, 1958. Burke's celebrated work on "the Sublime" provides useful evidence of the central place held by primitive poets, especially Job, in the esthetic theories at large of the eighteenth century; provides parallels with Lowth's "Sublime"; in Section V reflects the weakening of the role of memory in the use of words in sublime verse that we read about in Lowth's Lecture XVII.

BURNET, THOMAS. *Telluris theoria sacra.* 2 vols. London: W. Kettilby, 1681, 1688. Trans., T. Burnet, *The Theory of the Earth,* 2 vols., London: W. Kettilby, 1684, 1690. Reprinted, *The Sacred Theory of the Earth,* London: the Centaur Press, 1965. This influential work united the eighteenth-century "Sublime," of mountains and oceans and other great works of Nature in an eternal aspect, with the work of "Oriental" writers, Job and Moses for example, in a materialist account of Creation.

_____. *Archaeologicae philosophicae.* 2 vols. London: G. Kettilby, 1692. Trans., "Mr. Foxton" London: E. Curll, 1729. Reinforced this view of the primitive Oriental writers, by finding the "jewelled" vision of writers, such as Ezekiel, corroboration of the preexistence of matter.

BUTLER, CHARLES. *The English Grammar or the Institution of Letters, Syllables, and Words in the English Tongue.* Oxford: William Turner, 1633. Early seventeenth-century grammar, a copy of which is listed in the catalogue of Lowth's library, and whose views, reflected in

Lowth's *Short Introduction,* indicate its "primitive" content.

Catalogue of the Library of the Late Reverend Robert Lowth including the LIBRARY of his Father, the Celebrated Bishop of London, Author of the Hebrew Praelections, Translation of Isaiah, etc., which will be sold by Auction by Mr. Evans, at his House No. 93, Pall-Mall on Wednesday, January 15 and five following days. London: published by the bookseller, Evans, 1823. This catalogue, the only copy of which the author has seen is in the Bodleian Library, Oxford, is valuable in three particular ways. Its listing of Burnet, Hearne, and many volumes of Trapp, corroborates the view that Lowth's *Praelectiones* and *Isaiah* were indebted to the tradition of the earlier Oriental movement; the numerous titles of travelers to the Middle East at large reminds us that Lowth's *Praelectiones* and *Isaiah* did not represent the Old Testament poets as exclusively Hebrew, but as "Oriental"; listings of Chaucer, Gavin Douglas, as well as earlier grammarians, strengthens the view that Lowth, as attested by his *Grammar* as well as his *Wykeham,* was as vividly aware of, and learned in, the "primitive" era of his own nation, as the Oriental.

COOK, A. K. *About Winchester College.* London: Macmillan, 1917.

COWPER, WILLIAM. *Letters of William Cowper.* 2 vols. Ed., J. G. Frazer. London: Macmillan, 1912: contains surprising evidence that one of the eighteenth century's greatest poets considered Lowth's juvenile verse "sublime," and that Lowth, unlike himself, had "stepped into excellence at once."

DISRAELI, ISAAC. *The Calamities and Quarrels of Authors.* Ed., The Right Hon. B. Disraeli. 3 vols. London: G. Routledge, 1859. This work by the statesman's father contains a lively account of the Lowth-Warburton fight.

GIBBON, EDWARD. *The Memoirs of the Life of Edward Gibbon.* Ed., Birkbeck Hill. London: Methuen, 1900. Contains an appreciation of Lowth at Oxford; useful evidence of the closeness between Lowth's views and those of Gibbon.

GREENWOOD, JAMES. *An Essay towards a Practical English Grammar describing the Genius and Nature of the English Tongue; giving likewise a Rational and Plain Account of Grammar in General, with a Familiar Explanation of its Terms.* London: R. Tookey, 1711. 4th ed., 1740. Heavily indebted to the *virtuosi* of the Royal Society, Hickes, Mead, Wallis, and Wilkins, Greenwood's *Grammar* shows the relationship between the "scientific" study of language and the primitive nationalism of the early eighteenth century. The Medieval and Anglo-Saxon bias of Lowth's *Short Introduction,* which takes its positive sense of language from Hickes, *et al.,* seems to derive in part from Greenwood whose *Grammar,* with the exception of Butler's, is the only one listed in the catalogue of the Lowth library.

HALL, THE REV. PETER. "A Memoir." *Sermons and Other Remains of*

Robert Lowth. London: J. G. and, F. Rivington, 1834. Longest account of Lowth's life that there is; Hall's suffers from the mid-nineteenth-century sense of propriety of a country vicar. Even more impressive, perhaps, therefore, is Hall's sustained complaint that Lowth was not a "spiritual divine" but a man interested in the effects of "sublime" language and verse.

HEARNE, THOMAS. *Remarks and Collections of Thomas Hearne*. Ed., C. E. Doble, 2 vols. Oxford: Clarendon Press, 1886. Orientalism and the Professorship of Poetry are closely related from the beginning of the eighteenth century. Hearne's account of the foundation of this institution is, therefore, of more than incidental importance.

KENNEDY, ARTHUR G. *A Bibliography of Writings on the English Language*. Cambridge, Mass., and New Haven: Harvard University Press and Yale University Press, 1927. Useful sourcebook parallel with Alston; records the extraordinary popularity of Lowth, the grammarian, not only in England.

LOWTH, WILLIAM. *A Commentary upon the Larger and Lesser Prophets*. 3rd edition. London: J. and J. Knapton, *et al.*, 1730. Father's celebrated *Commentary* on the prophets occasionally anticipates Robert Lowth, notably in the awareness of the reality of their original era for the eighteenth century and the "sublimity" of Ezekiel.

MACCLINTOCK, WILLIAM DARNALL. *Joseph Warton's Essay on Pope, a History of the Five Editions*. Chapel Hill: University of North Carolina Press, 1933. This valuable little book underlines the emphasis on *particulars* in Spence and Warton; reminds us that Lowth's appreciation of the primitive Oriental poets' sense of Nature was part of a central mid-century development.

MOBERLY, GEORGE HEBERT. *Life of William of Wykeham*. Winchester and London: Warren, 1887. Moberly's *Life of Wykeham* is pious and amateurish; confesses an almost total dependence on Lowth's *Wykeham,* but lacks the elegance and wit of that work.

PATTISON, MARK. *Essays by the Late Mark Pattison*. 2 vols. Oxford: Clarendon Press, 1889. Pattison's account of Warburton contains the finest and most informative account of the Lowth-Warburton fight; most reliable impression of Lowth's achievement and nature.

SHAFTESBURY, ANTHONY, EARL OF. *Characteristics of Men, Manners, Opinions, Times*. 3 vols. 2nd ed. corr. London: J. Darby, 1714. Shaftesbury's "sublime" esthetics are highly relevant to the philosophical content of the primitive, Oriental movement, especially in the philosopher's account of Nature in her "original wilds" on the North African coast. It is suggestive that Shaftesbury should not only write a significant chapter about early eighteenth-century Orientalism but should have also suggested the view of abstractions recognizable in Lowth's Lecture XIII on personification in Hebrew poetry.

SMART, CHRISTOPHER. *Rejoice in the Lamb.* Ed., William Force Stead. London: J. Cape, 1939. The pioneer work which pointed to the use to which Smart had put Lowth's discovery of the "parallelism" of Hebrew poetry.

———. "Literary Observations; Further Remarks on Dr. Lowth's celebrated PRELECTIONS." *The Universal Visiter and Monthly Memorialist.* London: Thomas Gardner, 1756. Smart's review of Lowth's *Praelectiones* was highly enthusiastic. Its recognition of Lowth's translation of the fourteenth chapter of Isaiah into Alcaic ode non-caesural stanzas suggests a model in Lowth not only for Smart's *Jubilate Agno,* as Stead and Bond suggested, but also for *A Song to David.*

SPENCE, JOSEPH. *An Essay on Pope's Odyssey, in which some particular Beauties and Blemishes of that Work are Considered.* 2 pts. London: J. and J. Knapton, 1726, 27. Spence's *Essay,* which won him the Professorship of Poetry prior to Lowth, shows the extent of the Oriental movement even in Classical, or neo-Classical, criticism in the early eighteenth century. Spence uses Shaftesbury's account of Mt. Atlas to illustrate Homer, but, more excitingly, confesses his own coinage of a totally new literary term, "an *orientalism*" to describe an effect or technique of prophetic verse he finds in Homer and Ezekiel and which Lowth used in his poetry.

THOMAS, W. *Le Poéte Edward Young, 1683–1765, Étude sur sa Vie et ses Oeuvres.* Paris: Hachette et C$^{\underline{ie}}$: 1901. Laborious dissertation on Young which contains useful information on Wykeham's school at Winchester in the early eighteenth century.

TRAPP, JOSEPH. *Praelectiones poeticae in Schola Naturalis Philosophiae.* 3 vols. London: B. Lintot, 1711, 1715, 1719. Trapp's poetry lectures show that the Professorship of Poetry (of which he was the first incumbent) and the Orientalism of the eighteenth century flourished together. The first *Praelectiones* were translated by W. Clarke and W. Bowyer, *Lectures on Poetry,* by Joseph Trapp. London: C. Hitch and C. Davis: 1742. Like Lowth's, these have been reprinted (1969) by Georg Olms, Hildesheim, in their series, *Anglistica & Americana.*

TUVESON, ERNEST LEE. *The Imagination as a Means of Grace.* Berkeley and Los Angeles: University of California Press, 1960. Tuveson's account of the fortunes of "the Sublime" in the early eighteenth century is of particular interest.

WARTON, JOSEPH. *Essay on the Genius and Writings of Pope.* 2 pts. London: M. Cooper, 1756; J. Dodsley, 1782. Like Lowth, Warton was a Wykehamist and central to the "pre-Romantic" movement. Significantly, his criticism of Pope, in the *Essay on Pope* as in his edition of Pope's *Works* (1797), includes high praise of Lowth's work. (Usually given: '*Writings and Genius.*' The 4th ed., "corr." (1782) which I have used reads thus).

WARTON, THOMAS, THE ELDER. *Poems on Several Occasions*. Ed. Joseph
Warton. London: R. Manly and H. S. Cox, 1748. The Oriental and
Medieval verses of the second Professor of Poetry at Oxford are further evidence of the growth of these movements under the impulse of
the Poetry Professorship.

Index

211

DATE DUE
